Advance Praise for *Babe Ruth's Called Shot*

"Nothing makes for better reading than terrific reporting, and few singular moments in sports history have been debated, discussed, and researched with the fervor of Babe Ruth's Called Shot. It took place more than 80 years ago, but it is argued about as if it happened last week. Ed Sherman brings it into sharp focus in a uniquely entertaining and greatly detailed way."
—John Feinstein, author of the bestselling *A Good Walk Spoiled* and *Open*

"Sherman cuts through the hype and hyperbole to deliver the true history of the event, revealing not just what happened but how and why a single at bat became the stuff of legend."
—Glenn Stout, bestselling author of *Yankees Century* and *The Cubs* and series editor of *Best American Sports Writing*

"Ed Sherman has written with affection and charm about one of baseball's most intriguing moments. This is a wonderful look at Ruth, his team, and his time."
—Jonathan Eig, author of the bestselling *Luckiest Man* and *Opening Day*

"A fun and fascinating exploration of baseball's most famous and infamous home run. If there's such a thing as a sports archeologist, then Sherman is the tops in his field as he meticulously digs for the truth and uncovers little known and never-before-told factual gems. He examines this iconic moment from every imaginable point of view—players, spectators, sportswriters, and others who were there—and guides you, pitch by pitch, during the Babe's unforgettable at-bat. In this thoroughly enjoyable and incredibly informative book, Sherman does a yeoman's job of separating myth from reality and lays out compelling cases for those who believe in the Ruthian legend and those who don't. For any fan who loves baseball history and is looking for ammunition to use during the next sports debate of did-he-or-didn't-he, this is must reading."
—Allan Zullo, coauthor of *The Baseball Hall of Shame*

"Babe Ruth remains the singular colossus of American sport, and his home run in the fifth inning of Game Three of the 1932 World Series remains the most indelible moment of his career. Ed Sherman takes us back to that afternoon on the North Side, which for so long has remained shrouded in mystery, with this detail-rich biography of the most mythologized at-bat in the annals of the national pastime. Finally we have the definitive account of the so-called Called Shot."
—Jeremy Schaap, six-time Emmy Award winner and author of the *New York Times* bestselling *Cinderella Man*

"An exhaustive, delightful treatment of a fascinating moment in American sport . . . This brilliantly rendered account of Ruth's famous Called Shot and the decades-long debate brings to life the most celebrated athlete American sport has ever known at the very moment when he crosses that precipice separating man from legend. The moment is expertly captured and examined from all its many angles. Anyone who appreciates the lore, history, and, yes, mythology of America's game will delight in getting lost within these pages."
—Josh Pahigian, author of *The Ultimate Baseball Road Trip* and *101 Baseball Places to See Before You Strike Out*

"*Babe Ruth's Called Shot* sheds light on one of baseball mythology's great tales. Sherman does a terrific job of taking the reader back to the days when the iconic Bambino ruled baseball. Well written and quite entertaining—I couldn't put it down."
—Bill Chastain, author of *Hack's 191* and *100 Things Giants Fans Should Know and Do before They Die*

"Chicago sportswriter Ed Sherman, who has forgotten more about baseball than most people will ever know, dissects Ruth's Called Shot like a frog in a high school science lab—meticulously researched and reported and wonderfully written. Even the Bambino would buy this book."
—Gene Wojciechowski, author of the *New York Times* bestseller *The Last Great Game* and *Cubs Nation*

"Sherman gives us a flesh-and-blood Babe, a late-career legend who will forever be bigger than life no matter what he was specifically pointing at during the 1932 World Series. If you are going to pick one swing from one player, who better than someone who could turn a World Series sweep into a mystery still hotly debated four score and almost seven Octobers later because of a hand gesture? It's a Ruthian blast."
—Matt Silverman, author of *Swinging '73* and *100 Things Mets Fans Should Know and Do Before They Die*

"Ed Sherman's wonderfully entertaining dissection of Babe Ruth's most memorable World Series home run reminds us of the mythic power packed into baseball and its ability to help us see life in its most vivid colors."
—Edward Achorn, Casey Award–nominated author of *The Summer of Beer and Whiskey* and *Fifty-Nine in '84*

"A wonderful journey through a Depression-ravaged era when everything that happened in baseball—and particularly what Ruth did—mattered to a nation anxious for a diversion. So did the Babe really call his shot in Game 3 of the 1932 World Series? Perhaps we'll never know for sure, but Sherman expertly relives that magic moment in time and reminds us why we love baseball in the first place."
—Jim Reisler, author of *Babe Ruth: Launching the Legend*

The Sultan of Swat in 1920

BABE RUTH'S CALLED SHOT

The Myth and Mystery of Baseball's Greatest Home Run

ED SHERMAN

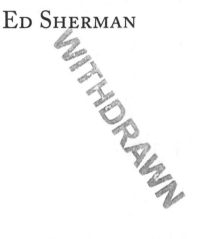

LYONS PRESS
Guilford, Connecticut
An imprint of Globe Pequot Press

To buy books in quantity for corporate use
or incentives, call **(800) 962-0973**
or e-mail **premiums@GlobePequot.com.**

Lyons Press is an imprint of Globe Pequot Press.

Frontispiece photo courtesy of the Library of Congress.

Project editor: Meredith Dias
Layout: Lisa Reneson, Two Sisters Design

Library of Congress Cataloging-in-Publication Data

Sherman, Ed.
  Babe Ruth's called shot / Ed Sherman.
     pages cm
  Summary: "Game 3 of the 1932 World Series between the Cubs and
Yankees. The legend of the Called Shot was born, but the debate over
what Ruth had actually done on the afternoon of October 1, 1932, had
just begun" —Provided by publisher.
  ISBN 978-0-7627-8539-1 (hardback)
  1. Ruth, Babe, 1895-1948—Anecdotes. 2. World Series (Baseball)
(1932) 3. Home runs (Baseball)—Anecdotes. 4. Chicago Cubs (Baseball
team)—Anecdotes. 5. New York Yankees (Baseball team)—Anecdotes. I.
Title.
  GV865.R8S44 2014
  796.357092—dc23

                                                        2013045433

Printed in the United States of America

10 9 8 7 6 5 4 3 2 1

To my wife, Ilene, my heart and soul,
and to Matt and Sam, my best friends forever.

And to baseball's historians,
for keeping the game's glorious past alive.

He first built up his act with a mixture of comedy and kidding, farce and humor, and then he turned it into drama. No one else in sport could have developed such a plot and then finished the story with such a flaming finale. He called the turn in advance, and then he put everything his 225 pounds carried into the most tremendous swing and lash his big bat had ever known.

—GRANTLAND RICE

Contents

CONTENTS

CONTENTS

Roster at Wrigley Field

NEW YORK YANKEES

Johnny Allen: Emerging as a key player on the 1932 team, he went 17–4 in his first year in the majors.

Earle Combs: Center fielder, he was one of the best all-time leadoff men, setting the table for Ruth and Gehrig, and had a career .325 batting average.

Frank Crosetti: A 21-year-old rookie in 1932, the shortstop eventually cashed 23 World Series checks as a player and longtime coach for the team.

Bill Dickey: Among the top catchers ever, he had a career .313 batting average.

Lou Gehrig: At age 29 he was taking over as the central figure on the Yankees in 1932. All told, he played in 2,130 straight games and hit 493 career homers.

Lefty Gomez: This wiry lefthander was the Yankees' ace during the 1930s. He posted four 20-win seasons.

Tony Lazzeri: A top run producer as a second baseman, he recorded more than 100 RBIs in a season seven times.

Joe McCarthy: Getting fired from the Cubs in 1930 proved to be the best thing that ever happened to him. Hired by the Yankees in 1931 to manage the team, he helmed seven World Series titles, tying for the record with Casey Stengel.

Herb Pennock: A longtime fixture of the Yankees staff in the 1920s and early '30s.

George Pipgras: A solid starter, he was the winning pitcher of the Called Shot game.

Red Ruffing: Picked up as a reject from the Boston Red Sox, Ruffing went on to win 273 games. Also a strong hitter, he had 36 career homers.

Babe Ruth: The one and only.

CHICAGO CUBS

Guy Bush: A 19-game winner in 1932, he had 176 career wins, yet like Charlie Root his legacy ties to Ruth's Called Shot.

Kiki Cuyler: The outfielder had four seasons in which he hit over .350, including .360 for the Cubs in 1929.

Burleigh Grimes: A winner of 270 games, he was 38 years old when he joined the Cubs in 1932. His best days lay behind him, though, as evidenced by his 6–11 record.

Charlie Grimm: A midseason replacement for Rogers Hornsby in 1932, Grimm managed the Cubs to three National League titles.

Gabby Hartnett: Catcher and the heart of four Cubs National League pennant–winning teams, he had a career .297 batting average.

Billy Herman: The second baseman was a 10-time All-Star during his prime years with the Cubs and later with the Brooklyn Dodgers.

Mark Koenig: A late-season pickup in 1932, his .353 average helped spur the Cubs' run to the pennant.

Charlie Root: Winner of 201 games, he will forever be remembered for one pitch.

Riggs Stephenson: At age 34 in 1932, the outfielder hit .324 for the Cubs.

UMPIRE

Bill Klem: "The Father of Baseball Umpires," Klem served from 1905 to 1941.

COMMISSIONER

Kenesaw Mountain Landis: A former judge, he became baseball's first commissioner and receives credit for saving the reputation of the sport after the fallout from the Black Sox scandal.

RADIO ANNOUNCERS

Bob Elson: Working with Husing for CBS, Elson became a longtime announcer for the Chicago White Sox.

Ted Husing: A major sports figure in the 1930s, he was on the call for CBS Radio.

Graham McNamee: One of baseball's first star announcers, he called his first World Series in 1926. He was on the call for NBC Radio.

POLITICAL FIGURES

Anton Cermak: Mayor of Chicago, he was shot and died following an assassination attempt on President Roosevelt in March 1933.

Franklin D. Roosevelt: He attended the game while on a campaign swing through Chicago as the Democratic candidate for president. His son, James, joined him.

PRESS BOX

Paul Gallico: This famous *New York Daily News* columnist later wrote *The Poseidon Adventure*.

Ring Lardner: He was the first widely acclaimed sports columnist and also a noted writer of short stories.

Grantland Rice: Generally regarded as the most significant sportswriter of all time.

Damon Runyon: He was the sports columnist whose short stories served as inspiration for the Broadway musical *Guys and Dolls*.

Red Smith: Just 27 at the time, the future legendary columnist covered the game for the *St. Louis Journal*.

FANS IN THE STANDS

"Little Ray" Kelly: Ruth invited him, as his young mascot, and Kelly's father to attend the game in Chicago.

Lincoln Landis: Ten years old at the time, he attended the game with his uncle, Commissioner Landis.

Amos "Loudmouth" Latimer: Some suspect that this heckler in the bleachers played a role in the Called Shot.

John Paul Stevens: Age 12 at the time, Stevens later served more than 30 years as a US Supreme Court justice.

INTRODUCTION

Supreme Witness

When the legend becomes fact, print the legend.
—Maxwell Scott in *The Man Who Shot Liberty Valance*

The line rang, and a woman answered.

"Hello, Justice Stevens's office," she said.

I introduced myself as a reporter for the *Chicago Tribune*. I told her that I was planning to be in Washington, DC, and wanted to set up an interview with US Supreme Court Justice John Paul Stevens. "I'd like to talk to him about Babe Ruth's Called Shot homer. The justice was at the game."

"This is about . . . what?" she asked.

It wasn't exactly a usual request that comes in to the office of a Supreme Court justice. I almost expected her, confused, to ask, "Who is Babe Ruth?" Her patience was quickly wearing thin, so I made a final pitch.

"The justice is very busy," she said dismissively. "I'll forward your request to him, but I wouldn't expect anything." The justice rarely grants interviews, so she no doubt thought there was no way I'd get an audience with him. I had a feeling otherwise.

US Supreme Court Justice John Paul Stevens, pictured here in 1976, was only 12 years old when he attended Game Three of the 1932 World Series. "It was quite a day," he said.

Sure enough, my phone rang a few days later.

"Yes, you have an interview with Justice Stevens on September 22 at 1:30 p.m.," his assistant said.

Smartly, I refrained from saying, "I told you so."

It didn't surprise me that Stevens wanted to talk. Several times during my years at the *Chicago Tribune*, I ventured to Capitol Hill to meet with senators and representatives about sports-related subjects. They were always willing to talk. Sports offers them a welcome diversion from the daily grind of running the country. They also like the idea of their names attached to sports stories. I figured Justice Stevens wouldn't be any different. He may not extend himself to discuss his views on court matters, but talking about witnessing Ruth's most famous homer firsthand? Of course.

Historians cling to eyewitnesses as events drift farther into the distance. Those observers offer a living connection to moments in time that become immortal—transformed into myth, if you will—by their magnitude. Listening to each story, we grab hold of each word as a bridge that transports us over the chasm from the past to the present. On a bright September day in 2008, Justice Stevens, then 88, was offered a bridge to one of the most vaunted and debated moments in sports history: the Babe Ruth Called Shot homer.

At the appointed time I was ushered into the justice's chambers. You never know what to expect when you meet someone of Stevens's magnitude, but there was a decent chance the justice was anticipating our meeting as much as I was, Babe Ruth our common denominator. Stevens greeted me warmly. For all the public formality of the nation's highest court, I was struck immediately by what I didn't see. Stevens wasn't wearing his trademark bow tie. Instead, he sported an open-collar blue shirt.

During the course of the interview, Stevens pulled out a Cubs bow tie. "My clerks gave it to me, and I wore it to a Chicago Bar Association meeting," said the Chicago native and lifelong Cubs fan. "I'm very proud of it. The funny thing is, most of the people I shook hands with were Sox fans—but there were enough Cubs fans, too."

Artist Robert Thorn left no room for debate in his rendition of the Called Shot.
Note the lemon in the foreground on the left.
IMAGE COURTESY OF NATIONAL BASEBALL HALL OF FAME LIBRARY, COOPERSTOWN, NEW YORK

For all that he has achieved in his life, Justice Stevens ranks throwing out the first pitch at a Cubs game among his biggest thrills. The stately justice walked to the mound wearing a Cubs jersey with pride. "I have a lot of grandchildren in Chicago, and they were all at the ballpark. On that day I was really a hero."

A putter and a wedge sat in the corner of his chambers. On his desk lay a bag decorated with the logos of all the Major League Baseball teams. "Do you have souvenirs in there?" I asked, thinking it might contain the bounty from a recent visit to a Washington Nationals game.

"No," he said. "My wife brought me over my lunch."

There's something refreshing in knowing that even a Supreme Court justice brown bags it—even MLB bags it.

Stevens actually had a formal brush with Major League Baseball. In the 1960s he represented Charlie O. Finley when the legendary A's owner moved the team from Kansas City to Oakland. Dealing with the mercurial owner never proved a dull experience. "He was a character," Stevens said, "a very interesting guy. He did some dumb things from time to time. We had our share of difficult moments. However, he was a man of his word. If he said he was going to do something, he did it. I enjoyed working with him."

Stevens devoted a corner of his chambers to sports memorabilia. He showed a signed picture from Michael Jordan as well as a signed photo of Casey Martin, the golfer with a severe leg ailment that prevented him from walking the course. Martin sued the PGA Tour for the right to use a cart in tournaments, and the case went all the way to the Supreme Court. Martin prevailed in a 7–2 decision.

"I wrote the opinion," Stevens said. "It was an easy call."

But it was a drawing depicting Ruth that formed the centerpiece of the collection, his right arm extended, two fingers pointing into the distance.

"It was quite a day," Stevens said.

These are the facts. On October 1, 1932, the New York Yankees and the Chicago Cubs played Game Three of the World Series at Wrigley Field. In the fifth inning Ruth at the plate faced the Cubs' Charlie Root, two strikes on him. Ruth, jawing with the Cubs dugout, held out two fingers. Ruth sent the next pitch soaring toward Lake Michigan. The ball whizzed just to the right of what now would be the iconic scoreboard in center field. The "Ruthian" blow, if ever there was one, traveled nearly 500 feet.

No one disputes that he hit one of the most majestic homers in World Series history. But the question is this: Did he call the shot, or was he merely gesturing in response to the Cubs bench jockeys? It remains one of the greatest debates in sports history, holding us captive as only Ruth can. Sports historians continue to look for clues that might reveal a true answer. From the moment it happened, opinions polarized.

"The more interesting angle is not what happened on the field," said John Thorn, official historian for Major League Baseball. "Rather, it's why do we care about it so much, and why has it produced so many co-conspirators who want to keep it alive?"

The incident provides a unique snapshot into the role that sports played during the Great Depression and the lengths to which the hungry and emerging sports media wanted to serve the country a legend of mythic proportions. None came bigger than Ruth. Nearly 80 years later, few people remain living who attended that game—let alone a Supreme Court justice. Stevens scores on both fronts.

His eyes brightened as he recounted a love affair with baseball that dates back more than three-quarters of a century. Born in 1920 to a wealthy family in Chicago (his father owned two hotels), he attended his first baseball game in 1929. It was Game One of the World Series between the Cubs and the Philadelphia Athletics. Sitting behind home plate, the nine-year-old had high expectations for his team. However, in the first of a lifetime of disappointments handed out by his favorite team, he watched Howard Ehmke, a surprise starter for the A's, strike out 13 Cubs in a 3–1 victory. "He threw a nothing ball up there," Stevens said. "My heroes struck out one after another. It was the saddest day of my life."

In 1932 Stevens attended another World Series game at Wrigley Field. Just over four decades later, President Ford appointed Stevens to the highest court in the land. He served during the administrations of seven presidents and under three Supreme Court chief justices. He ruled on cases that have altered and shaped the fabric of America. Yet witnessing the Called Shot clearly ranks as one of the great moments in his life. It appears in all the biographies of the justice. When *60 Minutes* profiled him as he stepped down from the Supreme Court in 2010, they recorded part of the interview at Wrigley Field, and Stevens talked about the homer.

In my interview Stevens went back in time, recalling when, as a 12-year-old boy, he thrilled at walking into the park with the other 50,000 people there that day. Not only was he seeing his team in a World Series again, it also was the first time he ever saw the Great Babe Ruth. "There was no television back then," Stevens observed. "You were able to listen to the games only on the radio, so to see this larger-than-life character for the first time made quite an impression on me."

Stevens sat in a box seat behind third base, overlooking the Cubs dugout. He heard the catcalls from the stands when Ruth stepped up to the plate in the first inning. Ruth immediately answered with a long, three-run homer to give the Yankees a quick 3–0 lead. That set the stage for what took place in the fifth inning. Looking back more than three-quarters of a century later, Stevens said, "You wonder what really happened, or is it the memories of your memories? I do have a clear recollection."

He continued, "During the game [Cubs pitcher] Guy Bush was razzing him. He and Ruth were in some kind of discussion back and forth. I heard years later it was over the Cubs being tightfisted and not giving a full share to Mark Koenig [former Yankee teammate who played for the Cubs in 1932]. I do remember Bush came out of the dugout and engaged in a colloquy with him."

"Colloquy"—now there's a colorful word that only a Supreme Court justice would use to describe the trash talking.

Ruth hit left-handed, so Stevens, sitting in a box seat along the third baseline, had a clear view of the man at the plate. He could see into his eyes and try to read his lips. "My interpretation was that he was responding to what Bush was saying. He definitely pointed toward center field. My interpretation always was, 'I'm going to knock you to the moon.'"

Stevens laughed. "That was a kid's reaction," he said.

So did it happen? According to a man who has sat on the highest court in the land adjudicating matters of national importance for decades, did Ruth call his shot?

"He definitely was arguing," Stevens said. "He definitely did point to something. I have no idea what he said or his motivation."

A diplomatic answer—but Stevens was more emphatic about Ruth's intentions to CBS's Scott Pelley than he was during my interview.

STEVENS: He took the bat in his right hand and pointed it right at the center field stands, and then of course the next pitch he hit a home run to center field. There's no doubt about the fact that he did point before he hit the ball.

PELLEY: So the Called Shot actually happened?

STEVENS: There's no doubt about that.

PELLEY: That's your ruling?

STEVENS: That's my ruling.

PELLEY: Case closed.

STEVENS: That's one ruling I will not be reversed on.

Undoubtedly, the glare of the camera's eye in a nationally televised interview prompted Stevens to be more dramatic in his assessment. He couldn't very well sit in Wrigley Field with *60 Minutes* and say he had no idea of Ruth's motivation, as he told me in his chambers. But it is telling that a sitting Supreme Court justice still gets caught up in the moment even years later.

There would be no doubt if the Called Shot occurred today. Television cameras and microphones would capture it from every angle. An on-field reporter would fill the telecast with exactly what was said during the exchange. After the game Ruth would sit behind microphones and answer repeated questions about the incident from a pack of reporters. His words would be carried live on ESPN, Fox, the YES Network, the MLB Network, WGN, and countless other outlets. In minutes the Internet would fill with accounts and analyses of what happened in the fifth inning of Game Three. Bloggers and Twitter would have exploded with commentary the moment the ball came crashing off Ruth's bat.

But none of that existed in 1932. Radio carried the game, but back then the play-by-play men delivered more or less a meat-and-potatoes account. There was no such thing as a color man providing analysis.

Fans in the stands that day did take amateur videos. Discovered years later with much fanfare, the grainy footage provides a different view than the newsreel cameras that missed the exchange between Ruth and the Cubs bench. However, that footage still can't provide definitive answers.

Many newspaper accounts initially made no mention of Ruth's so-called dramatic gesture. Grantland Rice perhaps the most famous sportswriter ever and certainly the poet of sports for several generations— omitted the detail of Ruth calling the shot in his first story about the game. In a second-day column Rice gave an embellished version of Ruth's feats. It's also quite possible that a headline in the *New York World-Telegram*, which ran on the same day as the game, helped give the story some traction: RUTH CALLS SHOT AS HE PUTS HOME RUN NO. 2 IN SIDE POCKET. It wasn't long before the story took on a life of its own.

The Called Shot homer occurred during a time when both baseball and the country were in transition. Ruth's great career was nearing an end. The Yankees no longer ranked as the dominant team in baseball. Indeed, the Athletics had won two of the three previous World Series titles. Ruth wasn't even the game's most feared slugger. Jimmie Foxx and Lou Gehrig did more damage at the plate. Baseball also struggled to maintain its standing during the height of the Great Depression. The game remained the most popular sport in the land, true, but, with so many unemployed, many fans could no longer afford to see games. Attendance sank, and teams cut back. Even Ruth, who hit .373 with 46 homers and 163 RBIs in 1931—incredible numbers in any era—suffered the indignity of a pay cut going into 1932.

The economic outlook was bleak, and the prospect for change in the White House loomed during the 1932 World Series. In a few short weeks, Herbert Hoover faced a challenge from Democrat Franklin Roosevelt. As fate had it, Roosevelt was in Chicago and had a private box for Game Three. No stranger to a good political scuffle, he was thoroughly engulfed in watching this real-life drama play out before him. When Ruth hit the homer, the future president let out a hearty laugh, savoring every minute of the show.

It was Ruth's final moment of greatness on the game's biggest stage. The homer was his 15th and last in a World Series. It also was his most memorable. Ultimately, the entire incident has fallen to interpretation, with both sides weighing in. For his part, Ruth only added to the mystery with his post-homer reactions. Initially he said he wasn't pointing to any particular spot. Knowing how the story could augment his legend, however, Ruth eventually played up the tale. He ended a detailed account of how he pointed by saying, "Well, the good Lord must have been with me."

True sports heroes are often recalled for that one perfect moment when all their talents coalesce in one tremendous burst of agility. Ted Williams went six for eight to secure his batting average over .400 in a season-ending doubleheader in 1941. Sandy Koufax threw a perfect game against the Cubs in 1965. Reggie Jackson launched three homers on three pitches during Game Six of the 1977 World Series. In other sports, Michael Jordan had his shot against Utah in the 1998 NBA Finals. Dwight Clark's famous catch of a Joe Montana throw propelled San Francisco to Super Bowl XVI. The mighty Secretariat defied reality, flying down the homestretch at the Belmont. Ruth gave Hank Aaron his iconic snapshot when the Braves star hit 715.

But of all the homers that Ruth hit, only one lives on in sports eternity. The Called Shot remains the defining moment in an incredible career. Ask most people what comes to mind when they think of the Babe, and most will raise an arm and point into the distance as if to a center field fence 400 feet away.

Indeed, set aside the debate over Ruth's intentions that day, and most people believe that, if one person in the history of baseball could have the audacity to point to center field and deliver on the next pitch, it was the Bambino. When Ruth walked to the plate, anticipation hung in the air that something big, maybe even magical, was about to occur. Ruth knew it. He recognized his role as a public entertainer and understood it well.

In the 1946 World Series, the Cardinals made a radical infield shift against Ted Williams. "They did that to me in the American League one year," Ruth told columnist Frank Graham. "I could have hit .600 that year slicing singles to left."

"Why didn't you?" Graham asked.

"That wasn't what the fans came out to see."

Robert Creamer was one of those fans. Like Stevens, he was a young boy discovering his love for baseball in the '30s. He later wrote the first definitive biography of Ruth, *Babe*, detailing his off-the-field excesses with women and booze. But those antics held no meaning to the young Creamer when he visited Yankee Stadium for the first time.

> *I saw Babe play at least one game in 1932, 1933, and 1934, his last three seasons with the Yankees, and each time I saw him hit a home run (a couple of times it was a doubleheader and he hit a homer in one of the games, but he hit one). In short, I have the thrill of remembering what a Ruthian homer looked like up close—simply gorgeous. That beautiful swing and Ruth's big face looking up watching it go as he starts to run. And the ball, already enormously high in the air as it floated past the infield. I mean, I saw Babe Ruth hit home runs.*

Even Ruth's statistics reach almost mythical proportions and perhaps even more so given when he played. When he retired with 714 homers—one of the most recognizable numbers in sports—his deputy on the list, Lou Gehrig, had yet to reach the 400 mark. Thanks to Ruth, the home run was just coming into vogue in the 1920s. He had seasons in which his mark for homers as an individual outnumbered the entire total of some teams.

Ruth once scored 177 runs in a single season, more than 1 run per game. In 1923 he had an on-base percentage of .545, and his career OBP was .474. That means he reached base nearly half the time he stood at the plate. For a slugger who often swung from the heels and went for the fences, remarkably he never had a season with 100 strikeouts.

Also consider this: His numbers would have been even more staggering had he not played his first four full seasons as a pitcher for the Boston Red Sox—and a good one at that. Ruth essentially accumulated his slugging statistics in 16 full seasons and part of 2 others as a hitter. Meanwhile, it took Hank Aaron 23 years to reach 755 homers, and Barry Bonds needed 22 years and some extra assistance to get to 762. It's little wonder that teammate Joe Dugan once said of Ruth, "He wasn't human. He fell out of a tree."

Ruth's fellow players, even the future Hall of Famers among them, stood in awe of his achievements. Charlie Gehringer, the great Detroit Tigers second baseman, didn't think it right to shake hands with the slugger after he hit a homer in 1933 All-Star game. "We all kind of looked up to him, you know," Gehringer said. "I didn't know him well, had never played with him, never had much in common with him. Nobody had much in common with Ruth, I guess. Funny, it just didn't seem right to shake hands."

"Some 20 years ago, I stopped talking about the Babe for the simple reason that I realized that those who had never seen him didn't believe me," said Tommy Holmes, a longtime outfielder for the Boston Braves.

Legendary pitcher Dizzy Dean, hardly a shrinking violet as one of the game's great showmen, felt the same. "No one hit home runs the way Babe did. They were something special. They were like homing pigeons. The ball would leave the bat, pause briefly, suddenly gain its bearings, then take off for the stands."

Before Major League Baseball retired Jackie Robinson's number 42, Frank Crosetti, the Yankee shortstop in 1932, thought the game should have honored Ruth's number 3. "Babe did more for the game than anyone ever," Crosetti said. "The game was crooked in 1920, and he single-handedly saved it. Only one number should be retired, and no one should ever wear it for any team, Babe's number 3."

Yet Ruth's impact went far beyond the field. A New York sportswriter who traveled with the Yankees, Richards Vidmar witnessed his popularity. "If you weren't around in those days, I don't think you could appreciate what a figure Babe was. He was bigger than the president. One time, coming North, we stopped in a little town in Illinois, a whistle stop. It was about ten at night and raining like hell. The train stopped for ten minutes to get water. It couldn't have been a town of more than 5,000 people, and 4,000 of them were standing in the rain, just waiting to see Babe."

Former teammate and Hall of Fame pitcher Waite Hoyt had this wonderful assessment of Ruth: "He was one of a kind. If he had never played ball, if you had never heard of him, and passed him on Broadway, you'd turn around and look."

David Halberstam, a Babe Ruth of journalists, enjoyed the diversion of writing books about sports during his long career. In one chapter from *Everything They Had*, a collection of his shorter sports publications, he summed up the aura of Ruth thus:

No one signaled the coming of power quite like Babe Ruth. He changed the very nature of sports. He was five years old when the century began. Because his deeds were so awesome, particularly when measured against the existing dimensions of what passed for power, his name was almost immediately turned into an adjective. Long drives, more than half a century after he played his last game, are said to be Ruthian.

He was the perfect figure about whom to create a vast assortment of myths and legends, some of them true, some of them not, though it meant little if they were true or not, because the ones which

had been made up seemed just as true as those which could be more
readily documented.

On learning of Ruth's death in 1948, Red Smith, a legendary sports-writer in his own right, wrote with simple grace, "Now that Babe is gone, what's to be said that hasn't been said? Nothing, when you come down to it. Just that he was Babe Ruth. Which tells it all, for there never was another and never will be."

Justice Stevens is proud to have a link to this moment in sports his-tory. He displayed a framed scorecard from the game, positioned by the Called Shot drawing on his wall. James Marsh, "a fine lawyer from Phil-adelphia," sent it to him. Marsh had kept score while listening on the radio. When the lawyer read that Stevens attended the game, he wanted the justice to have his scorecard. "Funny thing about it, he mixed up the pitchers," Stevens said, pointing to the scorecard. "He had Root pitch-ing for the Yankees and George Pipgras for the Cubs." But the gaffe only enhanced the treasured souvenir in Stevens's eyes. It provides some authenticity, he said.

Stevens doesn't have his own scorecard from that game he attended when he was 12 years old. Instead, he has his memories of seeing the great Babe Ruth hit a homer that we're still discussing generations later. "There probably are a million people who say they were at that game," he said before leaning forward for emphasis. "But I know I was there."

BABE RUTH'S CALLED SHOT

ONE

Transition

I don't think [they] realized that I had matured, was finally a grown man with family responsibilities and not the pipe-smoking playboy [Yankees owner Jacob Ruppert and general manager Ed Barrow] had pulled the covers off in that hotel room in 1919.
                                   —BABE RUTH, *THE BABE RUTH STORY*

When the Yankees' train pulled out of St. Louis at the end of the 1928 season, Babe Ruth had no idea that he would play in only one more World Series and that his team would have to wait until 1932 to play another game in October.

As he took another wild swig of champagne—some of it actually reaching his mouth—he wasn't thinking about how his body was feeling the effects of age, not to mention his hard lifestyle. Other, younger players would eclipse him in power if not prestige. One of them, Lou Gehrig, played for his own team, and their relationship soon deteriorated over a perceived slight about daughters and mothers.

When he let out a roar to make his presence felt, Ruth wasn't thinking that he would remarry and live a more domesticated life with his

3

Babe Ruth ruling the roost in the Yankees dugout.

new wife and two daughters. He could still break loose every now and then when it came to women and booze, sure, but he started to travel in a slower lane. Perhaps in his mid-30s he finally was starting to grow up.

As he wrapped his arms around his diminutive boss, the Babe also couldn't have foreseen that his longtime manager, Miller Huggins, soon would die suddenly. The death of Huggins heralded the most painful and frustrating moments of Ruth's career: his unfulfilled dream of managing a Major League Baseball team.

When he downed his fourth sandwich in the last hour, Ruth didn't have a clue that major life changes lay just over the horizon—and why should he? The Babe ruled baseball and anything it touched. For all the talk to come about the Called Shot in 1932, his greatest overall World Series performance came in 1928. The Yankees won their second straight World Series with their second consecutive four-game sweep. This time it was the St. Louis Cardinals who fell victim to their strength. Ruth, one year removed from his 60-homer season in 1927, "slipped" to 54 homers in 1928. But in the series he savaged the Cardinals, going 10 for 16 (.625), saving the best for last. In the Yankees' 7–3 victory in Game Four, Ruth dazzled onlookers with three homers, including an eighth-inning blast off future Hall of Famer Grover "Pete" Alexander.

This second three-homer performance in a World Series game made for an astounding show. Ruth even threw in a little defense, making a spectacular running catch off future Hall of Famer Frankie Frisch. As was already their custom, the scribes in the press box fell over one another in the collective effort to give proper magnitude to Ruth's feats.

James Harrison of the *New York Times* wrote after Game Four:

> *If there was any lingering doubt, if anywhere in this broad land there were misguided souls who believed that Babe Ruth was not the great living ball player, they should have seen him today.*
>
> *They should have seen him, hooted, and hissed, come to the plate three times, twice against Wee Willie Sherdel and once against the*

great Pete Alexander, and send three mighty drive whistling over that right-field pavilion. . . .

It was thus that the world's series of 1928 passed into history—with Ruth triumphant, with Ruth rampant on a field of green, with Ruth again stranger than fiction and mightier than even his most fervent admirers had dreamed he would be.

Naturally Ruth stood at the center of the team's wild party on their train ride back to New York. Prohibition? Forget about it. Champagne, beer, and other spirits—both liquid and emotional—flowed in tribute to the Yankees' third title with Ruth. It was a wonderful time. He was the country's biggest sports star, adored by all. Meanwhile, the Roaring Twenties were motoring along at full force, oblivious to the economic crash lurking around the corner.

Indeed, 1929 proved momentous not only for the country but also for Ruth. The flush of a joyous off-season ended on January 11, 1929. A fire broke out at a house in Watertown, Massachusetts, just outside Boston. A woman died in the conflagration. Initial reports identified her as the wife of a dentist named Kindler. However, it soon came to light that the victim was actually Helen Ruth.

Ruth hadn't lived with his first wife for years; they had married in 1914. He wasn't much of a husband, though, taking full advantage of the spoils that fame brought him when it came to women. Jimmy Reese was one of Ruth's roommates. "Actually I roomed with his suitcase," said Reese in the oral history book *Baseball Chronicles*. "Babe was hardly ever in the room, unless it was to enjoy a woman or to come in to change his shirt." In the book Reese repeated a favorite story: "Babe used to light a 'victory cigar' after every successful coupling. One time, I went down to pick up the paper and have breakfast. When I came back a few hours later, Babe, with a girl in his bed, was crushing out his seventh stogie."

Perhaps, like everything else about Ruth, the truth had been embellished a bit, but it doesn't change the point: Babe didn't simply hit homers, and he didn't simply go to bed with a woman. Everything in his life, it seemed, happened on a grand scale. For example, everyone knew that Ruth and Helen had had a daughter together, Dorothy. But Dorothy's daughter, Linda Ruth Tosetti, has since said that her mother came from Ruth's union with another woman. Helen left Ruth because of his many infidelities and moved in with Edward Kindler.

Even so, Ruth took her death hard. Reporters crowded his home, and, eventually letting them in, he read from a statement: "My wife and I have not lived together for the last three years. During that time, I have seldom met with her. I've done all I can to comply with her wishes. Her death is a great shock to me." Reporters tried to press him, but Ruth, emotional, shut them down. "I won't answer any questions. I won't say anything more."

Despite not seeing his wife for several years, Ruth did attend her funeral, to which Lou Gehrig and Miller Huggins sent floral arrangements in condolence. Two of Ruth's friends also served as pallbearers.

Helen's death paved the way for Ruth to marry Claire Merritt Hodgson. They had met in 1923, becoming more steady acquaintances in 1926. She was a model from Georgia with a three-year-old daughter at the time. Ruth often went hunting with her brothers and grew close to their mother. In his autobiography Ruth wrote, "Claire had many things I did not possess: culture, background, good looks." The relationship also gave him the family he never had.

On April 17, 1929, Ruth and Claire married at St. Gregory the Great Church on West 90th Street in New York City. The ceremony took place at 5:45 a.m. in the hopes of avoiding a large crowd. Still, hundreds of fans gathered at the church. A year later, Ruth formally adopted Claire's daughter, Julia, and Claire did the same with Dorothy, his natural daughter. The newly blended family took up residence in an 11-room apartment on the seventh floor of 345 West 88th Street.

In her book *Babe Ruth: A Daughter's Portrait*, Julia writes of domestic tranquility. She describes Ruth making Egg in a Basket, his favorite breakfast: Butter a slice of bread, brown in it a frying pan, cut a hole in the middle, turn it over, drop an egg inside, fry the egg, and add some bologna to go with it. (No wonder Ruth struggled with his weight.) Julia also writes of the Ruth home: "Daddy enjoyed having a family, a real family, where the parents and their children loved each other and enjoyed each other. Our home was so unlike what he had experienced as a boy."

Claire had a calming effect on Ruth. She took control of his finances, giving him $50 checks whenever he wanted to go buy cigars. *Chicago Tribune* columnist Westbrook Pegler noticed the change.

> *He has thrown confetti money to the winds, and he has had moods of remorse and moral stock-taking when he resolved to mend his ways, save his money, and live a finer life.*
>
> *And now that the end of his personal boom is approaching he reveals a quality of common sense. For all his spending and nonsense, the Babe has amassed some assets. He also has the vitality to go on and on, and is, as the statesman would say, fundamentally sound.*

Claire also traveled with him on many of the Yankees' road trips. Fellow players who knew better still ribbed him about his wife's presence: "Having a hard time dodging those old phone calls?" they asked.

Ruth lay at the center of attention as he prepared for the start of the 1929 season. Despite another big year in 1928, speculation was swirling that Ruth might be headed for a downward slide. Joe Williams of the *New York World-Telegram* wrote:

> *Mr. Ruth has arrived at a critical stage of his career. Early next month he will be 35 years old. He has been in the big leagues since 1914.*
>
> *With a top-heavy body perched perilously on pipe-stem legs the Babe, flaunting training rules, scoffing at accepted standards of health preservation and burlesquing all the quaint laws of the game, has thundered on from one epochal baseball accomplishment to another—a human Niagara charting its own course. But the time will come when ever the roar of Niagara will drop to a thin whisper.*

Maybe this will be another great season for him, and maybe it won't. Personally, I'd say the odds are quite against him. When you're 35 in baseball, you're pretty old.

Ruth actually was 34 going into the 1929 season—only later was it discovered that he was born in 1895 rather than 1894—but the writers and everyone else had reason to wonder if the player's mid-30s would start his decline. He was getting heavier and slower. His weight crested above 240 pounds in the early '30s. The famed Yankees pinstripes weren't just a design feature—owner Jacob Ruppert added them because the vertical stripes made Ruth look thinner.

Still, the new season couldn't have started better for the Yankees. Rain delayed the opener on the day of Ruth's wedding to Claire, so in typical fashion he and his entourage partied long and hard. Also in typical fashion, it didn't affect Ruth the next day. In his first at bat, he hit a homer and dedicated it to his new wife.

The Yankees won 13 of their first 17 games, and it looked as if they were going to run away with their fourth straight American League pennant. Then they lost five games in a row in May. Ruth injured his wrist and developed a bad chest cold. He was admitted to the hospital for a day in early June, and rumors flew that he had had a heart attack.

Ruth missed several games in June and played in only 135 for the season, his lowest number since 1925. But fans could forget about the possibility that he was slowing down when it came to a bat in his hands. The Colossus of Clout still clubbed 46 homers alongside 154 RBIs and a .345 batting average. On August 11 Ruth hit his 500th career homer, putting him more than two-thirds of the way to reaching the legendary figure of 714 regular-season homers.

But none of that was good enough for the Yankees in 1929. They never fully meshed as a team, going 88–62, finishing 18 games behind the Philadelphia Athletics—and it was the Athletics, not the Yankees, who now ruled baseball. They came of age in 1929, winning 104 games en route to the first of two straight World Series titles and three consecutive

American League pennants. Like the Yankees, the Athletics were loaded. Their leader, catcher Mickey Cochrane, once had a dropkick of 52 yards for Boston University. A great athlete and a standout leader, he had the complete package. Cochrane's play inspired a father in Oklahoma in 1931 to name his newborn son after him: Mickey Mantle.

Outfielder Al Simmons was a hitter who traveled in the same stratosphere as Ruth and Gehrig. He topped Ruth with 157 RBIs in 1929. The attack then was fortified by Jimmie Foxx. Only 21, Foxx had his first big season in '29 with 33 homers and a .354 batting average—and that was just the start. In 1932 he was going to threaten Ruth's mark of 60 homers, falling just short with 58. Considered "the right-handed Babe Ruth," Foxx weighed in at a powerfully built 195 pounds. One sportswriter remarked, "Even his hair has muscles."

However, also like Ruth, Foxx was a free spender and enjoyed too much of the nightlife. He was a heavy drinker, and he and his wife ran through all of their money; they employed a butler even during the height of the Great Depression. Even though he finished with 534 career homers, the consensus held that he could have done better if he had taken proper care of himself.

Lefty Grove led the Athletics on the mound. The 300-game winner won 20 games in 1929, 28 in 1930, and 31 in 1931. Grove was a hard thrower who eventually learned how to pitch, but his biggest asset may have been his mean streak. One writer described Grove as being "crabby all the time." He no doubt led the league in ripped uniforms and kicked-over buckets of water in the dugout. Hitters, though, remained leery of digging in against him. A fierce competitor, he once hit a teammate in the back after the player landed a homer off him in an intrasquad game. "You didn't hit that one, did you, busher?" Grove snarled.

Philadelphia sportswriter Al Horwits, who covered those Athletics and Grove, said, "He could pitch. He could really burn them in. Jesus, he'd knock you down, throw at you, do anything."

But if anyone could tame Grove, it was Connie Mack. He was baseball's stately gentleman at a time when the game had more than its fair

Yankees owner Jacob Ruppert (left)—standing in the dugout next to Commis-
sioner Kenesaw Mountain Landis in April 1923—built a stadium for Ruth but
never let him manage the team.
PHOTO COURTESY OF THE LIBRARY OF CONGRESS

share of rough edges. With a managerial career that spanned an incredible 53 years, Mack called the shots until the age of 87. Yet he never wore a uniform in the dugout. Instead, he guided his teams in a suit while waving a scorecard. Mack put together two of the greatest dynasties in baseball history. Prior to the 1929–31 Athletics lineups, he oversaw a great run in Philadelphia from 1910 to 1914, winning four pennants in five years. But Mack proved a better manager than businessman. On both occasions he had to break up those clubs because of financial problems.

Mack had complete respect from his players, who called him "Mr. Mack." He also liked to play his hunches as a manager. In 1929 Horwits did a story on Mack for the *Saturday Evening Post*, part of which discussed his choice of Howard Ehmke to start Game One of the World Series against the Cubs. At 35 Ehmke was winding down his career, appearing in only 11 games in 1929. Yet Mack went with Ehmke over his ace, Grove.

In the story Horwits writes that Mack told Ehmke he was going to release him in late August. The pitcher started to cry. "I've never been on a pennant winner before. I always dreamed I could pitch in the World Series," Ehmke said.

"Do you think you could pitch in the World Series?" Mack asked.

"There's one good game left in this arm," Ehmke replied.

Sure enough, Ehmke mowed down the Cubs with a World Series record 13 strikeouts in Game One, ruining the first game ever seen by future Supreme Court justice John Paul Stevens.

Meanwhile, the 1929 season ended on a tragic note for the Yankees. Miller Huggins, the manager who had guided the Yankees to their three titles, was in poor shape throughout most of the season. On September 20 he was admitted to the hospital. He was diagnosed with erysipelas, a serious bacterial infection. He soon developed a high fever, and the situation deteriorated quickly. On September 25, 1929, Huggins died at the age of 50.

Huggins's death rocked baseball. The American League canceled its games the following day, and the viewing of his body drew thousands of fans. The Yankees were shocked. "I'll miss him more than anyone,"

Gehrig said. "Next to my father and mother, he was the best friend a boy could have. He taught me everything I know." Ruth also took Huggins's death hard. He joined the ranks of the players in the clubhouse sobbing when they learned the news. "You know what I thought of Miller Huggins, and you know what I owe to him."

Huggins had been his only manager since arriving in New York in 1920. During those early years, it fell to Huggins to try to tame the wild young slugger. Ruth often resisted his manager's discipline. Huggins— just 5-foot-5 and soft-spoken—didn't inspire much fear in Ruth. When Huggins died some speculated that his troubles with Ruth may have taken five years off his life. Nevertheless, in his autobiography, Ruth appreciated what Huggins did and meant for him: "We were a hard-boiled bunch, at least on the field. Most of us had our scraps with Hug. We had cursed him when he tried to harness our energies, and he had cursed us. We had scrapped, but we had played for him, played up to the hilt for him."

The unexpected development left the Yankees reeling and looking for a manager for the first time since 1918. General manager Ed Barrow wanted future Hall of Famer Eddie Collins, but Collins wasn't interested. Art Fletcher, a longtime coach for the Yankees, also declined an offer to run the team. Ruth, meanwhile, had the perfect candidate in mind: himself. Why not? After all, he had been playing in the big leagues since 1914. He knew the game as both hitter and pitcher. Also, let's not forget: He had led the Yankees to their greatest glory, winning pennants and World Series titles and filling Yankee Stadium, which became known as "the House That Ruth Built."

"Hey, what's the matter with me?" wrote Ruth in his autobiography. "I had been with the Yankees organization 10 years; had been in baseball for 16 years; knew baseball." Ruth also saw other big-name stars—Ty Cobb, Eddie Collins, Rogers Hornsby, George Sisler, Tris Speaker—taking advantage of opportunities to become player-managers. Who was the biggest star among them? It was Ruth by a mile, of course. "I felt I had a better knowledge of the game than almost all of them," Ruth wrote.

Surely Yankees owner Jacob "the Colonel" Ruppert owed him this opportunity. Managing a big-league squad was the only thing he hadn't done in baseball. Not only was he qualified, but the position would serve as a payback for all that he had done for the franchise. Ruth pleaded his case. "I told him I knew how to handle young pitchers because I had been one myself. I knew how to handle hitters because I was one myself."

Ruppert resisted the idea. All those years of flaunting the team rules when he was younger, requiring both owner and manager to discipline the slugger, were coming back to bite Ruth. Ruppert, with his German accent, always pronounced the Babe's last name "Root." In turning him down, the team owner uttered the famous line that dogged the slugger for the rest of his baseball career: "You can't manage yourself, Root. How do you expect to manage others?"

Ruth had a comeback, though. He wasn't a kid anymore. He was about to turn 35. He had a new wife and was raising two daughters. Ruth tried to convince Ruppert that he had matured. His wild days lay behind him. Besides, he reasoned, who else better to know whether one of the players was getting out of line. "I know every temptation that can come by any kid, and I know how to spot it in advance," he said. "If I didn't know how to handle myself, I wouldn't be playing today."

Ruppert said he would consider it, and Ruth walked out of the meeting thinking that he had a chance. It turns out that he had zero chance. Not only did Ruppert not select Ruth, but the owner further offended his star by not personally informing him. Ruth learned that Bob Shawkey had filled the position through the newspaper, which he promptly threw across the room. That wasn't the end of the matter, however. Ruth writes that he "extracted revenge" from Ruppert by demanding a big salary for 1930. Initially he asked for $100,000, eventually settling for a two-year deal at an unheard-of $160,000. He also informed Ruppert that he wouldn't be as available to play in exhibitions during the Yankees' off-days, another big revenue source for the team owner.

Shawkey, meanwhile, had the task of getting Ruth and the Yankees back to the World Series after a one-year absence. Acquired from the

Athletics in 1915, Shawkey was a fixture on the mound in New York. He had four 20-victory seasons in a career that saw him win 195 games. A hard-throwing right-hander, he once fanned 15 batters in a single game. Shawkey retired in 1927 to coach for the Yankees. He wasn't the first choice to replace Huggins, but his name fell higher on the wish list than Ruth's.

Shawkey was doomed from the beginning, though. The Yankees opened the season with five straight losses and dropped eight of their first ten. By the beginning of May, they already were seven games behind the first-place Athletics. Shawkey was floundering in his attempt to establish himself. At the end of May, he told his former teammate and future Hall of Famer Waite Hoyt, "You'll pitch the way I tell you to, or you won't pitch for me at all." Hoyt was traded to Cincinnati.

The Yankees did mount a surge in June and July, pulling to within one game of first. Ruth, at 35, continued to roll along with 49 homers, 153 RBIs, and a .359 batting average, but the Yankees sputtered during the second half of the season, finishing in third place behind Philadelphia and Washington. Shawkey paid the price. He was fired and eventually replaced by Joe McCarthy. Shawkey remained bitter about getting only one year to prove himself. He told Marty Appel, author of *Pinstripe Empire*, "I got screwed. They gave Huggins four years before he won his first pennant. They gave McCarthy two. Me, I had one year, and they fired me. I would have won in '31. I would have won all those pennants McCarthy won, and I'd still be going."

Shawkey's firing also proved to be another source of frustration and embarrassment for Ruth. Again, the slugger went to Ruppert, asking to be manager. He pleaded his case for a second time. "I don't think [they] realized that I had matured, was finally a grown man with family responsibilities and not the pipe-smoking playboy [Yankees owner Jacob Ruppert and general manager Ed Barrow] had pulled the covers off in that hotel room in 1919," Ruth wrote in his autobiography. Ruppert, though, recalled those moments and used them once again to deny Ruth the job. "He recited a long list of my early mistakes—he had somebody look them up—and at the end he shrugged. 'Under those circumstances, Root, how can I turn my team over to you?'"

Ruth believed that if McCarthy hadn't become available, he might have had a decent shot at the position. After leading the Cubs to the National League pennant in 1929, McCarthy was fired when the team came up short in 1930. Even so, Ruth wrote of yet another snub: "It still hurt," and that hurt lingered for the rest of his life. He desperately wanted to be a manager. Ruth wanted the authority. He wanted to show that he could be a leader of men.

But no one had faith in him to do so. In 1933 he fumed when the Washington Senators named Joe Cronin as a player-manager. Cronin was all of 26 years old. "It made me scratch my head and wonder if I'd ever be mature enough to become a manager," Ruth snarked. He also wrote that Detroit owner Frank Navin had asked if he might be interested in managing the Tigers after the 1934 season. Ruth said yes and asked if they could talk after he returned from a barnstorming commitment in Hawaii. Navin was put off by Ruth's inclination to honor his commitments. Instead, after spending $100,000 to buy Mickey Cochrane from Philadelphia, Navin made the catcher the new manager. "In looking back, I can't help but wonder whether those pennants would have gone to me instead of Mickey if I had run out of the first part of my Hawaiian contract," Ruth wrote.

Ruth was so desperate, he even signed with the lowly Boston Braves in 1935 because of a promise that he would become manager. He soon realized, though, that the Braves had no intention of letting him run their team. Jilted and with his skills totally gone, Ruth retired after playing only 28 games.

Even in retirement, while other former stars were tapped to become big-league managers, Ruth's phone never rang. The only offer he ever received was from Ruppert—to manage the Yankees' minor league team in Newark. So why didn't Ruppert give him the chance? Ruppert gave his thoughts on the matter to sportswriter Dan Daniel for an autobiography that never was finished.

Ruth could have remained with the Yankees forever. Even if I had any idea of letting him go, I could not have fought public opinion so strongly.

When Miller Huggins died in 1929, I did not make Ruth the manager because I felt as soon as he got the reins he would look for an easy seat on the bench and retire as a player. I know that when you make a great player a manager he gets lazy. You lose a great player and get an indifferent leader.

Later on, I asked Ruth to go to Newark and work into the trick of running a ballclub. But he unwisely refused, and then asked me to release him to the Boston club of the National League. That was the biggest mistake of Ruth's life. It was not my fault.

Given all the epic failures of managers in baseball history, it seems ludicrous in hindsight that Ruth never got the opportunity. He couldn't have done any worse, right? Just prior to his death in 2012, Robert Creamer addressed the issue in an interview. "I'll add that I think Ruth was unfairly judged," Creamer said.

No doubt he drank and caroused, but I can't see character resolutely determining a manager's odds for success. There have simply been too many exceptions to this throughout baseball history, the Boston Red Sox new hire Bobby Valentine only the latest example. In earlier years, John McGraw was a wild young manager with the New York Giants, Leo Durocher returned from a gambling-related ban to lead New York to multiple World Series, and Billy Martin won and drank everywhere he went. Even Casey Stengel told his players not to drink at the hotel bar "because that's where I do my drinking."

Although the one hole on his baseball résumé dogged him, Ruth certainly didn't let it affect his play on the field. He continued to astound. At the end of the 1930 season, he did something truly amazing, and it had nothing to do with his bat. In a meaningless late-September game against Boston, Ruth went to the mound for the first time since 1921. He had been quite the pitcher in his younger days, compiling a 65–33 record during a three-year stretch with the Red Sox. Who knows? He might have gone down as one of the best pitchers of all time. Now, age 35 and despite rarely throwing, Ruth went the distance in a 9–3 victory. He scattered 11 hits and started two double plays by handling hot smashes back to the mound. Ruth pitched in only one more game. At the end of the 1933 season, Ruth, 38, again went all nine in a victory over the Red Sox. However, he said he was "exhausted" at the end of the game and vowed never to pitch again.

iiiiiiiiiiiiiiiiiiiiiiiiiiiiiii

The Yankees, meanwhile, began 1931 with their third manager in three seasons. The team got off to another mediocre start and after late June never pulled within 10 games of the dominant Athletics, who won their third straight pennant with a 107–45 record. The Yankees did close with a 21–6 surge in September, lifting them to 94–59, good enough for second place. The strong finish gave the team some confidence going into the 1932 season.

Ruth spent the off-season making some instructional baseball movies in Hollywood and hunting in North Carolina. He enjoyed Christmas with his family. His daughter Julia said it was his favorite time of year. He would be 37 when he faced his first pitch in 1932. His skills definitely were eroding—yet neither he nor anyone else had any idea that the most memorable moment of his career was yet to come.

TWO

Depression

The lack of money gave the game a measure of intimacy, a kinship with the people that it hadn't had before and hasn't had since.

—ROBERT CREAMER, *BABE*

The Babe was angry. He paced around his hotel room in Florida, occasionally reaching for the glass of bourbon sitting on the table.

All winter, he had been fuming about the Yankees salary offer for 1932. Now spring training had begun. Ruth reported to camp, but he didn't have a signed contract.

"A pay cut?" he said repeatedly to his wife, Claire. "Can you believe the Colonel?"

This wasn't the first time that Ruth had bumped heads with Yankee owner Jacob Ruppert. Like Ruth, the Colonel was a compelling figure in his own right. Think of him as the original George Steinbrenner. He laid the foundation for the most successful franchise in sports history.

Surprised? Don't be. Ruppert's impact at large was greatly overlooked until 2012, when he finally was elected to the Baseball Hall of Fame on the pre-Integration ballot. Two other owners, Tom Yawkey of the Boston Red Sox and Charles Comiskey of the White Sox, had long since been enshrined despite having much less success than the Colonel—and Comiskey's record had the stain of the 1919 World Series, when the "Black Sox" revolted against him and threw the showdown. "We were surprised to learn Ruppert wasn't in," said former Yankees player and executive Bob Watson, a member of the 16-person election committee.

Ruppert, who never married, was a four-term congressman from New York, but people called him the Colonel because of a short stint he did in the National Guard. His family's brewing company fortune gave him the capital to purchase the Yankees in 1915 for $500,000. At the time, the team was a struggling franchise, placing a distant second to John McGraw and the Giants in New York. The Yankees hit rock bottom in 1912 with a last place finish and a .329 winning percentage—the worst in team history. They finished seventh in 1913 and better by one place in 1914.

Ruppert, though, had big aspirations, setting the tone for a future Yankees owner named Steinbrenner. Under Ruppert's watch the Yankees won seven World Series titles between 1923 and 1939. Ruppert relished the dominance, once saying a perfect day at the ballpark was "When the Yankees score eight runs in the first inning and slowly pull away." He had a keen attention to detail, which he believed mattered greatly. "He insisted that everything he possessed in the world would be clean and well groomed," said Yankees Hall of Fame pitcher Waite Hoyt. "He was the first owner to buy four sets of home uniforms and four sets of road uniforms and insisted that they be dry-cleaned every day so his team would look like champions."

Ruppert also was a shrewd marketer. He knew he needed a star to make his team succeed in New York. He landed the biggest when he spent $125,000 to buy Ruth from the Red Sox in 1920. Ruppert capitalized on Ruth's greatness to build Yankee Stadium, the premier palace in the game. With the Yankees attracting more than one million fans per year, he cleared in excess of $1 million in profits during the 1920s—even as the nation slipped inexorably into financial ruin. He was also a firm negotiator, limiting player payroll for a team of huge stars to $300,000 per season. As a result, he often battled Ruth over contracts and other issues.

They had an erratic relationship. Ruppert sought to rein in his wild superstar. He disliked Ruth's drinking and carousing during his early years with the team. Ruppert even went so far as to hire a private detective to follow Ruth and other Yankees players and report back on their activities on the road. When manager Miller Huggins fined Ruth $5,000 and suspended him for drinking and general carousing at the end of the 1925 season, Ruth tried to get Ruppert to overturn the punishment. Not relenting, the owner backed his manager, even though benching his biggest star was going to hurt him at the gate.

"It is up to him to see Huggins, admit his errors, and apologize for his hotheadedness. It is up to him to reinstate himself," Ruppert said. The Colonel never had complete trust in Ruth, ultimately denying him his dream job: managing the Yankees. The discord ultimately led to Ruppert releasing Ruth from his contract in 1935, at which point the star played out the remnants of his career with the hapless Boston Braves.

Yet despite their disagreements, down deep, the two men actually had a fondness for each other. Ruth once referred to Ruppert as his second father. The Colonel, as we know, always called his player "Root." In fact, legend has it that the only time he referred to him as "Babe" was during a visit the night before Ruppert died in 1939.

Even though his star player had generated millions for the Yankees, Ruppert the businessman did his best to limit Ruth's salary. Two years earlier, in 1930, Ruth had held out at the beginning of spring training. He wanted $100,000, an unprecedented amount at the time. Ruppert countered with $75,000. Ruth came down to $85,000 but wanted a three-year deal. Ruppert remained firm. Eventually, Ruth grew restless and signed a two-year deal for $80,000 per season. That salary was more than twice as much as the next highest player earned.

The newsreel cameras were summoned to record the historic agreement. Ruth and Ruppert, sitting at an umbrella table in front of the team's hotel in Florida, were all smiles as the slugger signed the contract.

Afterward, Ruth learned that he would be earning more money than President Hoover. Brash as always, he uttered this immortal line: "Why not? I had a better year than he did."

Indeed, Ruth, living the high life of riches and fame, was nearly oblivious to the Great Depression. During the Babe's holdout in 1930, noted New York columnist Dan Daniel chastised him. Running into Ruth in the lobby of the Florida hotel, he lectured the star, waving his hands: "Did you know that yesterday in Union Square there was a riot? People were rioting for bread. There's a Depression, and you're holding out for $85,000 per year while people are starving."

Daniel was referring to one of the frequent eruptions that had to be quelled by police in Union Square in 1930, which had become a gathering point for unemployed workers and homeless people, whose anger boiled over during those hard times. Shamed, Ruth bowed his head. "Nobody told me," he said. The image of hungry people didn't have a lasting impact on Ruth, though. While much of the country suffered, he continued to down the finest champagne—Prohibition be damned—and puff on expensive cigars. That's why Ruppert's contract offer for 1932, a mere one-year deal for $70,000, took him aback.

Ruppert wanted to slash Ruth's salary by $10,000 even though he was coming off a season in which he hit .373 with 46 homers and 163 RBIs at age 36. Lou Gehrig may have equaled Ruth in homers and had an American League record of 184 RBIs, but Ruth still commanded the show. The Yankees continued to play to the game's biggest crowds on the road. Fans came out to see Ruth work his magic with his huge 42-ounce bat. They arrived early to watch him take batting practice. Rapid fire, one after another, Ruth took those soft tosses and dented seats in the bleachers. Then during the game, everything stopped in the ballpark each time Ruth came to the plate. Even then crackled the anticipation of seeing a moment that you'd tell your grandchildren about a generation later. More often than not, the Babe delivered just that.

Ruth fumed at the audacity of Ruppert's offer. He wanted another two-year contract at $80,000 per. When told times were tough, he snorted, "I haven't noticed the Yankees in any Depression." But by 1932 everybody in baseball, including the Yankees, was falling prey to the worst economic crisis in US history.

Life in America hadn't been the same since late October 1929. Just two weeks after the Philadelphia Athletics closed out the Chicago Cubs to win the World Series, the stock market crashed hard. In an instant the country plunged into unthinkable suffering and despair.

Baseball had been riding high when the Great Depression began. Back then, the Major Leagues consisted of two eight-team leagues. Only five teams had their towns to themselves: those in Cincinnati, Cleveland, Detroit, Pittsburgh, and Washington. New York, then with a population of seven million people, had three teams: the Yankees, Giants, and Dodgers. The jet age hadn't yet taken off, so teams still traveled by train and went only as far west as St. Louis. Trains also connected fans to the game. Doors opened, and subways and elevated rail lines deposited a convoy of fans just a few feet from the gates.

Baseball held the country's complete attention. Pro football barely existed, and few took notice. Notre Dame and fabled coach Knute Rockne put college football on the sports fan's agenda, but that only happened a few Saturdays in the fall. Baseball dominated not only the nation's headlines but also the vernacular. When Franklin D. Roosevelt was elected president in 1932, he used a baseball analogy: "I have no intention of getting a hit every time I come to bat. I just hope to have a high batting average."

In 1929 chewing gum magnate William Wrigley estimated his Chicago Cubs to be worth $4 million. He paid the Boston Braves $200,000 for superstar second baseman Rogers Hornsby. Wrigley's investment paid off handsomely as the Cubs won the National League pennant and set a record attendance of 1.485 million butts in seats.

The good times continued into 1930 despite what had occurred in the stock market the previous October. The Major Leagues reached an all-time attendance record of 10.1 million people, and owners remained confident they would weather the economic storm. "Former business depressions have not hurt baseball," said Detroit Tigers owner Frank Navin. "I do not think the present depression will materially affect attendance this year."

Either Navin was naive or, like Ruth and others, insulated against the worst of it, he had no idea of what was taking place around him. Total national income fell from $82.69 billion in 1929 to $41 billion in 1932—a decline of just over half. As the 1932 season was about to open, America, with its population of 122 million people, had as many as 20 million people without jobs, an unemployment rate of about 15 percent. Families and towns were devastated. For many, life became a matter of day-to-day survival. By 1931 New York hospitals were reporting many cases of malnutrition and even starvation.

In 1932 a housewife paid 65 cents for 24.5 pounds of Gold Medal flour; select corned beef was 12 cents per pound; a carton of Lucky Strikes cost $1.35. A month's rent at a downtown hotel set guests back $65, and a full dinner at Gimbels weighed in at 65 cents. Decades of inflation may make those numbers seem trivial now, but few people could afford such extravagances.

The full weight of the Great Depression did descend on Major League Baseball. Ticket prices typically ranged from 50 cents for the bleachers to between $1.50 and $1.75 for box seats, but very few people could afford the cost. The Yankees offered 20,000 cheap seats in an effort to stem the erosion in the box office. It didn't work. League-wide attendance dropped to 6.9 million by 1932 and then fell by another 600,000 in 1933, a decline of 40 percent from 1930. After drawing 1.169 million fans in 1930, the Yankees wouldn't crest above the 1 million mark again until the year after World War II ended.

But business for the Yankees was booming as compared to other teams. Connie Mack's Athletics, winners of back-to-back World Series titles in 1929 and 1930, saw attendance decline by 35 percent in 1931. It got so bad, in fact, that Mack began to break up one of the great teams of all time in 1933 because he couldn't afford to pay the salaries of his stars. He sold Al Simmons to the White Sox; Mickey Cochrane went to Detroit, and Jimmie Foxx and Lefty Grove wound up in Boston. Mack always saw baseball as a business first. In the 1920s he once said, "It is more profitable for me to have a team that is in contention for most of the season but finishes about fourth. A team like that will draw well enough during the first part of the season to show a profit for the year, and you don't have to give the players raises when they don't win." But after dismantling the Athletics powerhouse, Mack later admitted, "It has hurt me worse to break up my great teams than it has the fans."

In St. Louis the situation also looked bleak. The Cardinals, winners of the 1931 World Series, drew only 330,000 fans in 1932. That wasn't the worst of it, either. One year later, the American League St. Louis Browns attracted only 88,000 people for the entire 1933 season.

For those who could afford a ticket, baseball served as an escape. Longtime New York baseball fan Ray Robinson recalled in a 2009 interview that going to the ballpark took on an additional meaning during the Great Depression. "Like many recreational activities, people did go to the ballpark to get away from the economic horrors of empty wallets and ice boxes. I was very aware of the guys selling apples on street corners for a nickel. Along the Hudson River, you had some of these guys living in ramshackle huts in rags. So going to the ballpark was a big thing."

An Associated Press writer even suggested that people would buy tickets to the A's–Cardinals World Series in 1931 and "forego necessaries merely to experience the joy derived from a seat in the grandstand when the umpire calls 'Play ball.'" Some people did, but plenty of others didn't. Only 20,805 fans gathered in Sportsman's Park to watch the Cardinals win the title in Game Six.

Team owners knew they had to take measures to stanch the fiscal bleeding. They enjoyed overall profits of $1.35 million in 1929. By 1932 the Cubs and the Yankees were the only teams making any money, and both fell into the red the following year. The situation got so bad that Hoover stopped going to the ballpark after Philadelphia fans booed him when he showed up for a World Series game.

Owners met at the Drake Hotel in Chicago in the winter of 1931. As they gathered in lavish conference rooms with ornate light fixtures gleaming off the ceiling, the stewards of baseball targeted their number one expense: player payroll. First they decided to trim rosters from 25 to 23 players, eliminating 32 jobs at the big-league level. Then they sought to slash player salaries.

Washington Senators owner Clark Griffith, who two years later had to sell his star shortstop and son-in-law Joe Cronin to Boston, summed up the feeling of his fraternity: "The ballplayer alone has not felt the Depression." *Baseball* magazine editor F. C. Lane wrote, "This is the end of the golden age of inflated player income. When gigantic corporations everywhere are cutting salaries, baseball players can no longer look for immunity."

Eventually, most players saw their salaries cut by 25 percent or more. The average salary dropped from $7,500 to $5,000 in 1932. Brooklyn Dodgers pitcher Elbie Fletcher said that players had no choice but to accept the hard line from the owners. The reserve clause—standard in all contracts—bound the players and essentially meant that they remained the team's property for as long as it wanted. The Supreme Court further strengthened owners' hold on players when it ruled in 1922 that baseball wasn't violating antitrust laws. It wasn't until 1976 that players won the freedom of free agency, allowing each to play out his contract and sign with the team of his choice.

"They used to tell you what you were going to make," Fletcher said. "If you didn't like it, stay home. What the hell else could you do?" Veteran Philadelphia sportswriter Al Horwits sympathized with the situation. "Players were underpaid, and most of them were pushed around. They could be traded without notice and had to pay for their own travel expenses."

But no one else was about to shed a tear for the players. Average wages for the entire country fell by half. The players still had jobs, and a $3,000 sports salary was double what the typical industrial worker earned. Yankees pitcher Charlie Devens recalled, "With my salary and winner's share in the World Series, it amounted to about $10,000. That was the depths of the Depression. I thought I was the richest man in the world, and I think I damn near was."

The players understandably did everything in their power to keep those jobs. That often meant playing hurt. Detroit Tigers shortstop Billy Rogell once played on a broken leg. "In those days, you didn't want to get out of the lineup," he said. "Somebody might take your job."

Going beyond accidental injuries, baseball in the 1930s was often a rough and nasty undertaking, especially for young players trying to break into it. Future Hall of Famer Billy Herman recalled the initiation he received when he broke in with the Cubs in 1931. In his first game he faced Si Johnson, a pitcher who didn't like rookies. "My first time at-bat, I drove a single through the box," Herman said. "My next time up, he came right at me. I mean *right* at me. He threw a high fastball at my ear. *BAM*. I went down, and they carried me off the field, unconscious. I played the next day but didn't get any hits."

Three days later, the Cubs played the Reds again, in Cincinnati. "I faced Johnson again and went 3 for 3," Herman said. "He came in on each at-bat, but I guess I earned his respect by taking one in the ear, so he didn't hit me that day. He hit me later on, though."

Herman wasn't complaining, though. That's the way the game was played, he said. "There wasn't much comedy back then. We were serious; no wisecracks. We wouldn't look at or talk to anybody on the other team. It was all part of the game . . . tough. You ran out to center field; you slid hard."

Indeed, playing baseball made for a good life compared to the hardships endured by so many Americans. Lloyd Waner and Paul Waner were the best brother team in history. Growing up on a farm in Oklahoma, they both went on to have careers that landed them in the Hall of Fame. While playing for Pittsburgh in 1932, they lived in nice hotels and had first-class accommodations while traveling on trains during the season. It was easy to lose sight of all the suffering. However, in the off-season, when the Waner brothers returned to their home state, now a grief-ridden dust bowl, they saw the stark reality of the Great

Depression. "It made us realize how bad things were," Lloyd said. "The farms were abandoned, and the owners off to Lord knew where. Stores that had been doing business in the spring were boarded up. People were glum and poor. That was the real world."

The Depression forced baseball to react. The hard times sparked an era of unprecedented innovation in the game. Teams had to come up with new ideas—out of the box—in an effort just to survive in the years to come. Cubs president William Veeck wanted to exploit the new medium of radio. He placed Cubs games on four different stations in Chicago. Other owners in the 1930s didn't exactly embrace Veeck's idea with open arms, though. They argued that people wouldn't pay to go to the games in person if they could follow them for free by listening on a radio. "Colonel" Ruppert placed himself among the most vocal of opponents. He even banned the visiting teams in Yankee Stadium from broadcasting games back to their hometowns.

"Giving our details of games over the air to thousands of fans who would otherwise pay admission is a menace to the national game," Ruppert said. "All of the clubs in both leagues have invested heavily in real estate and in construction of modern ball parks. They are, like myself, battling with the times. Some of them must economize, which means reductions in salaries and other overhead expense. Now can you understand why club owners who want to save money are willing to let broadcasters give away their business for nothing?"

Veeck countered that just the opposite would occur. Fans would form a deeper connection to the team, making them more excited about taking a trip to the park. "Increased attendance, even in Depression times, reflects its value," he said.

Then came the first All-Star game, played in Chicago's Comiskey Park in 1933. Conceived as a onetime exhibition, the game proved to be such a big success that it became an annual fixture on the baseball calendar. Fittingly, Ruth hit the first homer in All-Star history.

The early 1930s also saw minor league teams experimenting with lights for night games. Again, tradition-bound owners scoffed at the idea.

Baseball, they maintained, was meant to be played during the day. Besides, who would want to go to a game in the evening?

Larry MacPhail, though, never went by convention. The general manager of the Cincinnati Reds thought night baseball would make it easier for fans to attend games. After all, most people worked during the day, didn't they? MacPhail had lights installed in Crosley Field, and on May 24, 1935, they lit up for a game against Brooklyn. The first night game attracted more than 20,000 fans, the biggest in years for the struggling Reds. Other owners took notice, and soon night games became the norm in baseball.

The one move the owners didn't make, however, was integrating the game. Baseball remained all white until Jackie Robinson made his debut in 1947. For their part, the Negro Leagues flourished, playing to occasionally big crowds during the 1930s. More than 50,000 fans once jammed Comiskey Park to see stars such as Satchel Paige and Josh Gibson, and no one could deny their immense talent. Like Ruth's Called Shot, tales of Paige's pinpoint control on the mound and Gibson's tape-measure power border on mythical as the stories are retold down the generations.

Those black players should have been playing alongside Ruth and Gehrig, and their exclusion was shameful. Yet the 1930s are regarded still as a terrific period for the Major Leagues. The decade featured huge stars and some of the most memorable baseball ever played. Other sluggers joined Ruth in thrilling the crowds with long homers. A fireplug at 5-foot-6 and 190 pounds, the Cubs' Hack Wilson hit 56 homers with 191 RBIs—still a baseball record—in 1930.

The entire National League hit .303 during the 1930 season. Bill Terry hit .401 for the Giants, becoming the last NL player to break the .400 mark. Several pitchers still managed to shine during the power barrage. Dizzy Dean made his debut in 1930 and soon became a master showman on the mound for the St. Louis Cardinals. The country boy from Arkansas liked to talk big. Once, he bet that he could strike out Joe DiMaggio's brother, Vince, four times in a game. After three strikeouts

Vince hit a pop-up to the catcher during his fourth trip to the plate. Wanting to win the bet, Dean yelled, "Drop it!" The catcher did, and Dean fanned DiMaggio for the fourth straight time. "It ain't braggin' if ya can back it up," said Dean, sounding very much like Ruth.

Dean became the big star on one of the most colorful teams in baseball history. The "Gashouse Gang" burst onto the scene by winning the 1931 World Series. A ragtag bunch, they often played in tobacco-stained, foul-smelling uniforms. Led by Pepper Martin, a wild and fearless runner on the base paths, the team from St. Louis quickly drew a huge national following.

Noted baseball writer Robert Creamer came to embrace the Cardinals growing up as a young boy in New York. "The Cardinals seemed to represent that era of Depression America," he wrote. "Henry Fonda as the undefeatable Tom Joad looked like a St. Louis Cardinal; lean; bony; hard; grim tight smile; defiance in adversity; spirit."

Creamer and his friends lived and breathed baseball. They played games for hours on end. They quickly wore out the ball, but nobody had the money to buy a replacement. Instead, the gang clanged down the stairs of somebody's cellar and wrapped the ball in black tape. Creamer said it eventually felt like "a chunk of cast iron."

Creamer also recalled running home after school in the early fall in anticipation of that day's World Series game. His mother turned on the radio prior to his arrival because it took so long for the machine to warm up. While he was listening to the game, out-of-work men knocked on their back door, looking to do any sort of odd job that might earn them some pocket change.

The entire dynamic produced an even tighter bond to baseball. "The lack of money gave the game a measure of intimacy, a kinship with the people that it hadn't had before and hasn't had since," Creamer wrote, and he was among the fans in the spring of 1932 who wondered when the Bambino was going to sign his contract.

The Colonel was standing firm. "Ruth hasn't a chance to get $80,000 in 1932 nor any other year in the future," Ruppert announced. "Never again will any player get that much money for a year's pay."

In the end Ruth had little choice. In the throes of the Great Depression, even the great Babe had to accept less money.

Ruth called Ruppert, and they agreed to meet at the Rolyat Hotel in St. Petersburg. They talked alone in front of a big fireplace, just the team owner and the superstar. Onlookers leaned in their direction in an attempt to catch a few words of their conversation. After 15 minutes the two men shook hands. Ruth agreed to a one-year deal for $75,000. The salary was more than double what any other player earned in the sport at that time. But there wasn't a player on the field who resented Ruth for making that kind of big money. They all recognized that he made them richer, too.

"You see, Ruth was one of the boys, but he knew he was great," said Yankees outfielder Ben Chapman. "A couple of times, he said to me, 'Chapman, if it wasn't for me, you wouldn't be making that lousy $5,000,' and he was right."

Summoned, the photographers had Ruth and Ruppert stand outside in front of a wishing well. Ruth pitched a coin into it and said, "I wish for another pennant so that I can play in 10 World Series." Ruppert, feeling the pinch of the Depression, dunked his coin in the water and said, "I wish I had the money in that well."

THREE

Motion Pictures

He had such a beautiful swing, he even looked good striking out.
—MARK KOENIG

When Babe Ruth finally arrived at spring training in 1932, he quickly made his presence known. Teammates greeted him with a loud chorus of "Babe!" as he entered the locker room. He shook hands with old friends and jabbed the needle at others. Infamous for not remembering anyone's name, he met both familiar faces and unfamiliar with his universal greeting of "Hey, keeed."

Ruth eventually settled in and started to put on his uniform. His teammates had a laugh when they saw him reach for his ever-present eye wash. "Babe had a superstition; he would always use this eyewash—it was called Eye-Lo—before every game," recalled shortstop Frank Crosetti. "He'd set it on the bench, and before his first at-bat he'd wash his eyes out. Usually he'd lose track of it, and part of his ritual was to say, 'Where's the Eye-Lo?' Someone would give it to him.

"Well, one day, [Tony] Lazzeri took the bottle, dumped it out, and filled it with water. Babe sees Lazzeri with the bottle and says, 'Gimme.'

Lazzeri says, 'No, gim*me*,' and proceeds to drink it. Babe is astonished. He says, 'Don't do that, it'll kill ya. Let me get you to a hospital.' But before he does anything, he goes for the Eye-Lo and washes his eyes out; he'd never vary from the routine."

Ruth eventually sauntered onto the field. At age 37 it took him much longer to feel loose and ready to play than it had when in his younger days he could stay out all night and still feel spry the next morning. Ruth was feeling anything but spry on this day. Gingerly taking a few practice swings, his bat felt like 42 pounds instead of 42 ounces. It also felt strange to put his hands on the bat. He hadn't touched one since the end of the 1931 season. His off-season exercise routine consisted of golf, hunting, and fishing, not swinging a bat.

A player's first workout hardly makes for much of an attraction—that is, unless his name is Babe Ruth. An estimated 5,000 fans showed up at Crescent Lake Park with nothing more on the agenda than watching Ruth take batting practice. But for those fans, a chance to see the great Bambino with a bat in his hand was more than enough.

Even after 18 years in the majors, the opening of a season required a reset of Ruth's brain. With everything feeling a bit more difficult than it had in the past, he had a brief moment in which he wondered whether he had crossed some threshold since his last game, leaving his skills on the other side. He faced nothing more intense than batting practice soft lobs, but his first few swings looked more like awkward lunges. He made weak contact, slapping a few grounders and barely piercing the damp March air with some feeble shallow flies.

Eventually, though, everything fell back into place. The old instincts rose up and locked into place. Ruth started to feel the pulse. The fans and even his own teammates stopped what they were doing to watch him put on his first show of the new season. He lofted a few balls deep over the fence, prompting everyone to use their mental calculators in an effort to gauge how far his shots had traveled.

It was a familiar scene to the people who watched Ruth perform his extraordinary feats on a daily basis. Even if you saw him only once, the memories of Ruth at the plate soon became indelible. "He had such a beautiful swing, he even looked good striking out," said Mark Koenig, the shortstop on the 1927 Yankees who eventually served as the catalyst for Ruth's Called Shot homer.

Yet those of us in later generations not fortunate enough to behold Ruth swing a bat have little idea of how he actually did it. We can visualize Carl Yastrzemski's distinctive stance, holding his bat up high. Who can forget Ernie Banks moving his fingers as if he were playing a piano while waiting for the pitch? A national television audience saw Hank Aaron hit number 715 in 1974, using those powerful wrists to pass Ruth's home run record.

But what did Ruth look like at the plate? How far did he stride? Did he hit off his front foot or back foot? Considering that he ranks as the greatest and most famous baseball player, it's somewhat remarkable that we have scant video footage of him. Old film clips appear grainy, often shot from a distance, and they hardly provide an appropriate perspective. Most avid fans can recite Ruth's core stats of 714 career homers, .342 career batting average, 60 homers in 1927—but few of us have a mental image of how he actually produced all of that magic. Indeed, it almost feels like he exists purely as a mythic figure, requiring people to use their imaginations to visualize him going deep, rather than someone who did so in front of millions of people.

Modern technology has opened a window onto the mystery of his magic if only just a little. Go to YouTube and type "Babe Ruth" in the video site's search engine, and several videos of the great slugger in action will appear. Many of them provide a closer look at how his natural gifts meshed in true baseball perfection. You can find one classic in which Ruth discusses his hitting philosophy—sort of. His business manager, Christy Walsh, arranged for Ruth to make some extra money by featuring him in a series of instructional films called *Play Ball with Babe Ruth*. The scripts had a kind of story line that required some acting skills on Ruth's part.

One of the more amusing videos features Ruth trying to teach members of a sorority how to play the game. After watching him hit a homer in a game, the girls in the stands call him over and ask if he will help them learn baseball.

"I've got to ask the manager," Ruth says before going over to his wife, Claire, who gives him the OK. She isn't about to leave Ruth alone with a bunch of sorority girls, however. During one of the "lessons," Ruth gets a bit too close while showing one of the girls how to hold the bat.

"Oh, Babe, don't you think the lady has the idea now?" Claire says perhaps a bit stereotypically but presciently, considering what we know now about Ruth's extracurricular activities.

Ruth is in his element in another film, the *Just Pals* short. In it kids swarm him when he arrives at an orphanage, a familiar place for him. He then serves as their umpire, working the game in his suit. One of the kids strikes out to end the game, incurring his teammates' wrath. The poor boy goes off and cries. Ruth, sensitive soul that he is, runs after the boy and brings him to the diamond for a baseball lesson and a heartwarming story of how he once struggled to find his swing.

Wearing a white baseball cap, Ruth begins the lesson by teaching the kid, of all things, how to bunt. "Bunting looks easy, but it is one of the hardest things to do correctly," he says. Ruth guides the youth's hands on the bat and taps out a bunt, even running out of the box. This is rare footage of Ruth laying down a bunt, although it wasn't uncommon to see him do so in a game. In 1930, when he hit 49 homers, Ruth racked up 21 sacrifice bunts. While it's mind-boggling to think that a manager would take the bat out of his hands, that's the way they played the game back then.

Ruth then tells the kid that there are two types of hitters: a choke hitter and a swing hitter. A choke hitter, he says, "swings flat-footed and just pokes at the ball." Ruth chokes up a few inches on the bat and slices at some balls.

Hardly a choke hitter himself, though, he tells the boy, "Swing hitting is the most popular style." He takes a few swings and knocks one over the fence. "Swing hitting depends on balance and timing," he teaches. "Note, the weight is on the left foot. As I start to swing, the weight shifts to the right foot."

Through the magic of Hollywood, the kid takes two swings and says, "I get it."

Next day, wouldn't you know it but the game comes down to Ruth's little protégé again. A teammate on the bench laments, "He'll just make another out."

Ruth encourages the boy, and sure enough he knocks it over everything. Ruth jumps out of his seat, shouting, "Look at it go!"

Meanwhile, the teammate who blasted him just a minute earlier says, "Didn't I tell you he can hit?"—clearly establishing himself as a future sportswriter.

If you examine it carefully, the video doesn't actually offer much detail on Ruth's philosophy of hitting. It's just generic advice: Shift your weight from the back foot to the front foot, and you, too, can homer like the Babe. If only it were that easy.

Ruth never articulated his approach to hitting in great detail. He once said that he emulated "Shoeless" Joe Jackson, the great hitting star disgraced in the Black Sox scandal. Perhaps—but it seems more likely that he simply relied on natural instincts and immense talents. He hardly was analytical about it elsewhere, either. "All I can tell them is pick a good one and sock it," Ruth once said. "I get back to the dugout, and they ask me what it was I hit, and I tell them I don't know except it looked good."

Then of course there's the classic quote on how to hit home runs: "I swing as hard as I can, and I try to swing right through the ball. . . . The harder you grip the bat, the more you can swing it through the ball, and the farther the ball will go. I swing big, with everything I've got. I hit big, or I miss big. I like to live as big as I can."

Clearly much more went into those 714 homers. Jaime Cevallos, a San Francisco Bay Area hitting instructor known as "the Swing Mechanic," broke down Ruth's swing from a video on YouTube. It features a rare slow-motion side view of Ruth at the plate with a camera angle similar to what you would see in today's video analysis of a hitter at work. Looking at his swing almost frame by frame provides a different perspective of his athleticism and raw power. "People often don't make the connection from great player to great swing," said Cevallos, who has worked with hitters at all levels, including several big leaguers.

As the video begins with Ruth's eyes focused on the pitcher, his stance is narrow, his feet almost touching. His weight leans to the left side. With his hands waist-high and close to his body, he's in a compact position. A modern comparison would be Ichiro Suzuki, who despite being a slap hitter can hit for power when needed.

In his first move or "forward swing," as Cevallos called it, Ruth takes a large stride with his front foot. The move creates tremendous momentum through his hips and core. The key, though, lies in his hands. They rise to just above shoulder level and push away from his body. According to Cevallos, this motion generates a tremendous amount of lag in his swing, allowing him to store up the energy that will be released on the ball.

Ruth keeps his back elbow bent as the rest of his body provides force and rotation. It's a key move. His "slot position" allows him to maximize his area of impact. "He centers the barrel for contact for a long distance," Cevallos said. "There's a large margin of error. It's twice as long as the regular hitter. His timing could be off a bit, and he still could square the bat to the ball."

Ruth's hands don't roll over. Cevallos pointed out that he's using his body to hit the ball by keeping his back arm bent. Then finally he snaps his front knee, whipping the bat through the zone. His weight moves completely to his front foot, with just the toes of his back foot meeting the ground. This stance runs counter to the prevalent hitting philosophy of staying back and firing from that position.

A couple of points stand out for Cevallos. While Ruth appears to have big, thick muscles, Cevallos believes he was very flexible, especially in his shoulders. That flexibility allowed him to achieve ideal angles and maintain them through the swing. Also, Ruth swung a heavy 42-ounce bat. Cevallos can't say for sure, but he theorized that the extra weight helped Ruth maintain better positions in his swing. In fact, he might have been prone to overswinging with a lighter bat.

When asked if he could improve one aspect of Ruth's swing, Cevallos indicated that it would be cutting down Ruth's stride. "I'd try to make it where he wasn't thrusting with so much weight going forward. He was out front for a lot of pitches. Maybe that was because of an overaggressive shift. In my eyes that's the only possible area where he could get better."

Then again, offering pointers to the Sultan of Swat would be like giving music advice to Mozart. Ruth was about as close to perfection as baseball has ever seen. How much better can it get than 714 homers and a .342 career batting average?

Cevallos said Ruth had the "best slot and impact position" of any player out there. It all adds up to "the best swing I've ever seen." How well would Ruth fare in today's game? Judging from what he saw on the video clip, Cevallos believes Ruth would torment pitchers in any era. "All the great hitters have the laws of physics working in their favor," Cevallos said. "Ruth had that. He had that consistency by having that slot position, by having the best impact position I've ever seen. You would have to think he would dominate today."

Beyond his pure physical strengths, Ruth also had superhuman hand-eye coordination, which he displayed even outside the baseball diamond. Bill Jenkinson, a baseball historian who has studied Ruth extensively, writes of Ruth on a hunting excursion. Alligators were the target, but the situation went amiss when, tables turned, his guide suddenly was attacked in the swamp by another kind of reptile.

While the others fled for their lives, Babe Ruth coolly raised his weapon and blew the head off the dangerous snake with a single shot. Nash [Ruth's guide] had hunted alligators for thirty-five years, claiming to have personally killed 2,000 of them, but had been rescued from disaster by a baseball icon. In fact, when the venturous foursome returned to dry land, [the guide] reported that Babe had bagged his 'gator with another single shot, this time with a direct hit through the left eye. During the hunt, Ruth had fired only three shots, but scored three bulls-eyes.

If Ruth were alive today, sports scientists would study him with the latest computers, metrics, and all sorts of other methods that would lead to increased understanding of his greatness. Ruth did submit himself to tests by the research laboratory of Columbia University's psychological department in 1921. Noted sportswriter Hugh S. Fullerton wrote about the findings in *Popular Science Monthly*. "They led Babe Ruth into the great laboratory of the university, figuratively took him apart, watched the wheels go round; analyzed his brain, his eyes, his ears, his muscles; studied how these worked together; reassembled him, and announced the exact reasons for his supremacy as a batter and a ball-player."

It was cutting edge back then, and the findings weren't surprising. Ruth's senses—especially his eyesight—ranked vastly superior to the norm. Fullerton wrote about a test in which a camera shutter "opened, winked, and closed at any desired speed." Cards placed behind the shutter were exposed to view for one fifty-thousandth of a second. When the cards marked with black dots were used, Ruth identified them correctly 12 of 13 times; the average was 8.

"The secret of Babe Ruth's ability to hit is clearly revealed in these tests," Fullerton wrote. "His eye, his ear, his brain, his nerves all function more rapidly than do those of the average person. Further the coordination between eye, ear, brain, and muscle is much nearer perfection than that of the normal healthy man." Tellingly, though, Fullerton made another more sociological observation: "If the results of these tests at Columbia are a revelation to us, who know Ruth as a fast thinking player, they must be infinitely more amazing to the person who only comes into contact with the big fellow off the diamond and finds him unresponsive and even slow when some non-professional topic is under discussion."

Indeed, the Columbia tests likely didn't mean much to Ruth. After all, he didn't use his brain for much else than baseball. Sportswriter Frank

Graham once wrote, "He was a simple man, in some ways a primitive man. He had little education and little need for what he had." All Ruth needed to know was how to hit a ball, and he did it better than anyone who played the game. That's why everyone in the park had locked onto Ruth on that warm March morning in 1932.

Ruth probably wasn't consciously aware of all the attention focused on him. It was part of his routine for nearly two decades. People watched; Ruth swung. Yet he likely had a sixth sense that told him that the curtain was up. Even in batting practice, Ruth always wanted to put on a show.

He took a few more swings, sending a handful of balls far beyond the outfield fence. When he had finished for the day, fans acknowledged him with polite applause as he walked back to the clubhouse. Ruth realized that it was just a start. He still had a long way to go to be ready. Still, he took heart knowing that he still had the swing at age 37. All the moving parts worked, and his natural instincts remained intact.

Opening day loomed just a few weeks away. The stage was being set for the greatest moment of Ruth's career.

Showtime.

FOUR

One Last Pennant

"Win as many games as you can by as many as you can."
—Sportswriter Tom Meany on the Yankees' strategy

The Called Shot almost didn't happen. If the timing had been different, Babe Ruth never would have made it to Wrigley Field for Game Three of the World Series.

As mid-September crawled along in 1932, Ruth wasn't capable of calling for a glass of water, much less calling a shot at Wrigley Field in a few weeks. At 37 he was starting to feel the effects of age. Twice during the season he had missed extended periods due to injuries. In July, trying to catch a fly ball, he tore a muscle in his leg and instantly fell in a heap. Carried off the field, he was out for two weeks. But that was nothing compared to what occurred one September day in Detroit. Ruth started to feel severe stomach pains. Traveling with his wife, Claire, Ruth quickly returned by train to New York City for treatment by his doctor.

"He was seized with pain," said team secretary Mark Roth.

Initially, it was feared that Ruth had developed appendicitis. Claire is even quoted in one story saying as much: "Oh yes, the pain he has suffered

Yankees manager Joe McCarthy (left, shaking hands with Bill Terry of the New York Giants in July 1937) had a cool relationship with Ruth.
PHOTO COURTESY OF THE LIBRARY OF CONGRESS

has been right there. It is appendicitis." Ice packs placed on Ruth's right side did little to alleviate his pain or high fever. "He did not rest at all last night," Claire said.

Ruth never underwent an operation, though. The exact nature of his ailment remains a mystery. Clearly, though, Ruth wasn't feeling good. With only three weeks left in the season, considerable doubt lingered about whether Ruth would be ready to play in the upcoming World Series. If it took place a few weeks later, he definitely would have to sit it out. Concern bubbled within the Yankees and among baseball fans all over the country.

General manager Ed Barrow tried to remain optimistic. He believed that baseball's most popular player "would stage his usual comeback" and appear in his 10th World Series. Ruth's ailment was the only obstacle in what otherwise had been an easy ride for the Yankees in 1932. The season offered a redemption of sorts for Ruth and his teammates. Across three long years they had watched Connie Mack's Athletics dominate with three straight American League pennants and two World Series titles. The Yankees and Ruth weren't used to playing second fiddle, nor did they like it. They went into the new season determined to regain their rightful place on baseball's podium.

Ruth was especially upbeat after an off-season full of golf. He often played 36 holes, even during the winter months in New York, walking the course at a brisk pace. He also worked out with trainer Artie McGovern. The golf and the exercises comprised his off-season conditioning program.

Ruth battled some nagging injuries during spring training but came through OK. Then in early April the great showman provided fans in Memphis with a day they'd never forget. During a game in the Yankees southern tour on their way back north, Ruth sat in the stands when the Yankees batted. He bought hot dogs and sodas for the kids, who were overwhelmed to be mixing with the great one. Then Ruth finished the show with a massive homer to center field.

Eventually the Yankees made their way to Philadelphia for the season opener on April 12. But this wasn't just any first game. No, this was a chance for the Yankees to make a statement by clobbering the Athletics. The Yankees never were in serious contention in 1931, but they had finished 21–6 in September. Ruth had a feeling that the team finally was coming together in Joe McCarthy's first season as manager. "We were going mighty good at the end of the season in 1931, and, with our pitching staff in much better physical condition at the start of the season than last year, I believe we have the stuff to beat the Athletics and Senators to the wire," he said.

Ruth backed up his comment with his first at bat of the 1932 season. Facing George Earnshaw, he slammed a mammoth homer, which landed on the roof of a two-story building across the street from the park. Ruth launched another blast in the seventh that traveled an estimated 480 feet. He had five RBIs that day as the Yankees pummeled Earnshaw in a 12–6 victory. Statement made.

But a crowd of only 16,000 people at Shibe Park witnessed the triumph. The small showing gave an early indicator to Mack that 1932 was going to prove a difficult season and that he soon would have to break up his great team.

The Yankees took two of three from Philadelphia in the opening series, scoring 34 runs. Ruth hit his third homer in a 14–4 mashing of the Athletics in the series finale. The tone clearly had been set. Ruth continued his assault on Philadelphia when the Yankees returned to New York for the home opener. Ruth went deep on future 300-game winner Lefty Grove in an 8–3 victory, thrilling the crowd of 63,000 fans at Yankee Stadium. Grove lamented, "No, sir, there's no good way to pitch to that fellow. All you can do is breeze it in there and hope he doesn't connect. If he does, it's likely to be a home run. He doesn't have to hit it square. Why, I've seen him knock them out of the lot with the handle."

The Yankees closed out April winning eight of nine games. Then they started to sprint in May with a nine-game winning streak. A 6–3 victory over Washington on May 20 pushed the boys from New York City back into first place. They remained there for the rest of the season.

⁙⁙⁙⁙⁙⁙⁙⁙⁙⁙⁙⁙⁙⁙⁙⁙⁙⁙

Yankees owner Jacob Ruppert was thrilled. Much as future owner George Steinbrenner would do in the 1970s, the Colonel had long since run out of patience after watching his team fall short to Philadelphia for three straight years. He dumped Bob Shawkey at the end of the 1930 season. The move coincided with the Cubs firing their manager, McCarthy. When Chicago sportswriter Warren Brown ran into Ed Barrow, he told him to move quickly. "You'll never get anybody better than McCarthy," Brown said.

McCarthy came up the hard way. He never played an inning in the majors. A native of Germantown, Pennsylvania, he bumped around in the minors after turning pro in 1906. He quickly realized, though, that he wasn't good enough to make it as a player. He made the transition to manager at Wilkes-Barre in 1913 at the age of 26. After a series of minor league stops, Bill Veeck Sr. hired him to manage the Cubs in 1926. McCarthy led the Cubs to the National League pennant in 1929. However, after losing to Philadelphia in the World Series and dipping to a second-place finish in 1930, the Cubs let him go. They parted ways with the manager who went on to win seven World Series titles with the Yankees and sport a .614 winning percentage—the highest in Major League history. It was yet another huge mistake in a century-plus of futility for the Cubs.

The Yankees quickly cashed in with McCarthy. It was difficult for him at first in New York, though. Ruth, as we know, thought that he himself should have been offered the manager's job, and many of his teammates agreed with him. Initially, Ruth had little respect for McCarthy, whose short and squat stature hardly made him an imposing figure. Why should the Babe take advice from a career minor leaguer and a manager from the inferior National League? Ruth wrote diplomatically in his autobiography, "I worked under McCarthy for the next four seasons. During that time, there never was the intimacy between us. Our paths rarely crossed off the field."

McCarthy did get Ruth's and all the Yankees' attention early on, nevertheless. Discipline had grown lax in 1930 under Shawkey. Only a few years earlier, he had sat beside them on the bench as a pitcher on the 1920s teams. He wasn't up to the task of setting rules in the clubhouse as a manager. McCarthy had no such connections and no misgivings about letting the team know who was boss. Prior to a game in 1931, he saw a bunch of players engaged in a heated game of cards. McCarthy promptly smashed the table. Ruth remembered his manager saying, "This is a clubhouse, not a clubroom. I want the players in here to think of baseball and nothing else," and even Ruth grudgingly admitted that "Joe was right."

McCarthy had a vision of how the game should be played. He let the players know his 10 commandments of baseball:

1. Nobody ever became a ballplayer by walking after a ball.
2. You will never become a .300 hitter unless you take the bat off your shoulder.
3. An outfielder who throws in back of a runner is locking the barn after the horse is stolen.
4. Keep your head up, and you may not have to keep it down.
5. When you start to slide, slide. He who changes his mind may have to change a good leg for a bad one.
6. Do not alibi on bad hops. Anybody can field the good ones.
7. Always run them out. You can never tell.
8. Do not quit.
9. Do not fight too much with the umpires. You cannot expect them to be as perfect as you are.
10. A pitcher who hasn't control hasn't anything.

Lou Gehrig, a no-nonsense fellow, lapped it up. He loved rules. He told catcher Bill Dickey, "I like this McCarthy."

McCarthy's work ethic also went beyond the field. The team had to dress appropriately at all times. McCarthy insisted that the players wear jackets even to breakfast. "We didn't make a farce out of the game," said shortstop Frank Crosetti. "We didn't fool around. Manager Joe McCarthy wouldn't stand for it. Once the game started, it was all business."

Despite all the discipline, McCarthy did fight for his players with Ruppert. He insisted that the players travel first-class on trains. In McCarthy's view they should do everything in a first-class manner if they wanted to be first in the American League. "I'm not a second-division manager, and I won't stand for second-division baseball," he said.

McCarthy's Yankees dominated baseball. The arrival of a young player named Joe DiMaggio helped the team and McCarthy win four World

Sitting on deck, Lou Gehrig had an up close view of the antics that took place during Ruth's famous at bat. There are conflicting views on whether Gehrig believed Ruth called his shot.

PHOTO COURTESY OF NATIONAL BASEBALL HALL OF FAME LIBRARY, COOPERSTOWN, NEW YORK

Series in a row from 1936 to 1939. The team had so many stars that some discounted McCarthy's impact. The rap was that anybody could win with this crew—but the players knew otherwise. DiMaggio once said, "Never a day went by when you didn't learn something from McCarthy."

Still, it helps to have talent. The team consisted of a dynamic mix of older veterans from the legendary '27 team and younger players who formed the core of the Yankees' dynasty in the late '30s. In 1932 you could say that the team was loaded. The team featured eight future Hall of Famers: Ruth, Gehrig, Dickey, Tony Lazzeri, Earle Combs, Lefty Gomez, Red Ruffing, and Herb Pennock. The number grows to 11 if you include McCarthy, Barrow, and Ruppert, who also have plaques at Cooperstown.

That season marked Frank Crosetti's debut. The shortstop eventually spent nearly 40 years with the Yankees as a player and coach, cashing 23 World Series checks as part of teams that featured DiMaggio and Mantle. But he had no idea what lay ahead in 1932. Only 21 at the time, he was thrilled to be wearing the same uniform as Ruth, and the leftfielder set the ground rules for the new shortstop. (Ruth, who played right field most of his career, eventually moved to left field to lessen the demands on his aging body.)

"Remember, when you hear me boom, 'My ball,' get out of the road," Ruth said.

"Yes sir, Mr. Babe," replied the rookie, who knew his 135-pound frame wouldn't do well in a collision with the burly Ruth.

The other half of the double-play combination, Lazzeri, was only 28 in 1932, but he already was playing in his seventh season. The Yankees spent $50,000, an unheard-of sum, to purchase him after he hit 60 homers in one season for Salt Lake City in 1925. "Buy him," a scout said. "He's the greatest prospect I've ever seen." The second baseman thrived in the big leagues despite suffering from epilepsy. His affliction caused other teams to pass on him. But he never had an episode while playing in a game. Lazzeri anchored the Yankees infield and proved a terrific hitter, eclipsing 100 RBIs in a season seven times during his career. He was also the game's first big Italian star, often a guest at Italian-American clubs when the Yankees were on the road.

Dickey always comes up when conversation turns to the greatest catchers of all time. A left-handed hitter, he had a career .313 batting average with a career-high .362 in 1936. He was a rock, catching more than 100 games for 13 straight seasons.

Only 25 years old but a key player in the Yankees' emergence in 1932, he blossomed as a star, hitting .310. He played in only 108 games, but it wasn't because of injury. A quiet man off the field, Dickey became a fierce competitor when he donned his catching gear. On July 4, in a game against the Senators, Carl Reynolds crashed hard into Dickey on a play at the plate. The next day, Dickey was still feeling the effects of being knocked unconscious, so he wasn't going to let this assault go. Enraged, the catcher—tightly muscled at 6-foot-1 and 185 pounds—delivered a punch that broke Reynolds's jaw in two places. Dickey paid the price for his anger, though. He was suspended for 30 days and fined $1,000, a significant sum in those days.

Dickey handled pitchers excellently, so concern emerged that the staff might suffer in his absence. Johnny Allen contributed to that concern. At age 27 he finally made the big leagues in 1932, and he made the most of it, sporting a 17–4 record. However, Allen wasn't a pleasant person to be around, and he lasted only four seasons with the Yankees. A teammate said, "He was just plain mean. You never wanted to go near him anytime anything went wrong."

The opposite held true for another young Yankees pitcher: Vernon Gomez, better known as "Lefty." The San Francisco native still rates as one of the most popular Yankees players of all time. A quirky sort whose other nickname was "Goofy," Gomez once stopped during a World Series game to watch an airplane fly overhead. He also had a penchant for one-liners. Late in his career, he said, "I'm throwing as hard as I ever did. The ball's just not getting there as fast." He and DiMaggio were longtime roommates and best friends. It was an odd pairing, given DiMaggio's stoic personality. However, the Yankee Clipper enjoyed having someone around like Gomez, who didn't take life too seriously.

Gomez was a rail at 6-foot-2, 160 pounds. Ruth, who had no trouble packing on the pounds, thought Gomez needed fattening up. Ruth wrote in his autobiography, "When we first saw him at St. Pete, we wondered how such a skinful of bones could have so much stuff. The club's first challenge was to fatten him up. We turned him loose on a herd of cows and told him to drink all the milk he could. He drank a ton and gained two pounds." As usual, Gomez delivered what soon became a classic line: "Nobody can fatten up a greyhound," he said.

Despite his slim stature, Gomez threw a blazing fastball thanks to a whiplike delivery. After going 21–9 in a breakout season in 1931, the 23-year-old was nearly flawless at the beginning of 1932. He exploded out of the gate with a 13–1 mark and eventually finished 24–7 for the season.

⸻

The rise of young players like Gomez and Dickey changed the look of the team from the dominant rosters of the 1920s. Yet the two biggest pieces of the Yankee success story remained in place: Ruth and Gehrig. In 1932 they were playing in their eighth full season together. As people, though, the two superstars made for a remarkable study in contrasts. Ruth's mother abandoned him, dumping him in an orphanage; Gehrig's mother played a big part in his legend for her doting and at times overbearing nature. Mama Gehrig almost didn't go to her son's wedding because she didn't want to accept that another woman had come into his life. Ruth didn't have any use for education; Gehrig was an Ivy Leaguer from Columbia. Ruth was supremely confident, feeling that he could do anything; despite his talents, Gehrig was unsure of himself. In fact, he had an inferiority complex, according to those who knew him well. These key personality differences showed: Ruth was effusive, loud, and boisterous; Gehrig was shy and quiet.

Teammate Bill Werber said of Gehrig, "He wasn't as outgoing as Ruth or Lazzeri or Combs. He didn't make a great effort to be friendly. It wasn't the nature of the man. I wouldn't say he was timid. He had the heart of a lion. But he was aloof." Gehrig once confided in sportswriter Fred Lieb, one of his closest friends, "You know, when some of the writers come up to me and ask me questions, they think that I'm rude because I don't answer right. But I'm so scared I'm shitting in my pants."

Their lifestyles were also vastly different. While Ruth liked to drink and carouse, Gehrig mostly kept to himself. "I'm just a plain, comfort-living citizen who likes to go to bed early and take life at a slow pace," Gehrig once wrote in a magazine piece. "I smoke a little, drink a little beer, like fishing and ice skating, and just recently I've begun to go for golf. I'm no Good-Time Charley, in other words."

It showed when they put on their uniforms. Ruth, who always looked puffy, had a paunch that stretched his Yankee pinstripes. Gehrig, meanwhile, was a model physical specimen. Famous shots show him taking batting practice without a shirt. The muscles in his back and shoulders look as solid as concrete.

Many have speculated about their relationship over the years. Ruth, who was seven years older, played a lot of cards with Gehrig and often was a guest at Mama Gehrig's home. She loved that Ruth talked German to her. Somewhere along the way, the two men had a falling out. In ESPN's *SportsCentury* profile of Ruth, his granddaughter, Linda Ruth Tosetti, says that it hinged on an argument that somehow involved Ruth's wife and Gehrig's mother—but who can say for sure?

Lieb insisted that Gehrig had "an admiration for Ruth. He was comfortable being in his shadow." Gehrig knew his place on the Yankees and in baseball. "I could never be another Ruth if I lived to be 500 years old," he said. Gehrig went into more detail in a first-person piece for *Liberty* magazine following the 1932 season. "I have a pretty definite idea of my value and I know I can hit a baseball very hard and very far. The point is that I do this in a pretty matter-of-fact way, whereas Ruth hits them with a flourish of drama that is instinctive, natural, and all his own. In other words, there is only one Babe Ruth. So why argue with the facts?"

But there also was only one Lou Gehrig, and there was nothing matter-of-fact about the way he played. Like Ruth, Gehrig was devastating at the plate. In 1931 he drove in 184 runs, an American League record that still stands today. Gehrig was more than just a slugger, though. The stately way he carried himself on the field made fellow players and fans revere him. No play was routine, and he never went through the motions.

By 1932 the streak that ultimately defined Gehrig's career was beginning to come into focus. When he opened the season, he had played more than 1,000 consecutive games. People were starting to take notice. The streak ultimately hit 2,130 games before illness cut short his career and life. Noted sportswriter Paul Gallico summed it up thus: "There is no greater inspiration to any American boy than Lou Gehrig. For if this awkward, inept, and downright clumsy player that I knew in the beginning could through sheer drive and determination turn himself into the finest first-base-covering machine in all baseball, then nothing is impossible to any man or boy in the country."

Like Ruth, Gehrig also experienced the most memorable game of his career in 1932. On June 1 the Yankees arrived in Philadelphia for an important six-game series—yes, six games—against the Athletics. Philadelphia won the opener with an 8–7 victory in 16 innings. The game was noteworthy because Mack summoned Grove to pitch in relief in the ninth inning. He wound up going eight innings to record the win.

After losing again the next day, Gehrig led the charge on a Friday afternoon for the third game of the series. In the first inning he slammed a homer off George Earnshaw. Then he tormented Earnshaw with long blasts in the fourth and fifth innings. Shibe Park was buzzing when Gehrig came up in the seventh. Until that point no post-1901 player—not even Babe Ruth himself—had landed four homers in a game. Facing Roy Mahaffey, Gehrig, locked in like never before, swung hard and knew from the contact that he had his number four. While the pro-Athletics

Baseball's greatest showman, Babe Ruth always rose to the occasion. The Called Shot proved to be the defining moment in his career.

crowd cheered his feat, Gehrig trotted around the bases, head slightly lowered in true understated fashion.

Gehrig wasn't through, though. The game turned into a slugfest, with the Yankees eventually winning 20–13—which meant he still had more chances for a fifth homer. After grounding out in the eighth, Gehrig came up again in the ninth. Once again, he tore into the pitch, sending the ball to deep center field. Afterward, Gehrig said, "You know, I think that last one was the hardest ball I hit all day. Gosh, it felt good."

Trouble was, Gehrig hit it to the deepest part of Shibe Park, which stretched to 475 feet. Athletics center fielder Al Simmons raced back and made a leaping catch in front of the wall. If Simmons had missed, Gehrig's fifth could have been an inside-the-park homer.

As it was, Gehrig's four-homer game was one for the books, and on any other day it would have been the biggest story in baseball. However, June 3, 1932, also happened to be the day that John McGraw announced his retirement after 31 years of managing the New York Giants. Gehrig was overshadowed in the headlines again. "Somehow, the spotlight always seemed to miss him. He had all the talent in the world but little of the luck," wrote Jonathan Eig in his biography of Gehrig, *Luckiest Man.*

‖‖‖‖‖‖‖‖‖‖‖‖‖‖‖‖‖‖‖‖‖‖‖‖‖

Ruth, meanwhile, hit his 15th homer of the season during Gehrig's big day. Although he was showing the power, Ruth was hitting only .282 in early June, a poor average for him. But then Ruth heated up, going 9 for 15 with four homers in a four-game series against Cleveland. He even started a double play with a shoestring catch followed by a bullet throw to second to nail the runner. By July 1 Ruth had lifted his average to .310, and the Yankees were rolling with a nine-and-a-half-game lead and a 48–20 record. For their part, Philadelphia hadn't given up hope. Buoyed by three straight American League pennants, the Athletics felt that they still had plenty of time to catch the Yankees. Eddie Collins, the Hall of

Famer who served as Mack's third base coach, said, "We're trailing the Yankees now, but we'll catch them when class tells."

The Yankees offered Philadelphia a glimmer of hope by losing five of six during a stretch in July. Ruth then suffered the injury to his leg, which was expected to knock him out for three weeks. But like Barrow said, Ruth was a quick healer. He was back in the lineup on July 28 against Cleveland—and all he did was produce two home runs and seven RBIs in the Yankee victory. By the end of July, Ruth's average had leapt to a more Ruthian .337.

The Yankees continued to take care of business in August. By the time September rolled around, the only suspense hanging over the American League wasn't the pennant race but whether Jimmie Foxx would break Ruth's record of 60 homers in a season. He entered the month with 48 homers, well within reach of Ruth's milestone.

On Labor Day the Athletics arrived in New York for a doubleheader against the Yankees. The day served as a coronation for McCarthy's crew, who were sitting on a 12½-game lead. A massive crowd of more than 70,000 fans jammed Yankee Stadium. Even during the Depression, a Labor Day twin bill was still an enticing draw.

Even though Foxx went on to hit 58 homers, marking the first time that Ruth didn't lead the American League in homers since 1926, the Bambino showed who was king, at least in fans' eyes, that day. In Game One he hit a monster blast that almost reached the scoreboard in right-center. Estimates put the homer's distance at 485 feet. The huge crowd erupted as Ruth doffed his cap while trotting around the bases in celebration of his 40th of the year. The Yankees went on to sweep the Athletics as the countdown began for the World Series.

The following day, Ruth homered during an exhibition game in Binghamton, New York. All told, the Yankees played 12 exhibition games during the 1932 season. Most took place in small towns as Ruppert tried to make extra cash off the team's popularity. Thus off-days became working days for the players, who had little rights in the pre–Marvin Miller era. But the players were used to it, and all seemed well for Ruth and the

Yankees when he boarded a train for Detroit. Then Ruth took ill with severe stomach pains.

||||||||||||||||||||||||||||||||

Once he was back in New York, Claire and doctors tended to his care. He was packed in so much ice that he joked, "I haven't thawed out yet." The fever broke after a few days, but Ruth remained painfully weak. Just 10 days before the start of the World Series, he went to Yankee Stadium to take some batting practice. He didn't reach the seats once. Yet if Ruth had any concern, he didn't share it with reporters when he returned to action on September 21 in Philadelphia. "Feeling fine," Ruth pronounced.

But he didn't look fine. He managed only three hits in his last five games of the season. The illness, coupled with concerns about his age and the toll of a long season, prompted speculation that Ruth finally might have run out of gas in September. One Associated Press scribe wrote, "It was his apparent weakness in the field that made some of the boys traveling with the Yanks suspect that Ruth's appendicitis attack was just a myth and that the real reason for his layoff was to give his legs a chance to rest up after the wear and tear they suffered from April to the end of August." Even Ruth conceded in his autobiography that the years were catching up to him in 1932. McCarthy often took him out for a defensive replacement in the late innings. Ruth wrote, "My old legs were getting tired. I just couldn't get over the ground as well as I had only a few years ago."

Ruth went hitless in the season finale against Boston on September 25. The Yankees finished with a 107–47 mark, easily winning the American League by 13 games. While the '32 season often doesn't get mentioned with some of the other great Yankees lineups, it was a dominating run that saw McCarthy become the first manager to win pennants in both leagues.

The Yankees slaughtered their opponents at home. For the season, they were an astounding 62–15 at Yankee Stadium. It was a vintage Yankees performance. Sportswriter Tom Meany wrote, "The Yankee tradition, as engendered by Ruth, fostered by Barrow and enjoyed by Ruppert, wasn't a bad one at all. Boiled down, its slogan was: Win as many games as you can by as many as you can."

Ruth hit .341 with 41 homers and 137 RBIs in 133 games. That was the lowest number of homers and RBIs that he had managed since 1925. While some experts tried to point to those stats as a symbol of Ruth's decline, Westbrook Pegler of the *Chicago Tribune* reached for some perspective: "Those are not much for Babe, but a young player coming along who could do that well would be regarded as a marvelous athlete, and the papers would publish his face next to pure reading matter. They might even call him the new Babe Ruth."

The old Babe Ruth was still feeling as confident as always. Miss the World Series? Are you kidding? The World Series was his stage—big crowds, big games. He liked nothing better, and there was nothing better than homering in a World Series game. Ruth already had 13 of them in nine previous showdowns, and he was looking forward to adding to his record. Besides, Ruth hadn't played in a World Series since 1928. He knew at age 37 he wasn't likely to get many more opportunities. (He did not know that in fact it was his last.)

As the season neared its climax, Ruth was looking forward to Game One at Yankee Stadium. Then, for the first time, Ruth started to think about playing in Wrigley Field. He had played there only on one previous occasion and came away unimpressed with the relatively short fences. "Why, I could bunt homers into that right field bleacher," he told reporters. In his mind Ruth already was envisioning the bounty that awaited him in Chicago.

FIVE

Setting the Stage

So they're going to give you a half-share, are they, Mark? Well, you had better collect that five bucks right now.
—BABE RUTH TO CUBS SHORTSTOP MARK KOENIG

What caused the Called Shot homer in the first place? Why had such bad blood formed between the Yankees and Cubs going into the 1932 World Series? How did a late-season pickup for the Cubs, an oversexed shortstop, and a femme fatale serve as catalysts for the one of the most famous episodes in baseball history? Every story has a beginning. Follow the thread.

Billy Jurges was staying in a hotel room a few blocks from Wrigley Field on July 6, 1932. Just 24 years old, he was in his second full season with the Cubs. Born in the Bronx, Jurges was young and handsome, and now he was playing shortstop for the Cubs. All in all, a good combination when on the prowl in search of pretty women. His average with the opposite sex likely fared better than his early days at the plate, when he struggled to hit above .250.

Among his "acquaintances" was a young woman named Violet Popovich. She had quite the figure and wasn't shy about showing it. She enjoyed having a good time and was said to be popular among the ballplayers of that day. Jurges was a particular favorite. In a 1988 interview with Jerome Holtzman of the *Chicago Tribune*, Jurges, then 80, recalled what happened when Popovich rang his hotel room on that warm summer morning in 1932.

"She called me from the lobby. It's early in the morning, about seven o'clock, and she said, 'I'd like to see you.' I said, 'C'mon up.'

"When she came to my room I told her, 'I'm not going to go out on any more dates. We've got a chance to win the pennant. I've got to get my rest.'"

Popovich didn't react well to the declaration. According to Jurges, she pulled a gun out of her purse and started shooting. An Associated Press account at the time said that Popovich was trying to commit suicide and that Jurges was shot when he tried to grab the gun away from her. Jurges doesn't mention anything about a suicide attempt in the Holtzman interview, though. He said he was hit twice before he grabbed the gun, which went off a third time, hitting him in the palm.

Jurges had more than just his hand to worry about. He suffered a more serious wound to the right side of his chest, the bullet hitting a rib and ricocheting out of his shoulder. He ran out to the hall and saw Marvin Gudat, a utility outfielder on the team. "I said, 'Get a doctor,'" Jurges recalled. "I was bleeding like a pig, lying on the bed, this young doctor was working on me. I could hardly breathe.

"I asked him, 'Doc, how am I?'

"'I'll give you 20 minutes to live. You've got it bad.'"

Luckily for Jurges, the situation wasn't as dire as that. John Davis, the Cubs team doctor, happened to be nearby and diagnosed Jurges's injuries as less than fatal. In fact, they weren't even all that serious. He was out of uniform for less than a month.

The shooting, though, caused quite a furor in Chicago and throughout baseball. A few weeks later, Popovich's case came up in court. Jurges described the judge as a big baseball fan. "He said, 'Bill, what's the story?' I told him, and he said, 'What do you want me to do?' And I said, 'To hell with it, let's forget it.'"

Jurges decided not to press charges, and Popovich walked free.

"This case is dismissed for want of prosecution," Judge John Sbarbaro announced, adding, "and I hope no more Cubs get shot."

In a move that seems inconceivable today, Popovich actually capitalized on the incident. She signed a 22-week contract to sing and dance at various nightclubs in Chicago, billing herself as "Violet 'I Did It for Love' Valli—the most talked of girl in Chicago."

Jurges said he never saw Popovich again. However, he added this postscript in his interview with Holtzman: "Later I found that three or four years before she shot me she had plugged another guy. I was screwing her. So were other ballplayers. She was a beautiful woman.

"I took the rap for it, but she had gone to his [teammate and future Hall of Famer Kiki Cuyler's] room first. Kiki was a big ladies' man. She had the key to his room, but he wasn't there. She wrote a note and put it on the mirror. 'I'M GOING TO KILL YOU!'

"The police and the lawyer told me they found the note. That's the absolute truth."

Popovich thus became the first femme fatale in baseball history. Some years later, in 1949, a 19-year-old girl shot Eddie Waitkus, a young first baseman for the Philadelphia Phillies. Like Jurges, Waitkus survived and continued to play. The Waitkus incident quickly worked its way into the public imagination in Bernard Malamud's 1952 novel *The Natural*, which later served as the basis for the 1984 film starring Robert Redford.

Some have theorized that elements of Malamud's novel refer to the Jurges shooting, which meanwhile found its place in the legend of the Called Shot. Again, some distortion comes into play. The myth holds that the Cubs, in search of a shortstop, immediately replaced Jurges with Mark Koenig, who became the pivotal player in the Called Shot saga. But it didn't actually work out that way.

Despite being shot only weeks earlier, Jurges actually returned to the lineup on July 22. On August 5 team president Bill Veeck acquired Koenig as a roster replacement for recently fired player-manager Rogers Hornsby. However, it seems like Koenig already was on Veeck's radar, especially given the initial uncertainty over Jurges's status. In a few weeks Koenig found himself at the center of the bad blood between the Cubs and the Yankees that led to the circumstances surrounding the Called Shot.

||||||||||||||||||||||||||||||

Koenig's career definitely was in limbo at the time. He came up with the Yankees in 1925 at the age of 20 and soon worked his way into the lineup. Koenig was the shortstop for the great 1927 Yankees team. With so many bombers on the roster, he was there for his glove, serving as an anchor for the infield, and he could hit a little, recording a .313 average in 1928. "I was ordinary, a small cog in a big machine," said Koenig, the last surviving player from the '27 Yankees when he died in 1993.

In 1929 Leo Durocher took over as shortstop for the Yankees, and the next year Koenig was dealt to Detroit. Eye problems plagued Koenig, though, and he opened the 1932 season with San Francisco in the Pacific Coast League.

Though he was just 27, it looked like Koenig's career was over. However, after undergoing surgery on his sinuses, his condition improved. His play also improved. When the call came from Veeck, Koenig was thrilled. Not only was he getting a chance to get back into the big leagues, he also was going to be a contender. The Cubs ranked as one of the favorites to win the National League going into the '32 season. After winning the pennant in 1929, they slid disappointingly to second in '30 and third in '31. Still, they had many of the pieces in place, including a Hall of Famer as manager.

When the Cubs opted to fire Joe McCarthy at the end of the 1930 season, they gave his duties to Hornsby. One of the game's great hitters (.358 lifetime batting average), he had mixed success as a player-manager. He guided the Cardinals to the World Series title in 1926, beating the Yankees. However, he only went 39–83 during a stint as manager of the Boston Braves in 1928. Cubs owner William Wrigley spent an unthinkable $200,000 to purchase Hornsby from the Braves in 1929. The investment paid off, though, as Hornsby hit .380 in leading the Cubs to the pennant.

It was McCarthy who had lobbied Wrigley to acquire Hornsby. Little did he know that it would lead to his demise with the Cubs. Hornsby considered McCarthy "a busher" because the manager never played in the majors. Hornsby started to lobby Wrigley to let him run the show. Despite 56 homers and 191 RBIs from Hack Wilson, the Cubs finished second in 1930. Wrigley listened to Hornsby and fired McCarthy with four games left in the season. "McCarthy lacks enough desire for a world championship," said Wrigley of the manager who later won seven World Series titles with the Yankees, two of them at the Cubs' expense.

Wrigley decided to get his money's worth out of Hornsby and named him manager. Hornsby, known as "the Rajah," wasn't a pleasant man. One sportswriter once said of him, "He was frank to the point of being cruel and as subtle as a belch." Anthony J. Connor wrote in *Voices from Cooperstown*:

> *He was a real hard-nosed guy. He ran the clubhouse like a Gestapo camp. You couldn't smoke, drink a soft drink, eat a sandwich. Couldn't read a paper. When you walked in the clubhouse you put your uniform on and got ready to play. That was it! No more kidding around, no joking, no laughing. He was dedicated to the game and made sure you were too. A very serious person.*

The stern approach didn't go over well with the Cubs. The players bristled under Hornsby's harsh leadership. There was another problem as well. Hornsby liked to gamble, and he had debts everywhere, including with several Cubs players. The situation reached the point to where Commissioner Kenesaw Mountain Landis, acutely aware of baseball gambling issues from the Black Sox scandal, even conducted an investigation.

Finally, Veeck had had enough. With the Cubs underachieving at 54–46 on August 4, he fired Hornsby.

Veeck then tapped Hornsby's polar opposite as his replacement, Charlie Grimm. His nickname, "Jolly Cholly," says it all. A fun-loving first baseman, he joined the Cubs in 1924. He became an important person in the team's history, guiding the Cubs to three National League pennants, along with serving as manager on three different occasions. Whenever the Cubs were in trouble, it seemed as if all they had to do was turn to Jolly Cholly. He had such a tight connection to the Cubs that when he died his wife scattered his ashes at Wrigley Field.

Released from Hornsby's dour iron grip, the Cubs players immediately responded to Grimm. They won six of the first eight games under his command. A 3–2 win over Pittsburgh lifted the Cubs into first on August 11. On August 18 Koenig got a single as a pinch hitter. The following day, Grimm inserted him in the lineup as shortstop, where he went 2 for 4 in a 6–5 loss to the Braves.

Grimm decided that Koenig merited another start. In the next game, with the Phillies leading 5–3, Koenig came up with two on in the ninth. The fill-in shortstop promptly hit a drive that cleared the fence in left. The three-run homer gave the Cubs a dramatic 6–5 victory, sending the Wrigley faithful into a frenzy. In the joyous Cubs locker room, the players toasted the team's new and unlikely hero.

Koenig's big hit and comeback win filled the Cubs with confidence. They won their next game, then the next game, and the game after that. Their winning streak hit five when Charlie Root pitched the Cubs to a 7–4 victory over the Dodgers in Brooklyn. Koenig, who remained in the lineup at shortstop, had two hits to give the Cubs six in a row with a 9–3 win over Brooklyn.

But the Cubs were just getting started. Soon their hot streak heated to 10 consecutive wins with a 5–4 victory over the Giants. Koenig stayed on fire, lifting his average to .405 with two more hits. The streak looked like it would end at 11 when the Giants scored four in the top of the 10th to take a 9–5 lead. But the Cubs weren't about to be stopped. They roared back with five runs in the bottom of the 10th to secure a thrilling 10–9 win. Koenig homered again the next

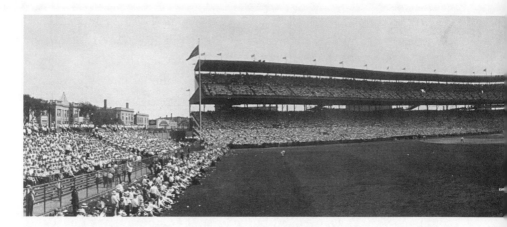

day as the streak hit 13. The Cubs then recorded their 14th in a row with a 6–5 victory over St. Louis in 11 innings. Ultimately, it took the Cardinals' future Hall of Famer Dizzy Dean to put the clamps on the Cubs, stopping their run with a 3–0 victory in front of 45,000 fans at Wrigley Field.

That 14-game winning streak gave the Cubs a vice grip on first place. With under a month to play, they now had a seven-game lead on the Pirates. Pennant fever started to overtake Chicago. The big day finally came on September 20. Nearly 40,000 fans packed Wrigley Field. Another 15,000 souls created a furor when they learned they couldn't get inside the ballpark. Police had to come and calm them down. Everyone wanted to be part of the celebration, which occurred when pitcher Guy Bush closed out the Pirates with a 5–2 victory.

The Cubs had captured their first National League pennant since 1929. However, a bittersweet development soured the party. William Wrigley, the chewing gum magnate who owned the Cubs and put his name on the iconic ballpark, suffered a stroke, eventually dying on January 26, 1932.

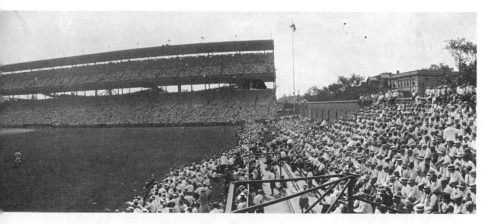

Wrigley Field in July 1929, nearly a decade before the signature ivy was planted.
PHOTO COURTESY OF THE LIBRARY OF CONGRESS

||||||||||||||||||||||||||||||

Wrigley had put his unique stamp on the team. He invested heavily in renovating and maintaining Wrigley Field. He wanted fans to enjoy the game in a clean and pleasing environment. It's one of the main reasons that the original park has survived for more than a century. Wrigley also embraced Veeck's vision for putting Cubs games on radio. Nor was he shy about spending money for players, as evidenced by his purchase of Hornsby.

Wrigley loved the Cubs and loved the game. "Baseball is too much of a sport to be a business and too much of a business to be a sport," he once said. The story goes that on his deathbed he told his son, Phillip, never to sell the team. Phillip wasn't a baseball fan, but out of loyalty to his father the Cubs remained in the family's hands until 1981.

When Wrigley finally succumbed, Veeck said, "It's a terrible shock. It's like losing a parent. Mr. Wrigley was the finest man that ever lived." Wrigley had changed Veeck's life. The latter man had been a Chicago sportswriter, often penning his stories under the pseudonym Bill Bailey.

Veeck met with Wrigley regularly to discuss the Cubs and baseball. Eventually Wrigley asked him to run the team.

A visionary, Veeck became the driving force behind the Cubs extending their reach beyond Wrigley Field by putting their games on radio. He also instituted other promotions, such as Ladies Day. His ideas had a profound effect on his son, Bill Jr., who went on to become perhaps baseball's most colorful owner. "Unlike me, my father was far too dignified a man to pull promotional stunts. But he was a man of imagination and easily the greatest innovator of his time," wrote Veeck Jr. in his autobiography, *Veeck—As In Wreck.*

It was Bill Jr. who installed the famed ivy at Wrigley Field as a young team executive in the late 1930s. Unfortunately, his father didn't have a chance to see his son's brilliant idea. Diagnosed with leukemia in 1933, Veeck Sr. died in October of that year. It was said that the last thing he tasted was a few sips of Al Capone's champagne.

Capone himself was in jail by that point, but not long before he had ruled Chicago. When he wasn't creating mayhem, Capone enjoyed watching games at Wrigley Field, and he went out of his way to befriend the players. "Capone was a big baseball fan," recalled Cubs second baseman Billy Herman. "He'd walk into the ballpark like the president walking in today, with bodyguards all around him. Once [Cubs catcher Charles] Gabby [Hartnett] posed for a picture with Capone. And the next year (Kenesaw Mountain Landis, the first baseball commissioner) made a rule that ballplayers couldn't talk to anyone in the stands."

Hartnett lay at the heart of the Cubs. The oldest of 14 children, he joined the team in 1922. His nickname was an exercise in irony—he was the opposite of gabby as a young player. He was so quiet that his teammates rode him with the nickname, and it stuck. But Hartnett quickly made noise as one of the game's biggest stars. In 1930 he had his greatest season, hitting .339 with 37 homers and 122 RBIs. Yet there was more to Hartnett than just his bat. He had a terrific throwing arm. Herman recalled: "He'd holler at pitchers, 'Let 'em run.' Gabby wanted to throw them out. He loved it when they tried to steal on him."

McCarthy, who saw much of Mickey Cochrane in the American League and managed Bill Dickey, called Hartnett "the perfect catcher." Hartnett was one of four Hall of Famers on that Cubs lineup. Herman, a rookie in 1931, began to establish his credentials in 1932, hitting .314 with 206 hits. He went on to become a 10-time All-Star, spending a decade with the Cubs before being traded to the Brooklyn Dodgers in 1941.

Burleigh Grimes earned his trip to Cooperstown by winning 270 games, mainly with Brooklyn and Pittsburgh. His career was sliding downward when he posted a 6–11 record with the Cubs in 1932, at age 38. However, he still played a role in Ruth's Called Shot.

Kiki Cuyler, elected to the Hall in 1968, was a fixture in the outfield. Acquired from Pittsburgh before the 1928 season, he hit .360 in 1929 and .355 in 1930. He also could run, stealing a league-leading 43 bases in 1929. A broken foot kept him out of action for a third of the 1932 season, but when he returned he played a huge part in the team's August surge. He hit the walk-off, three-run homer in that big extra-inning victory over the Giants. In *Veeck—As In Wreck,* Veeck Jr. recalled that the only time he saw his father lose his dignity was during the celebration of Cuyler's homer. The elder Veeck was sitting next to Landis at the time. According to the younger Veeck:

> *The ball was still climbing over the fence when William Veeck Sr. let out a rebel yell and vaulted over the railing. Marsh [Bill Jr.'s friend] and I had leaped out toward the railing, too, but we were somewhat delayed because we had to untangle ourselves from the harrumphing Commissioner. By the time we got onto the field, my father was in the very center of a mob scene, grabbing for Cuyler's hand.*

Such heroics were expected of Cuyler. Koenig, though, offered a complete surprise. After the big homer on August 20, the shortstop remained in the lineup the rest of the way. He hit a robust .353 in 33 games with 3 homers and 11 RBIs. As a bonus, he played superb defense in the infield as well. Koenig lit the unexpected spark that the Cubs needed as they closed with a 37–18 record after Grimm took over as manager. They probably couldn't have won the pennant without him. "We wouldn't be in first place if it wasn't for Mark," Grimm said.

⸻⸻⸻

What happened next is where the roots of the Called Shot firmly take hold. The threads of this chapter—from the young stud shortstop getting shot by a crazy lady to the Cubs picking up of an out-of-baseball infielder—all lead to the pivotal moment in our tale.

After the Cubs locked up the pennant, they gathered to divide up the bonus money for the World Series share. Remember, this was long before seven-figure salaries. Most players weren't even making five figures, and in the depths of the Great Depression money was even tighter. The prospect of making an additional $4,000 to $5,000 was a big deal for a player struggling to stay ahead in that economic climate.

Obviously the Cubs were going to award full shares to players who played for the entire season. But what about the guys on hand for only part of the ride? The players decided to snub Hornsby completely, even though he had managed them for the first 100 games and had seen action on the field in 19 games. But as the Cubs' second-half surge showed, Hornsby had proven to be an impediment as a manager. Besides, most of the players hated the snarly SOB. Nothing for him.

The Cubs awarded 22 full shares and 5 partials. Koenig fell into the latter category, ultimately cashing in $2,122.30 for a half-share of the World Series pot. Koenig's teammates thought they had justification for their reasoning. Koenig had played only 33 games. He hadn't been on the team for even two months. How did he deserve to get the same financial treatment as a full-season player? If anything, the Cubs felt they were being magnanimous in their treatment of Koenig. "It was all fair," said third baseman Woody English. "He did a great job for us but only played in 33 games and joined us in August when we had already been playing for four and a half months. On that basis, we gave him a

68

half-share. It could have been a quarter-share, but we didn't want to go that low."

Koenig wasn't thrilled, but he accepted the decision in stride. "I was disappointed, but the Cubs players were like that. Hey, they didn't vote Rogers Hornsby any money at all."

The Yankees didn't see it that way. Koenig was a former teammate. He had been part of the World Series winning teams in 1927 and 1928, and they knew that Koenig had helped the Cubs down the stretch. In their minds the Cubs couldn't have come as far as they had without his contributions. So they started to howl about the injustice of Koenig not getting a full share. The biggest yeller was Ruth. It wasn't like Ruth and Koenig were great friends, though. In fact, according to Leigh Montville's biography *The Big Bam*, the pair engaged in a locker room fight in 1929 when Koenig made a disparaging remark about Ruth's wife, Claire.

Ruth had either forgotten or forgiven the incident by the time the 1932 World Series rolled around. He led the chorus blasting the Cubs for their unfair treatment of the former Yankee. "Without Koenig's inspired play, I don't believe the Chicago club could have won," Ruth wrote in his autobiography. "But the Cubs went mercenary and only gave Koenig a half-share."

Ruth wasn't quite as diplomatic when he saw the Cubs in person. He admitted to calling the Cubs "a bunch of cheapskates, nickel-nursers, and misers." When Koenig took the field for Game One, Ruth shouted out, "Why do you associate with a bunch of bums like that?" Yankees pitcher Charlie Devens recalled Ruth piling it on. According to Devens, Ruth called out to Koenig, "So they're going to give you a half-share, are they, Mark? Well, you had better collect that five bucks right now."

The Cubs, meanwhile, fired back, telling Ruth and the Yankees to mind their own business. This had nothing do with them. The players thought they had been fair to Koenig. They rode Ruth about not being able to fulfill his dream of being able to manage. The Cubs jabbed him by saying he wasn't smart enough. Ruth wrote that the Cubs called him "grandpop." He didn't descend into name-calling, which for him crossed the line.

Koenig understandably found himself in an awkward position. He had played most of his career with the Yankees. Now, though, he was a Cub. "My heart still was with the Yankees," Koenig said. "Those were my buddies over there, but I was a member of the Cubs and wanted us to win."

Players of that era were rough around the edges, always cruising for a good fight. They didn't need much of an excuse. The Koenig flap riled up players on both teams. There was plenty of bad blood to go around prior to Game One. "We felt we had several scores to settle, and we wanted to embarrass them," said Yankees shortstop Frank Crosetti. "They had fired Joe McCarthy a year before, even though he was 22 games over .500, and we were lucky enough to get him as our manager for '32. And because of the Mark Koenig thing. We felt a nice guy like Mark deserved better. We hated that town and the team so much."

All that friction, burning hotter and longer, set the stage for the dramatic event of Game Three at Wrigley Field. But first, the Yankees had to take care of business during the first two games at Yankees Stadium.

||||||||||||||||||||||||||||||

Built in 1923, the grand facility already had fulfilled Yankee owner Jacob Ruppert's vision in less than a decade. The vast stadium, not a quaint ballpark like Wrigley Field, reached high into the sky, mimicking the city itself. Its distinctive facade, a white frieze running along the bleacher billboards and scoreboard, gave the stadium an air of dignity. It quickly became an iconic symbol for the ages, passed along when the new Yankee Stadium was built in 2008.

The original Yankees Stadium featured three tiers, a first in the United States. Ruppert knew fans would flock to see Ruth, and his business acumen met handsomely with crowds that reached upwards of 70,000 people on big days. The stadium was set to stage its fifth World

Series in just nine years. Normally, tickets would be at a premium. But these weren't normal times. In 1932, tickets, priced between $3.50 and $16, cost too much when many were having trouble putting bread and milk on the table. Fans could still walk up to the box office and buy tickets for Game One on September 28, but many passed on the opportunity. With a crowd of just 41,000 people, Yankee Stadium had plenty of empty seats. Overnight rain and overcast skies also dampened the mood.

On the field, however, the players on both sides couldn't wait to get started. They had been preparing for this day for weeks as they closed out the regular season with meaningless tune-up games. This was the World Series, the ultimate goal of every player. Ruth was playing in his 10th showdown, yet even he was hardly jaded. He knew how special these games were by the nerves gurgling in his stomach. As he was introduced in the pregame ceremonies, he waved his cap with a certain pride, know-ing that he had reached baseball's pinnacle again.

The pre-Series write-ups noted how the Cubs had the edge over the Yankees in pitching. The *Chicago Tribune* reminded readers that "There is an old belief, and it is a good one when it works, that pitching decides a short baseball series." However, the Cubs soon discovered that those old beliefs didn't work as well when their pitchers faced a lineup that included Ruth and Gehrig.

The Yankees took the field, and fans braced for the first pitch from Red Ruffing. They cheered when his fastball to Herman was a called strike.

Ruffing's career eventually landed him in the Hall of Fame, but he had to overcome adversity early in his life. He lost four toes on his left foot from a hunting accident. Despite that considerable handicap, he made his Major League debut with the Boston Red Sox in 1924. He did not look particularly bound for Cooperstown when he went a combined 19–47 in 1928 and 1929.

The Yankees nevertheless picked up Ruffing in 1930, and immedi-ately his fortunes turned. Pitching in front of a solid team, he gained confidence and started accumulating victories—273 overall. After going

18–7 in 1932, the 28-year-old Ruffing got the Game One assignment even though Lefty Gomez, only 23, had been more dominating at 24–7. McCarthy preferred Ruffing's experience, thinking him better suited to handle any opening game jitters.

The move didn't look good early on, though. Herman led with a single and then quickly scored when Ruth, playing right field, mis-handled a single from Woody English. The Cubs roared in delight, convinced that all the pregame banter had distracted Ruth. Chicago added another run, giving their starter Guy Bush a 2–0 lead before he threw his first pitch. Bush, who soon became a central figure in the Called Shot saga, had a bulldog mentality. Nicknamed "Missis-sippi Mudcat," he paced the Cubs pitchers in 1932, sporting a 19–11 record. He had heard all the hype about the great Yankees—but it didn't bother him. If anything, it gave Bush even more incentive to stuff it to Ruth and Gehrig.

Early on, that's exactly what he did. Bush retired the first nine Yankees with relative ease. However, it was a much different story for his second time around the lineup. Earle Combs opened the bot-tom of the fourth with a walk and advanced to second on Joe Sewell's grounder. With one out, Ruth drew his first blood of the series, hit-ting a liner past Grimm at first for a single to right, driving in Combs. Sensing that the Yankees had awoken, the crowd thundered as Gehrig stepped to the plate.

Like Ruth, Gehrig anxiously wanted to play in his first World Series since 1928. He wasted little time, launching a Bush screwball into the right field stands for a two-run homer. Ruth shook Gehrig's hand as he crossed home plate. Suddenly, the Yankees were up 3–2.

Bush completely unraveled in the sixth, starting with a leadoff walk to Sewell. Perhaps unsettled by what Ruth and Gehrig had done to him in the fourth, he walked them both to load the bases. In the modern era the starter usually gets pulled after issuing three straight walks in the sixth. It didn't work that way back then, though, as Grimm stuck with Bush. The move didn't work. With one out Bill Dickey singled to center, driving in two runs. The assault reached a fever pitch, as the Yankees scored five runs in the inning to take a commanding 8–2 lead.

The Yankees kept hammering. Even though he wasn't sharp, Ruffing went the distance for an opening 12–6 victory. Ruth walked out of the Yankees locker room content that the tone had been set for the series.

The Cubs, meanwhile, suffered a loss beyond the confines of the game. Koenig, who had been so strong down the stretch, injured his wrist and missed the rest of the series. As a result, the man who catalyzed the Called Shot watched the famous homer from the dugout rather than the field.

〰〰〰〰〰〰〰〰〰〰

The weather was brighter the next day for Game Two. A few more fans found their way to the Bronx as a crowd of 50,000 people filled Yankee Stadium a bit more. Gomez drew the starting assignment against the Cubs' Lon Warneke, a 22-game winner in 1932. After Game One Bush tried to remain optimistic, saying, "All we gotta do is stop two men—Ruth and Gehrig—and we'll do that all right."

American League pitchers no doubt had a good chuckle over the naiveté of Bush's remark. Not only does nobody stop Ruth and Gehrig, but the rest of the lineup featured the likes of Combs, Lazzeri, and Dickey. No, the Cubs weren't going to be "all right."

Sure enough, the Yankees got to Warneke early. Gehrig and Dickey drove in runs in the first, and Ben Chapman's two-run single in the third, scoring Ruth and Gehrig, gave the Yankees a 4–2 lead. That was more than enough for Gomez, who settled in and cruised through the Cubs lineup during the last six innings. With the crowd on its feet, Gomez struck out Rollie Hemsley in the ninth to close out an easy 5–2 victory. Just like that, the Yankees held a commanding 2–0 lead in the series.

Ruth credited McCarthy, who knew exactly how to dissect his former team. "If there was a certain tension between Joe McCarthy and me, it certainly didn't affect our having a grand 1932 World Series," Ruth wrote. "I don't know which one of us got a bigger kick out of it."

Gehrig had paced the Yankees with three hits in Game Two, and Dickey logged two RBIs. Meanwhile, Ruth's only noise in that game came in the seventh when he hit a line drive off the right field fence. Slowing down, Ruth was held to a single.

Ruth had only had two singles in the first two games. Still, he scored four runs thanks to the Cubs pitching around him with four walks. Charlie Root, the Cubs starter in Game Three, watched how cautiously his teammates pitched to Ruth. They were reeling as they boarded a train to shift the scene of play to Chicago, and Root decided he wouldn't pitch around Ruth at Wrigley Field.

SIX

Game Three

I heard things you can't print in a family newspaper. They sure were giving it to the Babe.

—Cubs PA announcer Pat Pieper

Babe Ruth knew it was going to be a good day when he woke up on the morning of October 1, 1932. He had a feeling that something special was going to happen. He could sense it in the air. As he prepared in his suite, knotting his tie, wiping a speck of dust off his shoes, Ruth felt ebullient—and why not? The Babe was back where he belonged, back in the spotlight. Ruth lived for these games: big crowds, nationwide radio broadcasts, everything on the line. He loved nothing more than to come through when everyone was focused on him. Ever the showman, Ruth never wanted to disappoint.

So what if Jimmie Foxx had hit 58 homers, thereby knocking Ruth off his pedestal as the game's most feared hitter? Foxx wasn't playing in Game Three today, was he? Maybe Foxx would be listening on the radio.

The Yankees were already halfway there after winning the first two games. Now Ruth faced the prospect of two games at Wrigley Field.

Even more, he wanted the opportunity to stick it to those Chicago fans. You see, there was more on Ruth's plate on that October morning than just getting ready to play. The Cubs and their fans had committed a fatal mistake: They had made him mad.

A day earlier, more than 5,000 fans had thronged the LaSalle Street station when the trains for both teams arrived. The mob grew so thick and unruly that Ruth and his wife, Claire, had to be escorted to a freight elevator and then to a cab. To compound matters, a woman spat at them when they entered their hotel. Not the kind of reception committee that the Ruths had been expecting.

"I've seen some nutty fans in my life, but never quite like those girls," Ruth wrote. "When Claire and I reached the Edgewater hotel, we were forced to run a gauntlet of two lines of hysterical, angry women. Most of the wrath was directed at me, and during that rough trip I heard some words that even I had never heard before. But what annoyed me was their spitting and their bad aim. Poor Claire received most of it." The unfriendly welcome he received that day only fired him up more. "I'll belt one where it hurts them the most," wrote Ruth, determined to exact a measure of revenge in Game Three.

People craned their necks as he made his way through the lobby of the hotel. You couldn't miss the game's biggest star. He smiled to himself at the sound of a few catcalls as he walked through the hotel's doors and climbed into a waiting car. Ruth didn't head directly to Wrigley Field, though.

A few days earlier, Leo Wilbur Koeppen, only 16, had been blinded during the gangland bombing of the home of a local judge. Learning of the incident, Ruth went to see the boy in the hospital. The slugger knew the impact that such hospital visits had on the children, and he rarely passed up an opportunity to help out. It's hard to imagine a current mega-star athlete doing the same on the day of a World Series game, but it was a different time then, and Ruth, for all his flaws, had a huge heart, especially when it came to kids.

Ruth did make his way to Wrigley eventually, and Cubs fans gathered early to watch his arrival at the ballpark. It was hardly the first time Ruth had played in Chicago, however. The American League White Sox drew their biggest crowds of the year when the Yankees visited the South Side at Comiskey Park. But those were regular-season games against the lowly Sox. This was the World Series against the powerful Cubs.

Wrigley Field pulsated like never before on that October morning. The ballpark, built in 1914, wasn't as picturesque as it would become in future years, its now-signature ivy on the outfield walls not planted until the late 1930s. With no real center field bleachers to speak of, the scoreboard sat at ground level, the flagpole located just to the right side. Cubs owner Phillip Wrigley spent $40,000 to install additional grandstands in the outfield that day, making the legendary ballpark look almost freakish. The extra grandstands swelled the park's capacity to more than 50,000 seats, every one of them needed. They easily could have sold more than 500,000 tickets.

Bleacher seats priced at $1.10 went on sale at 6:30 a.m. on the day of the Game Three, and another 2,500 tickets were sold at $2.50. So many buyers congested the ticket booths that many fans missed the first pitch.

The crowd included Franklin Roosevelt, Democratic candidate for president, who sat with Chicago mayor Anton Cermak. Roosevelt chatted with Yankees manager Joe McCarthy before the game. He even pointed to the right field bleachers, perhaps predicting the destination for balls hit by Ruth and Gehrig. Close by sat Judge Kenesaw Mountain Landis. Major League Baseball's first commissioner brought his 10-year-old nephew, Lincoln, to the game with him. Decades later, Lincoln provided eyewitness testimony to the events of that day. And of course, behind the Cubs dugout sat an eager young fan named John Paul Stevens, who became one of the longest-serving justices on the US Supreme Court.

Roosevelt's presence in the stands so close to the election offered a nice distraction, but everyone at Wrigley Field that day was there to see Ruth, and the Bambino knew it. He was bigger than Roosevelt or any other president during the 1920s and '30s. Ruth felt good as he donned his uniform, the familiar gray threads billowing over his increasing paunch.

He didn't feel like a man approaching 40. He seemed spry, loose, almost like a kid again.

As he emerged from the runway, he felt the soothing air of a cool, refreshing fall day in Chicago. His spirits brightened considerably when he spotted the flags on the pole. The wind was blowing toward Lake Michigan. Ruth didn't need any additional help, but the direction of the flags meant that it was going to be a hitter's day at Wrigley. Light-hitting pitcher Lefty Gomez cracked, "With that wind, I could hit a home run today."

The jeering commenced as the Yankees and Ruth took the field for batting practice. The fans threw lemons at Ruth, who, a fun-loving soul, playfully tossed them back into the bleachers. In a way, those Cubs fans were actually doing him a favor. They were providing him with extra inspiration, added oomph to cream the Cubs.

"You mugs are not going to see the Yankee Stadium any more this year," Ruth called out for everyone to hear as he walked past the Cubs dugout. "The World Series is going to be over Sunday afternoon. Four straight."

The crowd ate it up and collectively leaned forward in their seats as Ruth and Gehrig stepped into the cage. That alone would have been enough to satisfy the fans. The Yankees sluggers put on a show, engaging in a home-run derby that thrilled the crowd. One after another, Ruth and Gehrig handled the soft tosses and transformed them into majestic shots that pierced the Chicago sky. All in all, Ruth hit nine balls into the stands, Gehrig seven. The fans were almost breathless while watching the display. Gehrig had seen this show before from Ruth, but even he noticed that his teammate was in particularly fine form.

"The Babe is on fire," Gehrig said. "He ought to hit one today. Maybe a couple."

Gehrig tried to focus on the game. We might forgive Ruth's legendary teammate if he was a bit distracted, however. The night before, he had attended a party at which he met a woman named Eleanor Twitchell, daughter of the Chicago parks commissioner. In less than a year, the mama's boy was going to become a married man.

Charlie Root won more games than any other pitcher in Cubs history, but he lamented that his legacy hinges on "something that never happened."
PHOTO COURTESY OF NATIONAL BASEBALL HALL OF FAME LIBRARY, COOPERSTOWN, NEW YORK

Ruth, meanwhile, took the occasion to ride the Cubs even more. As he lofted yet another ball into the stands, he yelled, "I'd play for half my salary if I could hit in this dump all the time." His antics whipped Wrigley Field into a frenzy. After losing the first two games, the Cubs and their fans desperately wanted to turn the tide in the series. "The Cubs fans simply would not believe how severely or decisively their champions had been manhandled by the mighty Yankees in the East," wrote John Drebinger in the *New York Times*.

Pregame festivities featured players from both teams carrying an oversized American flag. A Marine Corps band playing patriotic music joined them. Leaning on his son James, Roosevelt threw out the first pitch from box 76, midway between the screen and the first base dugout.

The ballpark exploded when the Cubs took the field. Today was going to be different for Chicago. The fans knew that Charlie Root would put the Yankees in their place. Now in his seventh full season with the Cubs, Root anchored the pitching staff. Age 33, he won 15 games in 1932, making it the sixth time in seven years that he had hit or exceeded that victory total. He was a fierce competitor and earned the nickname "Chinski" for knocking hitters off the plate.

Always confident, Root thought he had the right approach for Game Three. Writing a first-person column for the *Chicago American,* he talked about the mistakes that Guy Bush and Lon Warneke had made in the first two games. "They were too careful. The way to pitch to the Yankees is not to be over-awed by their reputations, but to throw caution to the wind."

It didn't take long for the Yankees to make Root eat his words. In the first, Earle Combs, the Yankees' leadoff man, reached first base on an error by shortstop Billy Jurges, who had returned to the lineup after Mark Koenig hurt his wrist in Game Two. Root also appeared flustered, issuing a walk to the second hitter, Joe Sewell.

Two on with nobody out, and up to the plate stepped Ruth. The Cubs didn't allow him much leeway in the first two games, walking him three times. The big hitting star was Gehrig, who homered in Game One and had three hits in Game Two. Ruth knew, though, that Root couldn't pitch around him in this situation. As he walked from the on-deck circle to the batter's box, the boos rang through Wrigley. Again, a few lemons flew out from the stands. Ruth, dragging his bat, moved slowly, milking the moment for all the drama it was worth.

Meanwhile, the Cubs players were standing on the top steps of their dugout, led by pitcher Guy Bush. Known for having a tart tongue, Bush had won 176 games during a 17-year career—but like Root, Bush's legacy eventually tripped on failing to win his battles against Ruth. Fans within earshot heard Bush unleash a torrent of slurs at Ruth.

Ruth absorbed them, electing not to take the bait this time. Instead, he focused squarely at Root. With the count at 2–1, Root, not wanting to walk Ruth and leave the bases loaded for Gehrig, delivered a fastball that caught too much of the plate. Ruth knew immediately when he made contact where the ball would land. He still was standing in the batter's box when the ball finally arced down in those bleachers in right-center field.

While a mad scramble for the ball ensued in the stands, the remainder of the crowd marveled at the force of the blow . . . before they started booing again as Ruth toured the bases. Ruth could barely contain himself. It was sweet revenge for the spitting to which the people of Chicago had subjected him and his wife. The best, though, was yet to come.

Suddenly, the Yankees were up 3–0. The Cubs and their fans reeled. Maybe this game wasn't going to play out any differently than the first two. Nobody at Wrigley Field was in the mood to endure another blowout.

The fans breathed a sigh of relief when the Cubs got a run back in the first. Then, after Gehrig hit a long homer in the third to give the Yankees a 4–1 lead, the Cubs found life—with some help from Ruth. After Chicago scored two runs in the third to trim the deficit to one, Jurges opened the bottom of the fourth with a sinking line drive to left field. Ruth broke for the ball. Maybe in his younger days he would have made the catch, but with his legs mostly gone his gait looked almost like a waddle. He awkwardly lunged, trying to make an ill-advised shoestring catch. The ball slid past him for a double, and Jurges eventually scored the tying run.

The Wrigley crowd roared, taking enormous pleasure in watching the big oaf botch the play. The bleachers taunted Ruth once more, shouting at him to go eat some more hot dogs. They thought they were wearing him down, but really they were only raising Ruth's drive higher.

In the second inning Ruth had barely missed his second homer, sending a Root pitch to deep right field. Ruth didn't hammer quite all of it, though, and the ball was caught in front of the wall. The Cubs fans were relieved; Ruth gently kicked the dirt and turned to the dugout. Now with the game tied at 4–4, the Chicago faithful were back in full throat, feeling extremely cocky again. The Cubs also sensed a shift in the air, an energy returning to their dugout. Perhaps they could turn this series around. The stage for the fifth was set.

With the exception of the homer to Gehrig in the third, Root appeared to have settled down. In the fifth, Jurges energized Cubs fans even more when he went deep in the hole at shortstop to nail Sewell for the first out. Next up: Ruth.

‖‖‖‖‖‖‖‖‖‖‖‖‖‖‖‖‖‖‖‖‖‖‖‖‖

Now we lay our scene: Top of the fifth during Game Three of the World Series at Wrigley Field. One out and the score tied at 4–4.

Ruth already had done so much in his great career that it didn't seem likely that the slugger could eclipse his other achievements. Yet his next at bat delivered the defining moment of Ruth's life in baseball. That one swing landed a legendary blow, dissected and debated quite literally for generations, a symbol in itself of the mythical powers that the man possessed.

The anticipation of another showdown with Ruth transformed the stadium again. These weren't fans; they were an angry mob, rocking the ballpark with pent-up fury aimed squarely at Ruth. He may have thought that he had seen and heard it all over the course of his long career, but he never had experienced anything like this. The noise grew so loud that he almost didn't hear the slurs coming from the Cubs dugout—almost.

Ruth's ears couldn't help but funnel the barbs coming his way. Again, the players stood on the top steps, led by Bush and future Hall of Famer Burleigh Grimes. They called him a busher, a fat slob, and other terms not suitable for some of the young kids sitting within earshot.

Pat Pieper, the longtime Cubs public address announcer, was sitting behind home plate. "I heard things you can't print in a family newspaper," he said years later. "They sure were giving it to the Babe. Especially Guy Bush. Guy was really jockeying from the dugout. He'd cup his hands and holler insults to Ruth. I hoped that Commissioner Landis couldn't hear him because if he did Bush wasn't going to get any World Series check." Edward Burns of the *Chicago Tribune* wrote that the abuse hurled at Ruth "probably will go down as one of the classics of baseball razzing."

Frank Crosetti, the Yankees' young shortstop, recalled that Ruth's teammates also were taking full part in the volleys of nastiness. "He'd already hit one home run, and while he's up the Cubs in the dugout are really razzing Babe," Crosetti said. "In our dugout, we're really giving it back to the Cubs."

Ruth's animated reactions further spurred the Cubs and the crowd. "Shut your traps, you bums," Ruth is quoted as firing back at the Chicago dugout—although we can safely assume that he used more colorful language.

Meanwhile, standing on the mound, Root also wished—albeit privately—that his teammates would keep quiet. Hadn't they seen Ruth go deep on him in the first and almost take him out again in the second? The last thing Root wanted was the big guy getting an additional dose of motivation.

Ruth took the first pitch for a strike, much to the fans' delight. Then Root threw two pitches for balls. What happened next became the seminal moment of Ruth's career, the lead anecdote in the litany of his vast success.

With the count at 2–1, the razzing from the Cubs dugout now intensified. Bush and several teammates even went so far as to jump onto the field, badgering Ruth with increased vigor. Egged on by Bush's antics, the crowd had grown so loud that even Root barely could hear himself think.

Then Ruth extended his arm and appeared to wave his hand. Was this when he motioned to center field and called his shot, or was he pointing at the Cubs players, directing them to get their behinds back in the dugout?

This much is certain: If you were at Wrigley Field that day, you saw Ruth make a grand gesture of some sort with the count at 2–1. Players on the field, fans in the stands, and writers in the press box all saw him do something unusual following that last pitch. Everyone leaned in to see how the drama would unfold.

To clarify things: This gesture didn't occur on the pitch just prior to Ruth hitting the famous homer. It was after a Root delivery that skittered away from Cubs catcher Gabby Hartnett. The future Hall of Famer fired the ball back at Root. The pitcher tried to collect his thoughts. It was a hitter's count, but he didn't want to give Ruth anything to hit. Root took a couple steps, toed the rubber, then tried to block out the commotion swirling around him. He went into his windup and delivered.

Ruth shifted his weight as if he might swing. Instead, he let the ball whiz past him. The home plate umpire, Roy Van Graflon, raised his right arm and signaled strike two. Wrigley Field erupted. Chicago was thrilled that Root wasn't going to back down from facing the Yankees slugger. No, old Charlie was going to fight back with his best stuff. He was only one good pitch away from striking out the bum, the unsuspecting crowd thought.

As Hartnett returned the ball to Root again, Ruth cocked his arm and, his hand at chin level, extended one finger of his right hand. Again, what was he doing? What was the meaning of that gesture, which was subtler than the first one?

According to Hartnett, Ruth said, "It takes only one to hit it." Gehrig is quoted as saying that Ruth called out to Root, "I'm going to knock the next one down your goddamn throat." Umpire Van Graflon said that he heard Ruth announce rather primly, "Let him put this one over, and I'll knock it over the wall out there."

From his seat behind the Cubs dugout, Stevens, the future Supreme Court justice, took it all in. Only 12 years old at the time, Stevens was yelling at Ruth to quit clowning around. After all, he was a Cubs fan.

In his private box Governor Roosevelt also saw Ruth's antics. No stranger to a good political scuffle, the president-to-be was watching in rapt attention this contest of a different sort play out in front of him.

Up in the press box sat Grantland Rice, the poet laureate of sports-writers and a witness to most of Ruth's previous magical moments. As Rice intently watched the byplay between the Cubs and Ruth, he had an inkling that the Sultan of Swat was about to add to his legend.

Over in the dugout Yankees manager Joe McCarthy wondered what Ruth was doing. A stern man who didn't have much tolerance for nonsense, McCarthy worried that all the bluster from the Cubs might have distracted Ruth. But there was little he could do to rein in his wild star. Events had already played out too far to turn back now.

Nor was Commissioner Landis amused. Sitting close to the Cubs dugout he felt his ears burn—to say nothing of his sense of propriety—at the torrents of obscenities crisscrossing the field between Ruth and the Cubs dugout. Landis was even more acutely aware of it because his young nephew was sitting right there beside him and could hear it all, too. What kind of example were these players setting for him? The commissioner, who ruled the game with a tight fist, had had quite enough. After the game he decreed that anyone caught using foul lan-guage in the remainder of the series would be fined $500.

Kneeling in the on-deck circle, Gehrig smiled slightly, unsur-prised. After all, this was the World Series, and Ruth was trying to show up the Cubs. It was something that the reserved Gehrig would never do.

But what exactly did those hand gestures mean? Was Ruth spotlight-ing Bush, telling him to get back into the dugout? Was he emphasizing his message to Root? Was he announcing that he only had two strikes on him? Or was there more? Was he really pointing to center field, calling his shot like a pool hustler?

Talk about audacity. Ruth had hit more than 600 homers at this point in his career and had performed feats of power that shattered the boundaries of baseball fans' imaginations. But to predict a homer and then point to its ultimate destination? Certainly Ruth was smarter than to attempt that cheap trick.

As Root went into his delivery, the crowd roared yet again, this time in anticipation of Van Graflon recording Ruth's third strike. Despite the tumult, Ruth's instincts locked in on the pitch. It was a change-up curve, low and away, only a foot off the ground. Root later said that no other player in the game would have been able to do anything with what should have been ball three.

Ruth's right foot moved forward while he built power by keeping his hands back. His strong arms propelled the bat swiftly through the zone. At the exact moment of impact, leather compressed against wood—and then the ball began its journey into history.

When the ball first reversed against the bat, sportswriter Tom Meany thought that Cubs second baseman Billy Herman had a chance to catch the line drive. The ball kept rising, though, as if launched from a cannon. Cubs center fielder Johnny Moore took a few steps back and then stopped, giving up the futile chase. Improbably the ball still appeared to be ascending as it passed over his head. This wasn't going to be some wind-blown chip shot that barely made the seats. No, this homer was about to demonstrate the essence of what sportswriters like Rice had defined as a "Ruthian" blast.

The ball whizzed past the right side of the center field fence and kept flying. Nobody had ever reached that neighborhood at Wrigley Field—not even Cubs slugger Hack Wilson, who pounded out 56 homers in 1930. Estimates placed the homer's distance at nearly 500 feet. According to reports, seven different fans outside the stadium all said that they caught the ball.

Elation surged through Ruth in the instant that he made contact with the ball. He knew that he had airmailed a souvenir to the bleachers. "You lucky bum," Ruth said to himself as he headed to first base. "You lucky bum." As talented as Ruth was, he also realized that he had gotten away with a fast one. Regardless of whether he had pointed to center field, all of his antics called for a dramatic ending to that at bat—one way or another. He could have cut a meek grounder, a soft pop-up, or the air-piercing strikeout that the stadium wanted. Instead, he stunned the crowd, and even himself, with one of the longest homers that he had ever bashed.

By the time Ruth reached first base, he literally had become giddy over his accomplishment. Typically, Ruth's homers preceded a long, languid trot around the bases, extending his version of an encore. But not for this homer. Ruth was so excited that he practically sprinted around the bases. Even his own teammates cracked that they hadn't seen him run that fast in quite some time. Picking up speed, he gestured wildly, flashing four fingers at the Cubs infielders and their dugout. He was letting them know—in no uncertain terms this time—that this series was going to be over in four games.

"Squeeze the Eagle Club!" he shouted at the Chicago dugout, referring to their tightfistedness ("Squeeze the eagle [on the quarter] until it screams" went the saying) at awarding only half a share to Koenig of the 1932 World Series bonus.

The crowd was stunned. Ruth's bat, in addition to hitting the ball, had also delivered a blow to the hopes and dreams of the 50,000 fans at Wrigley Field. They had come to beat Ruth, and he beat them. Governor Roosevelt let out a hearty laugh, savoring every moment of Ruth's show.

Ruth couldn't recall ever feeling this good after a homer. As he was greeted by teammates, he let out a triumphant chant: "Did Mr. Ruth chase those guys back into the dugout? Mr. Ruth sure did!"

Rattled, Root nervously paced the mound, hoping—probably begging—that this nightmare somehow would fade. He couldn't believe that Ruth had victimized him again. Little did he know that the home run he had just allowed would define his own career as well. Gehrig came up next and hit Root's next pitch into the right field bleachers for his second homer of the day. Root was done. Cubs manager Charlie Grimm quickly yanked him and put him out of his misery. So much for his pregame edict of "throwing caution to the wind."

After Pat Malone recorded the final two outs in the inning, something amazing happened. As Ruth trotted out to left field for the top of the sixth, the same Cubs fans who had been pelting him with abuse just a few minutes earlier rose to their feet. Ruth actually received a standing ovation in a visiting ballpark during a World Series game. All the fans in Wrigley Field on October 1, 1932, knew that they had witnessed a majestic display of athleticism from the greatest player ever to play the game. It was perfection—from a large man swinging a piece of wood.

Ruth acknowledged the crowd's cheers with a soft tip of the cap as he took his position. Then he tried to calm his brain and focus on the task at hand. Ruth's blow had sapped all the juice from the Cubs. Still, the Yankees needed to finish them off. The remainder of the game proved anticlimatic. Both teams added meaningless runs in the ninth, with Yankees reliever Herb Pennock closing out the Cubs to seal a 7–5 victory.

Ruth could hardly contain himself during the celebration in the locker room. Meanwhile, in the Cubs locker room, Bush, who had led the verbal assault on Ruth, had to admit, "That boy sure can take it." The loser in Game One, Bush started Game Four. The Yankees had no intention of playing a Game Five.

Everyone knew the series was already over when they arrived at Wrigley Field the next day. Even Cubs fans were still buzzing at the power play they had seen from Ruth and Gehrig the day before. The Yankees all but chirped during batting practice—especially Ruth. In a fine mood, he knew that another World Series title lay just nine innings away. Meanwhile, the Cubs tried to convince themselves that they could make history by becoming the first team to rally from a 3–0 deficit. It was a futile effort.

Bush had his pride on the line, though. He wanted to make the Yankees, especially Ruth, eat their own words. But he had a problem.

As he stepped to the mound to make his first pitch, Bush was distracted by what had happened the day before. He hadn't forgotten Game Three. He gave up back-to-back hits to Combs and Sewell to open the game, and then Ruth stepped up to the plate. Bush needed an out. Instead, he was out for revenge. He wound up and fired at fastball directly at Ruth. This wasn't a pitch that got away; this was Bush's own version of a called shot.

The ball struck Ruth on his right wrist. He tried to brush it off as he trotted down to first. "Hey, lop ears, was that your fastball?" he called out to the pitcher. "I thought it was a gnat."

In reality, though, Ruth was hurt. After the game Ruth wrapped his aching wrist in hot towels. Some doubted whether he would have been able to play if the series had extended beyond four games.

But there was little chance of that happening as the Yankees zeroed in on the kill. The Cubs got off to a fast start, knocking out Yankees starter Johnny Allen with four runs in the first. It only delayed the inevitable. Gehrig and Lazzeri led the assault with seven RBIs combined. The Yankees scored their own four runs in the seventh and then put the game away with another four-spot in the ninth, with Pennock pitching the final three innings to wrap up the 13–6 victory.

The Yankees outscored the Cubs 37–19 in the sweep. It was a complete massacre, about which Grantland Rice grimly wrote: "The bitter anguish of Cub pitchers is over at last, but the nightmare will linger on. Their dreams for many a week to come will still be haunted by heavy thunder and the rush of spiked feet around the bases. They will wake up at night to see the leering specters of Ruth and Gehrig looking out from the shadows, with mocking smiles." But the real goat of the series was Bush, not Root. He talked big, but he couldn't back it up. He lost Game One and only got one out in Game Four before being lifted.

In the Yankees locker room at Wrigley Field, the beer flowed, and the players hugged anyone in sight as they celebrated their first title in four years. The sweep proved especially sweet for McCarthy: His new team had obliterated his former team. McCarthy made the Cubs look foolish for firing him. "I'm the happiest man in all the world," he said. "I figured we could do it. We simply had too much power for them. I am proud of the Yankees; proud of them as players and proud of them as men."

Even Ruth, who still chafed that Ruppert had selected McCarthy to manage the club, put aside any hard feelings. "Boy, what a victory," said Ruth, shaking McCarthy's hand. "My hat is off to you, Mac."

Ruth let out a piercing yell as the party got into full swing, the players basking in the victory with a massively out-of-tune rendition of "The Sidewalks of New York." Below the din Commissioner Landis and American League president Will Harridge congratulated Ruppert and McCarthy for a job well done.

The players changed quickly and raced back to the Edgewater Hotel. They stuffed their bags and dashed to the LaSalle Street station in time to catch the 6 p.m. train to New York. Iconic tap dancer Bill "Bojangles" Robinson came along for the ride. At every stop he and Ruth greeted the cheering crowds. Inside the train, Robinson danced, and the players drank—following Ruth's lead, of course.

Playing in what turned out to be his final World Series, Ruth hit .333 with two homers and six RBIs. Not bad, but Gehrig, who had blitzed the Cubs with a .529 average with three homers and eight RBIs in four games, outshone him. Gehrig had clearly demonstrated himself to be the most valuable player of this series. Yet as was the case so often, Gehrig found himself in Ruth's large shadow once again. Sure, Gehrig had put on a magnificent offensive display. But all anyone wanted to talk about was that one swing of the bat in Game Three at Wrigley.

And perhaps rightfully so. From the standpoint of statistics and strategy, Ruth's at bat in the fifth inning might have turned around the entire series. The Cubs had rallied to tie the game. Momentum was on their side. If Root had retired Ruth, especially with a strikeout, who knows what would have happened? Maybe the Cubs would have continued their surge, won Game Three, and rode the home crowd with a victory in Game Four. It would have been a case of anything goes with the showdown tied at 2–2.

But Ruth's monumental blow changed everything. The legend of the Called Shot was taking shape, and the debate over what the Bambino did on October 1, 1932, had just begun.

SIDEBAR

"Loudmouth"

There's another element in the story that we haven't considered yet. Some say that Ruth was targeting a heckler in the Wrigley Field bleachers that day.

According to black reporters covering the game, Amos Latimer, also black, drew Ruth's ire during Game Three. The reason lay in Latimer's nickname: "Loudmouth." Well known among visiting outfielders to Wrigley Field, he could deliver a nonstop torrent of abuse to distract visiting players and aid the cause of his hometown Cubs.

Game Three was the first time Ruth encountered Loudmouth at Wrigley Field since he had played in the American League. According to accounts that identify the heckler, Latimer was in fine fettle against the biggest star in baseball. After Ruth hit his three-run homer in the first, Loudmouth called him names, much to the delight of fellow fans in the bleachers. He even tossed lemon peels at Ruth. "Aw, the big bum, he ain't no good," Latimer shouted. "That [first inning homer] was just an accident. Get him a pair of crutches!"

Ruth had had enough, according to Alvin White, who covered the game for the Associated Negro Press. The slugger turned around and gestured at Latimer. The interpretation: "My next homer is coming your way."

When Ruth came up in the fifth, White reported that he doffed his cap in Loudmouth's direction. "The Babe held up one finger, signifying that it only took one swing to hit the apple," White wrote. Then the slugger hit his famous homer, which landed only a few feet away from Latimer.

Was Ruth really aiming at Loudmouth? In all the coverage of the homer, Ruth never mentioned a heckler. But the story quickly circulated in the black community in Chicago and has been retold for generations, the legend of Loudmouth becoming part of the legend of the Called Shot.

SEVEN

Landis

He raised his arm up in the air and had one finger [pointing]. He
definitely pointed. Everyone saw him do it.
—LINCOLN LANDIS, WHO ATTENDED THE GAME WITH HIS
UNCLE, KENESAW MOUNTAIN LANDIS

He never intended to play the role. But as the years passed, taking with
them the spectators and participants on hand for Game Three of the 1932
World Series, Lincoln Landis became a self-appointed guardian of one of
the most important moments in baseball history.

During an interview on a chilly winter day early in 2013, Landis, now
90, reflected on being there at Wrigley Field that day. His voice was strong,
and so was his conviction. Yes, Babe Ruth called his shot, Landis insisted.
You bet he pointed, he maintained with firm certainty.

Whenever a modern sports historian calls the Called Shot a myth,
Landis pulls out his ultimate trump card: I was there; you weren't.

"Everyone in the stadium knew he pointed to center field," Landis said.
"No doubt about it."

Lincoln Landis (right, as a boy) was thrilled to discover a picture of him sitting with his famous uncle, Commissioner Kenesaw Mountain Landis, during Game Three of the 1932 World Series.
PHOTO COURTESY OF LINCOLN LANDIS

Landis relishes every opportunity to go back to the past and talk about attending his first Major League baseball game with his uncle in 1932. Of course, it wasn't just any baseball game, and his uncle wasn't just another fan.

Ten years old at the time, Landis received a phone call from his uncle, asking if he and his brother, Charlie, wanted to attend Game Three of the World Series between the Yankees and Cubs. Young Lincoln called him Uncle Squire, but the rest of the world knew him as Kenesaw Mountain Landis, the former judge whom President Theodore Roosevelt had appointed and who became baseball's first commissioner.

"He had white hair at an early age," Landis said. "He picked up the nickname [Squire] and never gave it up. It really fit his personality."

The commissioner and young Landis's father, Frederick, who served as a US congressman, were the only survivors of five brothers. Young Landis remembered visits from Uncle Squire during which the brothers sat on the front porch, smoking cigars. The discussion always touched on politics rather than baseball. Nevertheless, young Landis always emphasized the baseball angle whenever he talked about his famous uncle to his friends.

"They were impressed," Landis said. "I was short, but having the commissioner as my uncle made me stand a little taller."

Growing up in Logansport, Indiana, Landis and his brother naturally were huge Cubs fans. They were overwhelmed when they saw Wrigley's green field for the first time. Landis remembered it as "a beautiful sunny day." He and his brother, along with the rest of the commissioner's entourage, sat in the commissioner's box just to the right of the Cubs dugout. Photographers snapped pictures as the number one man in baseball, with his distinctive white hair and piercing eyes, peered out over the field.

"This was really big-time," Landis said.

Back then, Landis had no way of knowing that one of those pictures would provide a sense of validation more than seven decades later.

Landis openly admits that he can't recall exact details of the game. For instance, he doesn't recall Ruth hitting a three-run homer in the first inning. That should have made for a searing memory in itself, considering that it was the first time Landis had ever seen the great slugger at the plate. But perhaps he was distracted by munching on a hot dog and soda or something else caught his attention. We can forgive him a little fuzziness of memory. After all, he attended the game more than 80 years ago.

Landis *is* certain about what he saw during Ruth's at bat in the fifth inning. "That event made such an impression on me," he said. What stood out for him was the fervor of the crowd. As Ruth walked to the plate, Wrigley Field boiled over in anticipation of his next confrontation with Charlie Root. Even at the tender age of 10, Landis knew this moment was different. "There was such an enthusiastic roar from the Cubs fans," he said. "They were really razzing him. . . . We were all yelling."

Sitting next to the third base dugout, Landis had a clear view of Ruth, who hit left-handed. Landis remembers the two strikes called on the slugger but not the two balls that Root threw. "After the first pitch he held up his right arm and raised one finger," Landis said. "Even as a kid, I knew he was saying, 'That was only the first one.'

"Then he turned around and took his stance again. After the second strike he raised two fingers. It doesn't take a genius to realize, 'That's only two strikes.' In my mind he's saying, 'Just wait and see what I'm going to do with the next one.'"

What about the moment of truth?

"Then he resumed his regular spot and pointed to center field. He raised his arm up in the air and had one finger [pointing]. He definitely pointed. Everyone saw him do it."

Landis remembers seeing the ball fly through the air. A novice fan, initially he thought it might be a high pop-up. He soon learned otherwise, however, as the ball soared over everyone and then the center field fence before disappearing into a throng of fans anxious for a souvenir.

What happened next, in Landis's view, proved to him that Ruth pointed. The Cubs fans, who had been riding him mercilessly just a few seconds earlier, suddenly started to cheer for the slugger and the deed they had just witnessed. There was such a commotion, Landis said, that fans didn't pay attention to the next batter, Gehrig, who homered on the first pitch.

"Everyone was standing up and waving their arms," Landis said. "This was not just another Babe Ruth homer. He was expected to hit homers. This was different. The fans went bananas. They were going crazy because of what they saw him do. It was: 'Wow, did you just see that? How could he do that? How did he hit the ball where he pointed to center field?'

"If anyone in the stadium doubted that he pointed and hit it there, I would be very surprised. All the fans knew it. That's why they were going nutty. They suddenly had a love for Babe Ruth. He pulled a good one on them. We were razzing him, and he stuffed it down our throats. There's absolutely no question that the fans were saying he pointed. And by golly, he did it. It was unbelievable."

\|\|\|\|\|\|\|\|\|\|\|\|\|\|\|\|\|\|\|\|\|\|\|\|\|\|\|\|\|\|\|\|

Those back-to-back homers by Ruth and Gehrig effectively ended the Cubs in Game Three. But Landis does have another lasting memory from that day.

Commissioner Landis asked whether his nephews wanted to meet one of the players. Sure, they said. They were Cubs fans, so they requested Gabby Hartnett. A few minutes later, they were shaking hands with the future Hall of Famer. That's the moment when it dawned on Landis that his uncle was a very important man. "We started thinking Uncle Squire must have a lot of power to get him to come and meet us."

Only later did young Landis discover that his uncle deplored the antics that had played out between the Cubs and Ruth during their big confrontation. The commissioner threatened to impose a fine on players if they misbehaved in Game Four.

"He could be persnickety," said Landis of his no-nonsense uncle.

After chatting with Hartnett the boys said good-bye to the commissioner and went back home. In the years following the game, Landis didn't think much about the Called Shot. He eventually attended West Point, served in the army for 20 years, and then worked for the government. After retiring in 1991 he kept himself busy by writing a book about his father, uncle, and their brothers.

But for Landis, Game Three of the 1932 World Series "always was in my blood." As the years passed, people tried to poke holes in the fabric of Ruth's famous homer, which upset the army man. So, along with the book about his family, he resolved to "straighten out the record about Babe Ruth."

Landis knew photographers constantly shot pictures of the commissioner, so he asked his son, Tim, an avid collector of baseball memorabilia, whether he could find a photo of him with his uncle from Game Three.

"Sure, Dad," said Tim. "I'll keep my eyes open."

In 2002 Tim spotted an interesting auction on eBay. It was a picture of Judge Landis, resting his chin on a railing, during the 1932 World Series. A familiar young face was sitting next to the commissioner. "I looked at it and said, 'Oh my God, that's me.' It was the greatest day of my life," recalled Lincoln. "To think that there was a picture of me with Uncle Squire."

Tim Landis bid $362.50 for the photo of his father and granduncle. In Lincoln's eyes it represented an important piece of evidence. The picture helped validate his position that Ruth had pointed to center field. "It shows that I was there and where I was sitting," Landis said.

Landis knows that some people doubt the veracity of his memory because he can't recall other aspects of the game, especially Ruth's three-run homer in the first. But so be it. It was the moment of a lifetime for the boy. "I feel so honored to have been there and to remember it so clearly," he said.

EIGHT

Witnesses

I'm not going to say he didn't do it. Maybe I didn't see it. Maybe I was looking the other way. Anyway, I'm not going to say he didn't do it.
—Yankees manager Joe McCarthy

More than 50,000 people attended Game Three of the 1932 World Series. The roll call included 14 future Baseball Hall of Famers, a soon-to-be president of the country, a future Supreme Court justice, the first commissioner of Major League Baseball, the premier sportswriters of the time (or any time, some argue), future Hall of Fame broadcasters, and thousands of fans.

It would have been a memorable day even without the Called Shot. Onlookers took in a terrific, intense game. Babe Ruth *and* Lou Gehrig each hit two home runs in a majestic display of power. If that alone wasn't memory enough for a lifetime, nothing would be. But Ruth's antics elevated the day to another level. This wasn't just another World Series game. No, this was the game in which Ruth hit the most debated homer in baseball history.

Did Ruth really call his shot?

Suddenly, all the people in the stands weren't just fans; they were witnesses. What they saw and how they interpreted it served as vital testimony in an age before ubiquitous TV cameras covered every possible angle in a World Series game. But as with so many controversial moments, what they had to say only muddled the picture and added further intrigue to the Called Shot.

The witnesses were split. The divide resembles a modern political map of Democrats and Republicans. Some maintain that Ruth did indeed point to center or right field on that fateful day. Others say not a chance.

Why the split? Perhaps those who affirmed the Called Shot fell victim to the mythology attached to the feat. They wanted to believe what they wanted to believe: *Of course it happened. I was there, so I saw it with my own eyes.* And what of the naysayers? Maybe they simply missed Ruth making his grand gesture. Maybe they lacked the imagination to believe that a player could pull off such a stunt—even the greatest player of all time. Perhaps pedestrian logic prevented them from acknowledging the extraordinary.

Several witnesses admitted their uncertainty. Long before he became an icon in his profession, Red Smith covered the game as a young sportswriter for the *St. Louis Journal*. Years later, he wrote:

> *I was there, but I never have been dead sure of what I saw. . . . Ruth made some sort of sign with his bat, some said, and their version has become gospel, that he aimed it like a rifle at the bleachers in right-centerfield.*
>
> *With all the dialogue and pantomime that went on, there was no telling what Ruth was saying to Root. When the papers reported that he had called his shot, he did not deny it.*

Ruth's manager, Joe McCarthy, remained coy when people asked for his account of that fabled day. McCarthy had an icy relationship with Ruth, though, remember, so perhaps he didn't want to burnish Ruth's legend. Happily, the pair did get a bit closer during the '32 World Series, both of them relishing beating up on the Cubs. "I'm not going to say he didn't do it," McCarthy said. "Maybe I didn't see it. Maybe I was looking the other way. Anyway, I'm not going to say he didn't do it."

Most of the witnesses, both famous and ordinary, adamantly held their opinions of what they saw. Regardless of their perspective, they all had one thing in common: There were there for one of the greatest moments in baseball history.

THE NAYSAYERS

Gabby Hartnett

Physically no one was standing closer to Ruth during that fateful at bat than the Cubs catcher. Squatting behind the plate, he could see everything and definitely heard the byplay between Ruth and his own dugout. That makes Hartnett a key witness to what transpired.

By all accounts a terrific guy, Hartnett had a high regard for Ruth. "In a World Series or just an ordinary game, Babe had class," Hartnett said. "You expected him to murder that ball, and he did. In that 1932 series, we tried every kind of pitch on him. It didn't make any difference. He rammed the ball down our throats. There'll never be another like him."

But Hartnett declined to endorse the Called Shot. After he retired he gave the following account of what happened.

"I don't want to take anything away from the Babe, who was and always will be the best in my book. But the truth of the story is this: The Cubs were riding Ruth something awful. . . . He came up in the fifth inning and took two strikes. After each one, the Cub bench gave him the business—stuff like he was choking and washed-up.

"Then Babe waved his hand across the plate toward the Cub bench on the third-base side. One finger was up. At the same time he said softly—I think only the umpire and myself heard him—'It only takes one to hit it.'

"Charlie Root then came in with a fast one and [Babe hit it] into the centerfield seats. That was it. It may have looked different to the press box and the grandstand because of the angle of Ruth's gesture.

"Babe didn't say a word when he passed me after the home run. If he had pointed out at the bleachers I would be the first to say so."

Mark Koenig

The player who triggered all the bad blood between the Cubs and Yankees was benched with an injury for Game Three. Even though his name forever interconnects with the Called Shot, Ruth's former teammate on the '27 Yankees disputed the tale.

"As far as pointing to center, no he didn't. You know darn well a guy with two strikes isn't going to say he's going to hit the next pitch for a home run.

"We never thought he pointed. It was more like, 'It only takes one.' But if we ever thought he pointed, he would have been thrown at. Even the pitcher, Charlie Root, told me, 'If that big monkey was pointing into the stands, I would have stuck the next pitch in his ear.' The fact that Root didn't throw at him proves Babe didn't point. But it was still a heck of a shot."

Bill Dickey and Shirley Povich

Like Red Smith, Povich was also a young sportswriter covering Game Three for the *Washington Post*. He went on to have a long and extraordinary career with the *Washington Post*, still churning out columns past the age of 90.

Povich doubted that Ruth actually pointed. In 1938 he wrote a column saying the tale was pure myth. He validated his view by getting the inside story from Yankees Hall of Fame catcher Bill Dickey. Povich wrote, "I was in Chicago's Wrigley Field on that day when Ruth brought everybody out of their seats with the damnedest demonstration you ever saw. Did he really call his shot? Baseball tradition says so, and tradition extended over a sufficient period of time tends to be regarded as fact. The real fact is that Babe Ruth's Called Shot homer run was no called shot at all."

Povich also detailed his exchange with Dickey:

DICKEY: Ruth just got mad about that quick pitch. . . . [He said,] "Don't do that to me anymore, you [bleep]."

POVICH: How do you know?

DICKEY: Because Ruth told us when he came back to the bench.

POVICH: How come you never told anybody?

DICKEY: All of us players could see it was a helluva good story. So we just made an agreement not to bother straightening out the facts.

Then Povich concluded, "They were right. It was a helluva good story. It has endured over the years, and nobody has been hurt. On the contrary, it has provided baseball with one of its classic folk tales. It just never happened, that's all."

Ben Chapman

The Yankee outfielder agrees with Dickey's version: "He was pointing at the pitcher. Someone asked him, 'Babe, did you call that home run?' Babe answered, 'No, but I called Root everything I could think of.'"

Frank Crosetti

The Yankee shortstop based his account on his conversation with Ruth. Crosetti interpreted Ruth raising his finger as saying, "I got one strike left," or "Lay one in I can hit."

Later, Crosetti said, "Never once in the dugout or even after the game until the writers asked him about 'pointing' did Babe ever say he pointed. I think he was theatrical and made up the story they wanted to hear, after they had already given him the details, just to have fun with them.

"After being grilled by the writers about his point into the stands, Babe sat down next to me and winked. He said, 'You know I didn't point, and I know I didn't point, but if those bastards [the writers] want to think I pointed to center field, let 'em.'"

Charlie Devens

The young Yankees pitcher initially believed, but Crosetti's story eventually swayed him. "Ruth was being ridden by the Cubs the entire series, and he would ride them right back. At the time, I did think

Babe was pointing to the bleachers, but Frankie Crosetti told me no, he put up one finger to indicate he had another strike coming. I think Frankie Crosetti was right, but Babe never denied that he was pointing to the stands."

Devens did believe Ruth made some sort of gesture, though. "It was quite extraordinary to see him point, then hit the very next pitch out of the ballpark."

Charlie Grimm

With the exception of Guy Bush, the Cubs all counted the Ruth story a myth. Grimm, first baseman and manager of the team, wrote about the Called Shot:

"I hesitate to spoil a good story, one that has been built up to such proportions down the years that millions of people have insisted they saw the gesture, but the Babe actually was pointing to the mound. I heard Ruth growl [to Bush], 'You'll be out there tomorrow, so we'll see what you can do with me, you so-and-so tightwad.'

"If he [Root] could have called any one of the thousands of pitches he made for the Cubs, the one Ruth picked on would have been his choice. Let's face it, though, a great guy hit that homer, the greatest slugger of all time. And if you want to believe he really planned it that way, you just go right ahead."

Woody English

The Cubs third baseman had a good perspective, looking straight in on the left-hitting Ruth.

"Ruth was up and I peered at him from third base. He was staring right at our guys in the dugout, and, boy, they were calling him every name in the book. I saw him hold up two fingers, meaning, 'That's only two.' He did not call his shot. He was looking at our guys, and his hand crossed the plate on his way back to the bat. Then he hit the ball very hard, and, although I'm sure he was trying to hit a home run, he never called it.

"That is the true story. I've been asked that question 500 times."

Billy Herman

The Cubs Hall of Fame second baseman was quite sure of what he saw.

"He really didn't do it. I hate to explode one of baseball's great legends, but I was there and saw what happened. Sure, he made a gesture, he pointed—but it wasn't to call his shot. Listen, he was a great hitter and a great character, but do you think he would have put himself on the spot like that?

"When he held up his hand, that's where the pointing came in. But he was pointing toward Charlie Root when he did that, not toward the centerfield bleachers. And then, of course, he hit the next pitch out of the ballpark. Then the legend started that he had called his shot, and Babe went along with it. Why not?

"But he didn't point. Don't kid yourself. If Ruth had tried that, he would never have got a pitch to hit. Root would have had him with his feet up in the air."

Burleigh Grimes

The Cubs pitcher goes along with the theory that Ruth's gesture represented one strike remaining. "What I heard, they [the Cubs bench] berated Ruth because he had two strikes. They said, 'What are you going to do now?' Then Ruth pointed his finger at the Cubs bench and said, 'I've got the big one left.'"

Edgar Munzel

The longtime baseball writer covered the game for the *Chicago Herald Examiner* and "thought Ruth raised his finger to indicate the number of strikes, and did not make a pointing gesture."

William Leonard

In 1957 Leonard, a Chicago baseball writer who covered the game, wrote a retrospective for the *Chicago Tribune* on the 25th anniversary of the Called Shot. He left little doubt on where he stood.

Just a quarter of a century ago, day after tomorrow, it didn't happen.

It never seems to occur to the folks who cling to the fairy tale that, if Babe had actually pointed to the center field seats and told the Cubs that's where he was going to hit it, Root would have put the next pitch right under his chin. Remember, there were two strikes and no balls on Ruth at the time!

Fairy tales won't die, but I was there too, that day, and I'll go along with Root, Hartnett, Herman and the rest. Day after tomorrow is the 25th anniversary of something that never happened.

It's worth noting, however, that Leonard got the count wrong. It was 2–2, not 0–2, so perhaps his memories of that day weren't as clear as he thought.

THE BELIEVERS

Lou Gehrig

Gehrig had an ideal view of Ruth during the fifth inning of Game Three. The younger slugger rested on bended knee in the on-deck circle, preparing for his turn at home plate. Their personal relationship may have been strained, but Gehrig still respected Ruth as a player and at times marveled at what the elder statesman of their sport could do. His testimony is telling in this instance.

At first Gehrig said he didn't see Ruth call his shot. More than 20 years after the game, New York baseball writer Joe Williams wrote a column that quoted Gehrig as saying, "The gestures were meant for Bush. Ruth was going to foul one into the dugout, but when the pitch came up big and fat, he belted it."

But another version of Gehrig's sentiments comes from sportswriter Fred Lieb, one of Gehrig's closest friends. The two had dinner after Game Three, and Gehrig made a believer out Lieb. "There was never any question that Ruth called the shot," Lieb said in Jerome Holtzman's *No Cheering in the Press Box*. "I had dinner with Lou the night of the game. Lou hit two home runs himself, but all he could talk about was: 'What do you think of the nerve of that big monkey calling his shot and taking those two strikes and then hitting the ball exactly where he pointed?'

"That's how Lou was. He was content to push himself backward and push the Babe forward." Those who support that Ruth predicted the homer still quote Gehrig's "nerve of that big monkey" line in their defense.

Lefty Gomez

The Hall of Fame pitcher signed an artist's drawing of the Called Shot that depicts Ruth raising his right arm and pointing to center field. Gomez wrote, "To Bill: Babe actually pointed and called the home run shot. I was there. Best regards, Lefty Gomez." Elsewhere the pitcher also clarified a key detail: "Ruth pointed with his bat in his right, to right field, not centerfield. But he definitely called his shot."

George Pipgras

The Yankees pitcher who started Game Three also supported the right field angle. "The Babe pointed out to right field, and that's right where he hit the ball."

Joe Sewell

The Yankees shortstop agreed. "Don't believe a word any of the writers have to say about the incident. Yes, he pointed to the fence, and I have a mental picture of the ball going out of the park in centerfield, through trees loaded with small boys seeing the game.

"Regardless of what anyone says or writes, that is the way I saw it all happen because I was in the game. I always will remember that series and that one special game."

Cy Perkins

The Yankees coach based his remarks on a postgame conversation with Ruth. "Don't let anyone ever tell you that Babe didn't point. In our hotel room that night Babe told me what a sucker he had been to point: 'Look how many ways they could have gotten me out.'"

Doc Painter

According to the Yankees trainer, "When Babe got back to the bench, [pitcher Herb] Pennock said, 'Suppose you would have missed. You would have looked like an awful bum.' Ruth laughed, 'I never thought of that.'"

Guy Bush

Of all people, Bush, the instigator in this saga, thought Ruth called his shot. In fact, he takes credit for riling Ruth up. "I'm going to be honest with you. I thought he pointed to the right-center or centerfield bleachers. Charlie Root pitched the ball just as soon as Ruth stepped back into the box, and when he did Ruth hit the ball clear out of the ballpark. . . . I believe Ruth meant to call the home run. He was so mad, see. I believe that he pointed, and I'll always believe that he pointed."

Pat Pieper

Pieper announced for the Cubs for 56 years. He called the starting lineups with his trademark, "Attention! Attention, please! Have your pencil and scorecards ready . . ." For Game Three he perched behind the plate, so he also had a clear view of Ruth during that at bat.

Pieper loved to tell his Called Shot story, giving this version to *Chicago Tribune* columnist David Condon: "Don't let anyone tell you that Ruth didn't call that shot. I was in a perfect position to see and hear everything.

"With two strikes, Ruth lifted his bat, pointed toward the center field flag pole, and dug in for Charley [*sic*] Root's next pitch. That was the most terrific home run I've ever seen. It went out of the park at almost precisely the same spot that Ruth had indicated. As far as I'm concerned, that ball is still traveling. You bet your life Babe Ruth called it."

Ford Frick

The future MLB commissioner was also Ruth's ghostwriter, and he worked hard to preserve Ruth's legend. As commissioner in 1961, Frick made the controversial decision to apply a "special designation"—later known as an asterisk—to Roger Maris's mark of 61 homers, noting that he accomplished that number in 162 games. Frick's resolution allowed Ruth to remain in the record book with 60 homers in 154 games. As a result of his bias, Frick likely had extra incentive to affirm the Called Shot. He wrote:

> *At that point, Ruth stepped from the box, dusted his hand, and then raised his right arm, with one finger extended, in the now famous gesture. . . . At that moment, there was no doubt in my mind, or in the minds of any of the writers who were covering the Yankees. The Big Guy had done it again. He had called his shot, and in the most spotlighted arena imaginable.*

Tom Meany

The longtime sportswriter who covered Ruth and wrote a biography on him had this to say on the matter: "Emily Post to the contrary, everyone agrees that Babe did point in the direction of the centerfield fence and that he did hit a home run there, and that's good enough for me."

Bob Elson

Elson was working on the radio team for the '32 World Series. Nicknamed "the Commander," Elson had a long and distinguished career on the radio with the White Sox. It's also important to note that Elson didn't resort to hyperbole when making his calls. "In 1932, I saw that Babe Ruth home run against the Cubs in the World Series, and I definitely know he pointed to centerfield. There was no doubt about it. He did call his shot."

Ray Kelly

"Little Ray" got to live out every kid's fantasy in the 1920s. After seeing Kelly playing ball with his father, Ruth decided to make him his mascot.

"Little Ray" Kelly and the Babe demonstrate their stances in 1922.

Ruth took him to Yankee Stadium numerous times, where he hung out with all the players. "I was just there to sit on the bench and look cute," Kelly once said.

Kelly and his father attended Game Three as Ruth's guests. Given his loyalty to Ruth, it comes as little surprise that he believed in the Called Shot. "He absolutely did it," Kelly said. "I was right there. Never in doubt."

"I've read many accounts that said he didn't point to the center field bleachers," said Kelly in a TV interview. "I was sitting in a box seat right alongside the Yankee dugout at ground level, and I saw him at one point raise his hand up. Not pointing at the pitcher, but his hand elevated.

"The first pitch Root threw was a called strike, and Ruth pointed a finger, as much to say, and I think he meant it, 'That's one strike.' Then he pitched another called strike, and Babe went 'two,' indicating—I assume what he meant was—'That's the second strike!' And then he yelled out to him, 'It only takes one!' That I heard vividly. The next pitch was a ball, and before the next pitch was when he pointed to the center field bleachers, and following that the pitch came in, and he hit one of the longest home runs that was ever hit in Wrigley Field."

James Roosevelt

One of Franklin Roosevelt's sons, James, attended the game with his father. In a 1982 interview with the *New York Times*, James recalled the reaction of his father, whom Ruth's antics clearly captivated. "I remember a lot of hoots and howls by Cub fans when Ruth came to bat. And I remember, with great deliberation, he [Ruth] pointed to the longest part of the park. There was no question what the gesture meant. And when he hit the homer, I remember Dad saying: 'Unbelievable!'"

John Carmichael

A longtime columnist for the *Chicago Daily News*, Carmichael later did a first-person piece with Ruth in which the slugger described his version of the Called Shot in vivid detail. "I thought he waved the back of his hand toward the fence, not in any particular direction, to indicate that the next pitch was going out."

Arthur F. Peterson

In 1983 Peterson read a story in the *Wall Street Journal* and the *Sporting News* that questioned the veracity of the Called Shot—but not a single doubt lingered in Peterson's mind. He had attended the game in 1932, and so he sent a letter to the *Wall Street Journal,* setting them to rights, and then a copy to the Baseball Hall of Fame in Cooperstown. Howard Talbot Jr., the Hall's director at the time, replied that the letter would make a "valued addition" to the Hall's collection on the Called Shot.

Peterson's letter said, in part: "Let me assure anyone who may be interested that there is, in fact, no cause for debate of it. I was there at that October 1, 1932, World Series game. A business associate of mine, Angus H. Taylor, and I had seats in the stands halfway between home plate and first base. . . . As Ruth stepped into the box, he raised his right arm and pointing momentarily . . . obviously pointing to the right field stands."

Peterson later writes that Ruth's gesture may have occurred so quickly that people might have missed it: "The foregoing description is not an opinion, myth, or legend. It is a statement of fact, an observation. I saw the performance. No doubt many in the stands, as well as the pitcher, did not see it because of heads turned or eyes shut momentarily at the moment of pointing."

Peterson concludes: "Ruth did call the shot by pointing to the right field stands. I was there, nearby with a good view of home plate. I saw the pointing clearly."

Paul Gallico

When the famed New York columnist decided to leave sportswriting in the late 1930s, he wrote a book, *Farewell to Sport,* which quickly became a classic. It featured a series of essays on his memories of the games and people he covered. Obviously it included a piece on Ruth, the most memorable figure of Gallico's tenure. Gallico finished his recollection of the slugger by discussing the Called Shot. Even if Gallico exaggerated the facts a bit, he wasn't about to dent the myth, and he told a great story.

Two balls, wide pitches, intervened. And at this point, Ruth made the most marvelous and impudent gesture I have ever seen. With his forefinger extended he pointed to the flagpole in center field, the farthest point removed from the plate. There was no mistaking his meaning. He was advising the crowd, pitcher and jeering Cubs that that was the exact spot where Root's next pitch would leave the park.

The incensed crowd gave forth a long drawn-out and lusty "Booooo!" Ruth made them choke on it by slugging the ball out of the premises at exactly that point, the centerfield flagpole, for his second home run of the day and probably the only home run in the entire history of baseball that was ever called in advance, as to both time and place.

Ruth could do those things, take those chances and get away with them, because he was The Babe and his imagination told him that it was a fine, heroic, and Ruthian thing to do. And he had the ability to deliver. I suppose in 50 or 60 years the legend will be that Ruth could call his shots at any time.

But once was sufficient for me, and I saw him do that.

Of course, two people in the ballpark that day had their own very specific interpretations of what occurred during the fifth inning of Game Three: pitcher and hitter. They alone could clear up the mystery—or not.

NINE

Pitcher

If he had pointed as they say, he would have been knocked on his fanny.
—CHARLIE ROOT

The typewritten letter is dated December 27, 1965. Two days after Christmas, James A. Bark from Racine, Wisconsin, wrote to Charlie Root. Here is Bark's note, unedited:

Dear, Mr. Root,

Since you were pitching when Babe Ruth hit his famous "called shot" home run in the '32 World Series I wonder if you could give me your comments on this home run. I read somewhere that he had merely pointed at the Cub's dugout indicating he would foul off the next pitch there. Is this true or did he really "call his shot?" I would appreciate an answer to this letter very much.

> *Sincerely,*
> *James A. Bark*

Root no doubt sighed as he read the letter. It had been more than three decades since Ruth hit the famous homer off him. The Cubs pitcher had aged into his 60s now, spending half a lifetime trying to tell people the correct version of what happened on that day in 1932. Yet the letters kept coming on a regular basis. A few arrived every month. The volume always picked up shortly after the World Series, when the Called Shot came up in various flashbacks.

Root gave a standard reply to these letters. He wrote in clear script under Bark's typed inquiry:

Babe Ruth did not call his shot. If he had pointed as they say, he would have been knocked on his fanny.

Charlie Root

The letter, subsequently obtained by the Chicago Baseball Museum, offers a snapshot of how Root felt about his role in the Called Shot and how he addressed it on a regular basis. He could have ignored the note like so much junk mail that filled up his mailbox. Instead, Root stuffed it into the stamped return envelope and sent it back to the gentleman in Wisconsin. Perhaps Root hoped that Mr. Bark would share his words with others and that his side of the story would start to take hold. The effort proved futile.

Root had no idea that when that fateful pitch left his hands during the fifth inning of Game Three, his entire legacy as a player suddenly adhered to Ruth's monumental blast. From that moment everything he accomplished during a highly successful 17-year career with the Cubs took a backseat to participating in one of the most memorable events in baseball history. Root became little more than a prop on Ruth's vast stage, yet another victim— perhaps the ultimate victim—of baseball's greatest showman.

Root protested loudly that the Called Shot was a myth. After he died in 1970, his widow, Dorothy, continued his cause. Then in 2009, almost 80 years after that game in Wrigley Field, a video appeared on YouTube, an interview with Root's daughter, Della, giving an emotional plea on behalf of her father. Roger Snell, who wrote *Root for the Cubs: Charlie Root and the 1929 Chicago Cubs,* conducted the interview. In the introduction of his book, he quotes Della, who attended the game as a 13-year-old girl: "If that big fat guy had pointed, you think we would have seen it." Here's what Della, then age 90, said on the video.

SNELL: Did Babe Ruth call his shot?

DELLA: No, Babe Ruth did not call his shot. There was nothing in the paper about the Called Shot until four days after that particular game.

SNELL: How much did it bother your dad?

DELLA: At first not at all. Right after the '32 World Series, we went to Australia and all through the South Pacific islands. We had a wonderful, wonderful time. When we landed in Australia, the paper said, "American baseballer shows up in Australia." So at the time it didn't bother him at all. But as he got older, that was all they ever asked him. He was a fine pitcher. There won't be another pitcher who wins 201 games for one team. Although he was a very humble man—I never heard him talk about baseball or "I did this"—it did bother him. [Tearfully] The day before he died, I was holding his hand. He looked at me and said, "You know, Della, I gave my life to baseball, and I'll only be remembered for something that never happened."

Della has since died. Snell spent quite a bit of time with her while researching his book. If anything, she was more bothered about the characterization of Ruth in the Called Shot than her father.

"She was obsessed about it," Snell said. "It never left her. There's a painting in the Hall of Fame of Ruth pointing. She was upset about it. Della wrote to the Hall. She wrote to players on the veterans committee. She didn't begrudge the painting being there. However, she felt there should at least be some documentation of the other side."

Indeed, Root is a key and ironically often overlooked character in this saga, and he and his family had good reason to defend his legacy. The reality is that Root ranked among the finest pitchers of his era.

A native of Ohio, Root had a brief fling with the St. Louis Browns in 1923 before joining the Cubs in 1926. He enjoyed immediate success with Chicago, sporting a 26–15 record in 1927. However, after falling back with 18 defeats in 1928, he feared that a sore elbow might end his career prematurely. In Root's biography, Snell writes that Root sobbed to his wife, "Dorothy, the doc says I'm through and I'll never pitch again."

Root's arm eventually bounced back, though, and he enjoyed another stellar season in 1929. His 19–6 record helped pace the Cubs to their first National League pennant since 1918.

Root relied on a fastball that he could locate quite effectively. But he could play wild when it suited his purposes. Root wasn't afraid to knock hitters off the plate. He even plunked them good if he really wanted to send a message—hence his nickname: "Chinski."

"I roomed with Charlie Root," said Cubs third baseman Woody English. "He was a nice guy, but when he was out on that mound, don't take too big a toe-hold on him. You'll get one right behind your ear. He was a sidearm pitcher, threw hard, and was a competitor all the way."

Root's bulldog mentality endeared him to then–Cubs manager Joe McCarthy. After McCarthy retired he was asked who would pitch on his dream team. He had Hall of Famers Lefty Gomez and Red Ruffing pitching for him during his days with the Yankees, but McCarthy chose Root. "He had the greatest heart I've ever seen," he said. "His determination and loyalty I'm very sure you'll never see again."

McCarthy called on Root to face the Philadelphia Athletics in Game One of the 1929 World Series. He pitched well, but Howard Ehmke threw better, striking out a Series record 13 Cubs en route to a 3–1 victory. But the Series turned in Game Four. With the Cubs trailing two games to one, McCarthy turned to Root again. The situation looked good for the Cubs as Root went into the bottom of the seventh with an 8–0 lead. However, in an incredible upset that foreshadowed decades of Chicago nightmares to come, the Athletics jumped on Root and subsequent relief pitchers for 10 runs in the inning. Lefty Grove closed out the victory for Philadelphia, who then won the Series in five.

Root continued to shine for the Cubs into the 1930s. With the exception of one year, he won a minimum of 15 games every season through 1935. In 1931 his salary stood at more than $20,000 per season, making him one of the top five highest-paid players in the game.

Root pitched in the majors until he was 42, bringing him through the 1941 season. But he didn't stop pitching. He went down to the minors, racking up more than 100 victories until he finally hung up his glove at the age of 49.

Root finished with a 201–160 record in the big leagues and a career 3.57 earned run average. More than eight decades later, Root still holds the Cubs record for most victories. After Ferguson Jenkins, who sports a Cubs cap on his plaque in Cooperstown, Root is considered the team's next greatest pitcher.

However, like the rest of his Cubs teammates, Root wasn't as successful in the World Series. He played on four losing teams: 1929, 1932, 1935, and 1938. Overall, he was 0–3 with a 6.75 earned run average in six appearances.

Of course, one World Series game always stood out. No one ever let him forget it. Perhaps the ultimate insult came when movie producers wanted to cast him as himself in the *Babe Ruth Story*. The epically horrible film starring William Bendix obviously was going to include a scene that depicted the Called Shot. The producers wanted Root to recreate his role as the pitcher. According to Root's teammate and manager, Charlie Grimm, they offered Root "a nice chunk of money" to throw a few pitches in the film. Root flat-out refused, though. "Not if you're going to show him pointing," he said.

Indeed, Root wouldn't tolerate anyone even joking about the Called Shot during his days as a coach. According to Snell's book, Warren Spahn, the great Hall of Fame left-hander, once pointed to center field while Root, then coach for the Milwaukee Braves, threw batting practice to him. Root shocked Spahn—and everyone else—by whizzing the next pitch by the star pitcher's head.

Snell recounts another story in 1961 about Root as a coach with the Cubs. During a tryout a young kid made the mistake of pointing. Not surprisingly, Root targeted a pitch at the guy—but he didn't stop there. He took all the balls in his pocket and threw them at the startled hitter. "OK, he didn't point!" the young kid replied in a tryout that he'll never forget.

Root's old teammates knew exactly how he felt on the subject. Given his "Chinski" nickname, they maintained that if Root saw Ruth pointing, the pitcher would have sent a clear message right back with the next pitch.

In a 1978 *Sporting News* column, noted St. Louis baseball writer Bob Broeg discussed the Called Shot and included this quote from Root:

I'm tired of being the goat. Hell, the Babe hit 15 World Series homers, so I wasn't the only guy he teed off on. But, no, he didn't take two strikes on purpose, and no he didn't point to the centerfield bleachers.

Our bench was getting on him, particularly Guy Bush, a pretty good jockey, and the Babe was letting 'em all know he had one strike left. I don't see where it's any discredit to Ruth to say he'd proved more than once that he knew what to do with one swing.

In 1957 Herbert Simons wrote a 25th anniversary piece on the Called Shot for *Baseball Digest*. He interviewed Root, then a coach with the Milwaukee Braves. Root talked about his only conversation with Ruth about their famous confrontation.

The only time I talked to the Babe after the game was before batting practice the next day. He was up at the plate, and I walked over and was looking at the bat he was using and asked him if that was the bat he had hit it with, and he said "yes" and handed it to me to feel. It was heavy—about 50 ounces I would say, and it was dark, a sort of hickory color; in fact, I think the wood was hickory. You know I had two strikes on him on fastballs right down the middle, belt high, in that fifth inning. Then I threw him a change-up curve, intending to waste it to get him off stride. It wasn't a foot off the ground and it was three or four inches off the outside of the plate, certainly not a good pitch to hit, but that was the one he smacked. So I asked him how he happened to hit such a pitch. "I just guessed with you," he told me. And that's all that was said.

But perhaps Root's most vivid account of that day occurred when he addressed a high school assembly in Los Angeles.

Sure, Babe gestured to me. We had been riding him, calling him "Grand-pop" and kidding him about not getting to be manager of the Yankees. We wanted to get him mad, and he was when he came to bat. As he stepped up, he challenged me to lay the ball in. After I had gotten the first strike over, Babe pointed to me and yelled, "That's only one strike."

Maybe I had a smug grin on my face after he took the second strike. But he stepped out of the box again, pointed his finger in my direction and yelled, "You still need one more, kid."

I guess I should have wasted the next pitch, and I thought Ruth figured I would too. I decided to try to cross him and came in with it. The ball was gone as soon as Ruth swung. It never occurred to me then that the people in the stands would think he had been pointing to the bleachers. But that's the way it was.

Despite his constant denials, the letters kept on coming. They reached him even in Hollister, California, where, after leaving baseball, Root owned a cattle farm and an antiques shop. With his family by his side, he died on November 5, 1970, at the age of 71.

|||||||||||||||||||||||||||||||||

With Root gone it fell to his family to tell his side of the Called Shot. In 1982, commemorating the 50th anniversary of the 1932 World Series, a reporter visited his widow, Dorothy, in Hollister. The piece, which appeared in the *Sporting News*, noted that Root's wife had sat in her regular seat for the game: box 58, tier 12. It lay on the third base side, just past the screen.

Dorothy, then 83, was described as "warm and friendly" and extremely active in the local community. She showed the reporter a mountain of newspaper clippings about her late husband that she had accumulated during his career. On her coffee table sat a bronzed baseball glove with this inscription: "To my wife on our 18th wedding anniversary. Used in 1929, 1932, 1935 World Series."

Dorothy knew why the reporter was there. She was also a witness on that day, and she knew what she saw. "Of course, I didn't see him point. Nobody else saw him point because he didn't. Charlie would have thrown it right at his head. I knew that, and so did all the ballplayers."

Dorothy also recalled her husband's reaction whenever somebody brought up the Called Shot. "There was always somebody who'd walk up to him and say, 'I saw Babe Ruth point.' Charlie would just walk away. He always was angry with that. It was a lie, and he knew it was a lie. I can't say we're bitter. That's not the word. I just think things should be accurate. I think when you do something to a man's reputation, you'd better be accurate. You'd better know the truth."

Dorothy concluded by vowing that Root's children, grandchildren, and great-grandchildren would continue to refute the story of the Called Shot "as long as there is one left."

Indeed, there's no joking about it in the Root family. In the *Sporting News* article, Root's son, Charlie Jr., recalled playing Wiffle ball with his family. The friendly mood turned when his wife came to the plate and pointed to center field. "I plunked her with the next pitch," Root Jr. said in a gesture that would have made his father proud.

For more than two decades, the Root family has had a personalized California license plate that reads BABEWHO. Car as commentary.

But let's be careful not to overstate the case. The Called Shot didn't torment Root. It didn't keep him up at night or throw him into a deep depression. It simply bothered him to be on the wrong end of what he considered a fable.

"Charlie pitched for 17 years and is in the top 100 for many pitching [records]," Snell said. "When you calculate all the pitches he threw, it's up there. Then for him to be remembered for one pitch, it's kind of sad."

Root knew during his final moments how his legacy would play out. "I gave my life to baseball, and I'll only be remembered for something that never happened." Moments after he died, his fears were validated. The obituaries could have focused on his 201 victories and his long career with the Cubs. But they didn't.

As in life, so in death. The first line of a wire service obituary defined Root's place in baseball history quite narrowly: "Charlie Root, the pitcher who served up the pitch Babe Ruth successfully predicted he would hit into the seats in the 1932 World Series, died today. He was 71."

TEN

Slugger

Well, the good Lord and good luck must have been with me because I did exactly what I said I was going to do.

—BABE RUTH

Nearly a century has passed since a young kid named George Ruth played his first professional game for the Baltimore Orioles, but the woman on the other end of the line is referring to him as "Daddy." The notion is almost mind-boggling. It doesn't seem possible that Ruth's daughter could still be alive in 2013, but thanks to longevity Julia Ruth Stevens, 96 years young on the day we spoke, is sharing memories of her father one more time.

I tell her what a thrill it is to be speaking to her.

"It's a thrill to me that I'm still here," she said, not missing a beat. "It's a thrill to me every time I wake up in the morning."

Charlie Root's family thought the Called Shot a myth, but Ruth's family has no such disbelief. While Ruth's own comments about what happened that day ranged all over the map, there's no doubt about it in the eyes of his daughter, grandchildren, and great-grandchildren. He definitely called his shot.

llllllllllllllllllllllllllllll

After he married his second wife, Claire, in 1929, Ruth formally adopted Claire's daughter, Julia, who has spent a good portion of her life talking about "Daddy" and his many deeds on the baseball field. Ruth and Julia had a warm, close relationship, and you still can hear the affection in her voice for a man who died in 1948.

"People always say, 'It's such an honor to meet you,'" Julia said. "I know they're saying that because I'm Babe Ruth's daughter and that's the closest they'll ever get to Daddy. I just enjoy meeting people, and a lot of them have stories about Daddy. I love to hear them."

Not many people are still alive who can recall witnessing her father hit home runs.

"It was always a thrill," she said. "I didn't go to all of the games, but I went to a lot with my mother. I wanted him to hit a home run every time. Everyone would start cheering when he came up. If he hit a home run, it was beautiful to see. He'd trot around the bases. Then when he got to home plate, he'd lift his cap to the crowd.

"I used to say, 'Hit the apple in the eye, you'll see how high it will fly.'"

Julia wasn't in Wrigley Field to see her father hit his massive homer during the fifth inning of Game Three. But she has seen footage and read countless stories about that memorable day. More importantly, she heard direct testimony from key witnesses at the game, including her mother and Cardinal Francis Spellman, the longtime archbishop of New York.

"Daddy certainly did point," Julia said. "He always seemed to rise to the occasion. He just wanted to beat the Cubs. If he had missed, he'd have been very, very disappointed, I can tell you. Cardinal Spellman just happened to be at the game. He said there's no question that he pointed. I'll take his word and my mother's."

Ruth's grandchildren and great-grandchildren second Julia's opinion. Brent Stevens, Julia's grandson, celebrates his great-grandfather's life with BabeRuthCentral.com, and Stevens doesn't waver when it comes to the Called Shot.

"The family's perspective is that he pointed to the outfield before that momentous pitch," said Stevens. "Whether he pointed to the exact location, as suggested by some of the media, is more questionable. However, he definitely indicated that he was going to hit a home run prior to that shot in Game Three of the '32 World Series."

Linda Ruth Tosetti also staunchly preserves her grandfather's legend. Her mother, Dorothy, was Ruth's natural daughter from a relationship he had with a woman whom he never married. Tosetti calls herself a "blood granddaughter" and proudly boasts of her resemblance to her forebear. Tosetti has her own website through which she savors the family connection, TheTrueBabeRuth.com.

Tosetti first heard of the Called Shot when as an eighth-grader she accompanied her mother on a trip to the Baseball Hall of Fame. "This player came up to us," she said. "I can't remember his name, but he was very loud about it. He said, 'Dorothy, don't let anyone say he didn't point. I was there, and I saw it. He pointed.' Later, I asked my mother, 'What's the Called Shot?'"

Tosetti soon learned more about the legend. Like her relatives, she maintains that it is true. "Yeah, I think he was bold enough to point," she said. "My grandfather was very confident in what he could do. Could he have done it? Most definitely."

But what about the man himself? What did Ruth have to say about the homer?

Surprisingly Ruth wasn't always as emphatic as his family about whether he pointed that day at Wrigley Field. Tom Meany, a sportswriter who knew Ruth well, noted Ruth's inconsistencies when telling the story. In his 1947 biography on Ruth, Meany writes that "Ruth had changed his version several times . . . and had grown confused, uncertain whether he had picked out a spot in the bleachers to park the ball, or was merely pointing to the outfield, or was signaling that he still had one swing to go."

If ever an episode deserved immediate reaction and commentary from the participants—from Ruth and Root to the jeering Cubs in the dugout—it was the Called Shot. However, it didn't work that way back in 1932. Sportswriters wrote what they saw on the field. Sports journalism didn't include working the locker room for quotes from the players and managers. As a result, dispatches went off to newspapers throughout the country following Game Three that featured flowery prose—but nary a quote about the showdown in the fifth inning.

Meany came closest to getting some sort of immediate reaction from Ruth. Writing for the *New York World-Telegram*, he told of visiting Ruth's apartment after the team returned to New York City on October 3. Meany asked him about the Called Shot.

> *Babe's interviewer interrupted to point out the hole in which Babe put himself Saturday when he pointed out the spot he intended hitting his home run and asked the Great Man if he realized how ridiculous he would have appeared if he had struck out?*
>
> *"I never thought of it," said the Great Man. He simply had made up his mind to hit a home run and he did. You just can't get around a guy like that.*

Unfortunately Meany didn't pursue the subject any further. It just wasn't done back then. As for Ruth's answer, you could interpret it a few ways: He confirmed that he did point, or he was just going along with the story, or perhaps he wasn't sure what Meany was talking about. Remember, this interview took place only a day after the Series ended. Ruth might not have had a chance to read the papers yet.

Ruth did a radio interview a few weeks after the game, in which he stated unequivocally: "I wanted to hit those two, and they are the only two home runs I care to remember." Later, he said, "That's the first time I ever got the players and the fans going at the same time. I never had so much fun in my life." He doesn't mention calling his shot or pointing to center field. All he wanted to do was to stick it to the Cubs.

On October 24, 1932, New York sportswriter Joe Williams attended a dinner at which Ruth addressed the two homers. Williams later wrote:

> *Earlier in his career Mr. Ruth used to say his greatest feat in base-ball was performed as a left-handed pitcher against the Tigers when they were the hardest-hitting team in captivity. He had shut them out 1 to 0, going into the ninth when they filled the bases with none out. The next three batters were Veach, Cobb and Crawford. Mr. Ruth struck them out on 10 pitched balls. But now he has made a revision in estimating his greatest contribution to baseball. Those two home runs made against the Cubs in the third game of the World Series this year . . .*
>
> *Mr. Ruth was asked if he really believed he was going to hit those home runs when he came to the plate.*
>
> *"I knew I wanted to hit them, but of course I wasn't sure. That's what gave me such a big kick—hitting 'em after saying I was going to. I've hit more than 650 home runs, but those two I hit off Charlie Root will always stand out above them all."*
>
> *As an afterthought, Ruth roared into the mike: "Can you imagine what a mug I would have been if I had missed them? Say, those people in Chicago would be laughing at me yet—and I wouldn't blame them either."*

Note that Ruth doesn't directly mention pointing of any kind. Perhaps he didn't want to look like he was showing up the Cubs by making such a grand gesture. Maybe in the immediate aftermath of the game, Ruth realized it wasn't the sportsmanlike thing to do.

Ruth's family insists that he was just being modest. Julia said she never recalled her father talking to her about the Called Shot. "It's not something he would do," Julia said. "He was very modest. He felt he was lucky to be in the position he was in. He always tried his best and wanted to be good for all the kids."

Tosetti offered a similar version: "He wasn't one to boast about himself. That's why his teammates loved him. Even though he was Babe Ruth, he never pushed that."

||||||||||||||||||||||||||||

But one quote in particular buoys the naysayers in this debate. It comes from an interview that Ruth did with Hal Totten early in the 1933 season. Totten, a Chicago broadcast pioneer who had been at the game, asked Ruth that next year if he had pointed to center field. Ruth replied:

Hell no. It isn't a fact. Only a damned fool would have done a thing like that. You know there was a lot of pretty rough ribbing going on both benches during the World Series. When I swung and missed that first one, those Cubs really gave me a blast. So I grinned at them and held out one finger and told 'em it only takes one to do it.

Then there was that second strike, and they let me have it again. So I held up that finger again, and I said I still had one left. Now kid, you know damn well I wasn't pointing anywhere. If I had done that, Root would have stuck the ball in my ear. I never knew anybody who could tell you ahead of time where he was going to hit a baseball. When I get to be that kind of fool, they'll put me in the booby hatch.

Well, there we have it—solid proof. Babe Ruth said he didn't do it. If he had pointed, Root would have beaned him. The Cubs pitcher is off the hook and doesn't have to endure an afterlife of questions about being the sap who gave up the famous homer.

It should have been that way, but it wasn't. If Ruth had made those comments today, the Internet would have exploded with the admission. End of story. But back then, Ruth's comments to Totten likely reached a limited section of people in Chicago. As a result, his revelation had a short shelf life.

Whatever the reason, Ruth's admission to Totten didn't become his definitive take on the subject. Far from it, in fact. The story of the Called Shot continued to circulate, and at some point Ruth jumped on the train. The theories are obvious: Why deny something you really did, or, if the public wants to believe in a grandiose gesture, why not let them?

"I think it got to the point where he was asked about it so many times," Tosetti said. "When they said, 'Hey, Babe, did you really point?' I could see him laughing it off and saying, 'Yeah, sure.'"

Ruth eventually went further than that. In *The Big Bam*, Leigh Montville details a conversation that occurred during a cocktail party thrown by famed sportswriter Grantland Rice in 1933. Ruth explained to the wife of columnist Walter Lippmann what happened on that day. (Rice gave an edited version in his autobiography, *The Tumult and the Shouting*, leaving decent blanks in the passage. Montville filled in the expletives in his book.)

"It's like this," the Babe said, dressed in white and waving his cigar. "The Cubs had fucked my old teammate Mark Koenig by cutting him for only a measly fucken half share of the Series money.

"Well, I'm riding the fuck out of the Cubs, telling 'em they're the cheapest pack of fucken crumbums in the world. We've won the first two, and we're in Chicago for the third game. Root is the Cubs' pitcher. I park one into the stands in the first inning, but in the fifth, it's tied 4–4, when I'm up with nobody on. The Chicago fans are giving me hell.

"Root's still in there. He breezes the first two pitches by—both strikes! The mob's tearing down Wrigley Field. I shake my fist after that first strike. After the second strike I point my bat at these bellerin' bleachers—right where I aim to park the ball. Root throws it, and I hit that fucken ball on the nose, right over the fence for two fucken runs.

"'How'd you like those apples, you fucken bastard?' I yell at Root as I run towards first. By the time I reach home, I'm almost fallin' down I'm laughin' so fucken hard—and that's how it happened."

Ms. Lippmann grabbed her husband and left the party.
"Why'd you use that language?" Rice asked Ruth.
"What the hell, Grant?" Ruth replied. "You heard her ask me
what happened. So I told her."

First, let's pause for a moment. Ruth, Lippmann, and Rice at the same party? That had to have been a pretty good party. But we can see from the conversation that Ruth didn't intend to play the bystander when it came to the homer in question. He was all in—at least for public consumption.

In 1937 Ruth appeared in a short film called *Home Run on the Keys*. It opens with Ruth returning to a log cabin after a day of hunting. He pulls off his coat, revealing quite a gut. Now retired from baseball, Ruth clearly was out of shape. He makes small talk with the guys, and one of them asks, "What hit gave you your greatest thrill?"

Guess which one Ruth picks.

"Well, I suppose that one out of Chicago in the World Series of 1932," Ruth replies. "The papers said it was the longest and most dramatic home run ever hit at the Cubs' park."

In the foreground Ruth tells his story. Meanwhile, in the background, inside the fireplace, with crude special effects, he appears in a Yankee uniform reliving this great moment. The flashback sequence even features actors playing the Cubs riding him from the dugout.

He says he let the first two pitches go by for called strikes. Ruth gets the count wrong, putting it at 0–2 instead of 2-2—and not for the first time. Ruth casts darting glances back to the umpire to express his disdain for the calls.

"Well, I stepped out of the box and looked over to the bench," he continues. "Then I looked at center field and I pointed. I said, 'I'm going to hit the next pitched ball right past the flagpole.'

"Well, the good Lord and good luck must have been with me because I did exactly what I said I was going to do. I'll tell you one thing: That was the best home run I ever hit in my life. . . . It was a pip."

The guys all lap it up, and then Ruth joins them in trying to figure out a song for that evening's entertainment. The short feels rather bizarre, but back then Hollywood looked for any reason to put Ruth on the big screen. It's important from a historical perspective, though. This is the clip of Ruth's voice often used in subsequent documentaries about the slugger when it comes to addressing the Called Shot.

Through the years, Ruth continued to field questions about the Called Shot, and we have evidence that he told a different version privately than he did to reporters. For his book *Wrigleyville* Peter Golenbock interviewed Ed Froelich, a trainer for the Cubs and later with the Brooklyn Dodgers. Ruth regularly went to Froelich for the treatment of various aches and pains, and Froelich recalled asking Ruth about the Called Shot when the Sultan of Swat was coaching for Brooklyn in 1938.

> *We got to talking one day. I said, "Babe, a lot of people in Chicago still say that you pointed toward the centerfield bleachers before you hit that home run there."*
>
> *He said, "Doc, can you hear me?"*
>
> *I said, "Yes."*
>
> *"A little louder," he said. "Can you hear me?"*
>
> *"Yes."*
>
> *He said, "You tell those people for Baby"—he always called himself Baby—"that Baby says they're full of crap right up to their eyeballs. I may be dumb, but . . . Root out there? On the next pitch, they'd be picking it out of my ear with a pair of tweezers."*
>
> *He said one final word, "No."*

That squares with Meany's assertion that Ruth was over all the place when it came to the Called Shot.

Yet in public, he wasn't about to prick his own legend. In 1942 writers visited with him in his hotel suite during a trip to Chicago. Ruth was 47 years old at the time and reportedly had "melted down to 223 pounds." He said that he had weighed 260 pounds in 1928. The writers found Ruth to be operating in fine spirits. They inquired once again if he had pointed 10 years earlier at Wrigley Field.

"Yes, I did, and it was a foolish thing to do," Ruth said. "I'd have looked pretty silly if Charlie had struck me out."

On August 15, 1947, a year and a day before he died, Ruth remained resolute about the Called Shot: "I was lucky," he said in a *Chicago Tribune* column penned by David Condon. "I would have looked like a damned fool if I missed, but luck was on my side. Sure I called my shot. And it only missed the flag pole by about four feet."

In 1948, shortly before the Bambino's death, E. P. Dutton published *The Babe Ruth Story,* cowritten with Bob Considine. It's hard to say how much Ruth was able to participate in the writing of the autobiography. According to Tosetti, the advancing stages of cancer made it difficult for him to talk in his final months. He might have nodded to indicate if he approved of how something was worded—if even that much.

Still, a line appears under his signature on the book's cover that reads, "My only authorized story." The book also features this dedication: "This book, the only authentic story of my life, is sincerely dedicated to the kids of America." The story is told in the first person, and the stories align with his career.

Ruth doesn't address the Called Shot until chapter 17. Tellingly, while his famous home run is all anyone talks about from that World Series, he opens by giving credit to Lou Gehrig for the sweep. Ruth might have been the only person who noticed. He wrote, "Lou was the solid man of the 1932 Series."

Ruth then sets up the Called Shot, discussing the hard feelings between the two teams that stemmed from the partial share awarded to Koenig. Ruth talks about the rude welcome that Chicago fans gave him and his wife, Claire, upon the Yankees' arrival for Game Three. "I guess it was while I was angry that the idea of 'calling my shot' came to me," he wrote.

But Ruth divulges that it wasn't the first time he had called a shot. In another chapter he discusses his fabled "homers-on-order" for Johnny

Sylvester, the sick kid in the hospital who suddenly got better when Ruth delivered on his promise to hit a homer for him in the 1926 World Series. Like the Called Shot, much debate has ensued over whether the Sylvester story was myth or reality. For his part, Sylvester insisted it was true.

Ruth also wrote of another episode, back in his early days with the Yankees, at the Polo Grounds. Ruth hit a ball down the right field line that home plate umpire Billy Evans called a foul. Evans told an irate Ruth, "It was an inch to the foul side of the line."

"Okay, watch this one," Ruth replied. "It will be an inch fair."

Ruth wrote that he hit the next pitch almost exactly where he hit the first one and then turned to Evans, who said, "It was an inch fair. Go ahead."

Ruth also claimed to have called a shot to assist traveling secretary Mark Roth one day in Chicago. The game was in extra innings, and Roth was nervous because the railroad was griping about holding a train for the Yankees.

"Why didn't you say that earlier?" Ruth asked him. "I'll take care of it."

Ruth did, hitting a homer to win the game.

Ruth wrote of yet another episode in which he helped Ford Frick, his ghostwriter and future commissioner of baseball, and his elderly father. "He was in his 70s and mighty brittle-looking," Ruth wrote of Frick's father, sitting in the stands on a hot day. Ruth told the younger Frick, "'I'll end it for your pappy so you can trot him and get your nap.'" In the distance a long train with open cars was passing. "See those cars, pappy?" Ruth yelled above the noise. "Watch."

"I hit one over the right-field fence and into one of those cars— which may still be traveling for all I know," Ruth wrote.

Ruth likely cited those examples to add to the credibility of his account of what happened in Game Three. In effect he was saying, "No big deal. I've done it before."

Yet Ruth and Considine get their facts wrong when they finally get into the Called Shot itself. His account has Ruth coming up in the fourth inning—but he came up in the fifth. It puts Earle Combs on base—but nobody was on. And of course, as in many retellings of the story, Ruth had the count at 0–2 instead of 2–2.

Ruth starts his account by recalling the abuse he was receiving from the Cubs dugout:

My ears had been blistered so much before in my baseball career that I thought they had lost all feeling. But the blast that was turned on me by Cubs players and some of the fans penetrated and cut deep. Some of the fans started throwing vegetables and fruit at me.

I stepped back out of the box, then stepped in. And while Root was getting ready to throw his first pitch, I pointed to the bleachers which rose out of deep centerfield.

Before the umpire could call it a strike, I raised my right hand, stuck out one finger and yelled "Strike one."

The razzing stepped up a notch. Root got set and threw again— another hard one through the middle. And once again, I stepped back and held up my right hand and bawled, "Strike two!" It was.

You should have heard those fans then. As for the Cubs players, they came out on to the steps of their dugout and really let me have it. I guess the smart thing for Charlie to have done on his third pitch would have been to waste one.

But he didn't, and for that I've sometimes thanked God. While he was making up his mind to pitch to me, I stepped back again and pointed my finger at those bleachers, which only caused the mob to howl that much more at me.

Root threw me a fastball. If I had let it go, it would have been called a strike. But this was it. I swung from the ground with every- thing that I had and as I hit the ball every muscle in my system, every sense I had, told me that I had never hit a better one, that as long as I lived nothing would ever feel as good as this.

I didn't have to look. But I did. That ball just went on and on and on and hit far up in the centerfield bleacher in exactly the spot I had pointed to.

*To me, it was the funniest, proudest moment that I had in base-
ball. I jogged down toward first base, rounded it, looked back at the
Cub bench and suddenly got convulsed with laughter.*

*You should have seen those Cubs. As Combs would say later: "There
they were—all out on the top step and yelling their brains out—and
then you connected and they watched it and then fell back as if they
were being machine-gunned."*

*That home run—the most famous one I ever hit—did us some
good. It was worth two runs, and we won that ball game, 7 to 5.*

Actually, it was worth only one run, making the score 5–4. It's surprising
that Ruth and his cowriter didn't have the facts right in his own book.
Then again, Ruth could barely remember anyone's name.

Perhaps Ruth's most interesting and famous comment on the Called
Shot came during a conversation with Frick. Several years after the game,
Frick tried to get a clear answer out of Ruth. "Did you really point to the
bleachers?" he asked.

Doubtless tired of answering yet another inquiry or maybe not wanting to lie to his friend, Ruth replied, "It's in the papers, isn't it? Why don't
you read the papers? It's all right there in the papers." But the papers only
added another layer of intrigue to the story.

SIDEBAR

"A Blankety-Blank Fool"

Chicago Daily News sports columnist John Carmichael interviewed Babe Ruth for the series "My Favorite Day in Baseball." Ruth naturally picked Game Three of the 1932 World Series. It appears Carmichael heavily edited this account, but he also used Ruth's vernacular to make it as authentic as possible. In this version, from the *Chicago Daily News*, Ruth leaves no question about his intentions during that day at Wrigley Field. Note, however, that he does say he wasn't pointing to an exact location.

‖‖‖‖‖‖‖‖‖‖‖‖‖‖‖‖‖‖‖‖‖‖‖‖‖‖‖

Nobody but a blankety-blank fool would-a done what I did that day. When I think of what a idiot I'd a been if I'd struck out and I could-a, too, just as well as not, because I was mad and I'd made up my mind to swing at the next pitch if I could reach it with a bat. Boy, when I think of the good breaks in my life . . . that was one of 'em!

Aw, everybody knows that game—the day I hit the homer off ol' Charlie Root there in Wrigley Field—October 1, the third game of the 1932 World Series. But right now I want to settle all arguments: I didn't exactly point to any one spot, like the flagpole. Anyway, I didn't mean to. I just sorta waved at the whole fence, but that was foolish enough. All I wanted to do was give that thing a ride . . . outta the park . . . anywhere.

I used to pop off a lot about hittin' homers, but mostly among us Yankees. Earle Combs and Art Fletcher and Frank Crosetti and all of 'em used to holler at me when I'd pick up a bat in a close game: "Come on, Babe, hit one." 'Member Herb Pennock? He was a great pitcher, believe me. He told me once, "Babe, I get the biggest thrill of my life whenever I see you hit a home run. It's just like watchin' a circus act." So I'd often kid 'em back and say, "Okay, you bums . . . I'll hit one." Sometimes I did; sometimes I didn't . . . but what the heck, it was fun.

One day we were playin' in Chicago against the White Sox, and Mark Roth, our secretary, was worryin' about holdin' the train because we were in extra innings. He was fidgetin' around behind the dugout, lookin' at his watch, and I saw him when I went up to hit in the fifteenth. "All right, quit worrying," I told him. "I'll get this over with right now." Mike Cvengros was pitchin' and I hit one outta the park. We made the train easy. It was fun.

I'd had a lot of trouble in '32, and we weren't any cinches to win that pennant, either, 'cause old Lefty Grove was tryin' to keep the Athletics up there for their fourth straight flag, and sometime in June I pulled a muscle in my right leg chasin' a fly ball. I was on the bench about three weeks, and when I started to play again, I had to wear a rubber bandage from my hip to my knee. You know, the ol' Babe wasn't getting any younger and Jimmie Foxx was ahead of me in homers. I was eleven behind him early in September and never did catch up. I wouldn't get one good ball a series to swing at. I remember one whole week when I'll bet I was walked four times in every game.

I always had three ambitions: I wanted to play twenty years in the big leagues. I wanted to play in ten World Series, and I wanted to hit 700 home runs. Well, 1932 was one away from my twentieth year, and that series with the Cubs was number ten, and I finally wound up with 729 home runs, countin' 15 World Series games, so I can't kick. But then along in September I had to quit the club and go home because my stomach was kickin' up and the docs found out my appendix was inflamed and maybe I'd have to have it out. No, sir, I wouldn't let 'em . . . not till after the season anyway.

The World Series didn't last long, but it was a honey. That Pat Malone and that Burleigh Grimes didn't talk like any Sunday school guys, and their trainer . . . yeah, Andy Lotshaw . . . he got smart in the first game at New York, too. That's what started me off. I popped up once in that one, and he was on their bench wavin' a towel at me and hollerin' "If I had you, I'd hitch you to a wagon, you pot-belly." I didn't mind no ballplayers yellin' at me, but the trainer cuttin' in . . . that made me sore. As long as they started in on me, we let 'em have it. We went after 'em, and maybe we gave 'em more than they could take, they looked beat before they went off the field.

We didn't have to do much the first game at home. Guy Bush walked everybody around the bases. I'll betcha ten bases on balls scored for us. Anyway, we got into Chicago for the third game—that's where those Cubs decided to really get on us. They were in front of their home folks, and I guess they'd thought they better act tough.

We were givin' them [the Cubs] hell about how cheap they were to [former Yankee] Mark Koenig, only votin' him a half-share in the Series and they were callin' me big belly and balloon-head, but I think we had 'em madder by givin' them that ol' lump-in-the-throat sign . . . you know, the thumb and finger at the windpipe. That's like callin' a guy yellow. Then in the very first inning I got a hold of one with two on and parked it in the stands for a three-run lead and that shut 'em up pretty well. But they came back with some runs and we were tied 4–4 going into the fifth frame. You know another thing I think of in that game was the play [Billy] Jurges made on Joe Sewell in the fifth . . . just ahead of me. I was out there waitin' to hit, so I could see it good, and he made a helluva pickup, way back on the grass, and "shot" Joe out by a halfstep. I didn't know whether they were gonna get on me anymore or not when I got to the box, but I saw a lemon rolling out to the plate, and I looked over and there was Malone and Grimes with their thumbs in their ears wiggling their fingers at me.

I told Hartnett, "If that bum [Root] throws me in here, I'll hit it over the fence again," and I'll say it for Gabby, he didn't answer, but those other guys were standing up in the dugout, cocky because they'd got four runs back and everybody hollerin'. So I just changed my mind. I took two strikes and after each one I held up my finger and said, "That's one" and "that's two." Ask Gabby . . . he could hear me. Then's when I waved to the fence!

No, I didn't point to any spot, but as long as I'd called the first two strikes on myself, I hadda go through with it. It was damned foolishness, sure, but I just felt like doing it, and I felt pretty sure Root would put one close enough for me to cut at, because I was showin' him up. What the hell, he hadda take a chance as well as I did, or walk me.

Gosh, that was a great feelin' . . . gettin' a hold of that ball and I knew it was going someplace . . . yessir, you can feel it in your hands when you've laid wood on one. How that mob howled. Me? I just laughed . . . laughed to myself going around the bases and thinking, "You lucky bum . . . lucky, lucky," and I looked at poor Charlie [Root] watchin' me, and then I saw [Yankee coach] Art Fletcher at third wavin' his cap, and behind him I could see the Cubs, and I just stopped on third and laughed out loud and slapped my knees and yelled, "Squeeze-the-Eagle Club" so they'd know I was referrin' to Koenig and for special to Malone I called him "meathead" and asked when he was gonna pitch.

Yeah, it was silly. I was a blankety-blank fool. But I got away with it and after Gehrig homered, behind me, their backs were broken. That was a day to talk about.

ELEVEN

View from the Press Box

His beaming countenance wore a broad grin. He then pointed to center field.
—Grantland Rice

Not all of the legends at Game Three of the World Series were on the field. Some were working the press box.

What those sportswriters wrote—or more importantly, what some didn't write—plays an integral part in making an ultimate verdict on the Called Shot controversy. Whether they wrote the truth, missed it, or simply contributed to the myth of the great slugger merits keen analysis. It is, after all, one of the most compelling elements of the story.

As morning turned to afternoon on October 1, 1932, the men—no women reporters back then—began to assemble in the Wrigley Field press box. For these sportswriters, covering the World Series represented the pinnacle of their careers. They had become the ultraelite in their profession. "The sportswriters were absolutely the best writers on the papers in those days, and baseball writing was the best of all jobs on a newspaper," said Marshall Hunt in Jerome Holtzman's *No Cheering in the Press Box*.

The lineup of writers covering Game Three certainly speaks to Hunt's claim. It was as powerful as any gathering ever for a sporting event.

Ring Lardner, one of the first acclaimed sports columnists and a master short story writer, walked into the press box. He listed F. Scott Fitzgerald among his friends, and his work influenced a young writer named Ernest Hemingway. As it turned out, 1932 was his last World Series. He died the following September, age 48, from complications due to tuberculosis.

Arch Ward greeted the writers. The young sports editor of the *Chicago Tribune* wanted to help celebrate the 1933 World's Fair in Chicago in his own area of expertise. He had the brilliant idea of an exhibition game featuring the best players of the American League facing the best players of the National League. Thus the first All-Star game came to pass, played in 1933 at Comiskey Park. Ruth fittingly hit the first All-Star home run.

The *New York Daily News* sports columnist Paul Gallico grew tired of sports in the late 1930s and turned his efforts to fiction. He wrote *The Snow Goose* and *The Poseidon Adventure*, the latter adapted into a 1972 hit movie starring Gene Hackman.

Surrounded by the clatter of typewriters, Damon Runyon made small talk in the back of the press box. He began his career as a sportswriter, but he went on to become a fixture on Broadway. His short stories provided the inspiration for the musical *Guys and Dolls*.

No one paid much attention when Red Smith entered the press box. But fame and notoriety soon came his way. He became one of America's most revered sports columnists. In October 1932, working for the *St. Louis Journal*, he was only a few weeks past his 27th birthday. The young redhead was just thrilled to be covering a World Series and quietly took his seat.

Smith no doubt took note of the many larger-than-life characters who filled the room. But one man stood out among the rest: Grantland Rice. Back in the 1920s and '30s, radio was still a fledgling medium, and television stood several decades away from hitting its stride. Fans got their sports news from the papers. As a result, sports columnists became huge celebrities, and none was bigger than the man from Tennessee.

An excellent athlete, Rice played football while studying at Vanderbilt University. After a series of jobs in the South, he eventually landed in New York just in time to participate in the sports boom of the 1920s. Besides Ruth, he covered Jack Dempsey, Red Grange, Bobby Jones, Knute Rockne, and many others. Rice's celebrity soon shone as bright as the stars he covered. He is easily the most significant sportswriter in history. Even today, his impact remains. When ESPN's Bill Simmons started a new website aimed at long-form sportswriting and thought-provoking columns, he named it Grantland.

Despite his fame, Rice was described as an extremely humble man. He introduced himself to awed reporters whom he didn't know by saying, "Hi, I'm Grantland Rice." He didn't seek special favors. Once, when he forgot his credential to a game, he bought a ticket, placed his typewriter on his lap, and wrote his column from the stands.

After Rice died in 1954, at the age of 73, Red Smith, now a major star in his own right, wrote, "Grantland Rice was the greatest man I have known, the greatest talent, the greatest gentleman. The most treasured privilege I have had in this world was knowing him and going about with him as his friend. I shall be grateful all my life. I do not mourn for him, who welcomed peace. I mourn for us."

Rice was doing what he did best—typing a column—when he suffered a fatal stroke. It couldn't have ended any other way, really. A one-man powerhouse, he was a prodigious writer. Estimates put his 53-year career output at 67 million words. That's an average of 3,500 words per day, and many of those words rank among the most fabled in the history of sports journalism.

Drawing on his classical education, Rice loved to write in verse, and he set the standard for the poetry of sportsmanship:

> For when the One Great Scorer comes
> To mark against your name,

He writes—not that you won or lost—
But how you played the Game.

He also penned the ultimate ode to the craft of sportswriting itself:

If somebody whispered to me, "You can have your pick,"
If kind fortune came to woo me, when the gold was thick,
I would still, by hill and hollow, round the world away,
Stirring deeds of contest follow, till I'm bent and gray.

But Rice is best known for writing the most famous lead to a sports story. In 1924 he covered the Notre Dame–Army game at the Polo Grounds in New York. Rockne was at the midpoint of creating his legend at South Bend. Much like Ruth's, some of the coach's feats, such as "Win one for the Gipper," became much-embellished tales. Rice made his contribution after Notre Dame's victory over Army, elevating its famous backfield into a mythical realm:

Outlined against a blue-gray October sky the Four Horsemen rode again.
In dramatic lore they are known as Famine, Pestilence, Destruction and
Death. These are only aliases. Their real names are: Stuhldreher, Miller,
Crowley and Layden. They formed the crest of the South Bend cyclone
before which another fighting Army team was swept over the precipice
at the Polo Grounds this afternoon as 55,000 spectators peered down
upon the bewildering panorama spread out upon the green plain below.

Rice's readers couldn't get enough. As he saw it, his job was not to write about sports but to celebrate it and the athletes he covered. He was, you might say, the anti–Howard Cosell. In *Sportswriter: The Life and Times of Grantland Rice*, Charles Fountain observed that

The twenties are the "Golden Age" of sport because Rice saw them as
golden. He was not a fool. He knew athletes and knew their failings.

He knew that Babe Ruth was a sot and that Ty Cobb was a boorish churl. But he chose instead to celebrate their enormous athletic gifts, and in Granny's eyes Ruth's dissipation was merely exuberance, Cobb's misanthropy dismissed as tenacity.

"If he couldn't say something nice about an athlete, he would rather write about another athlete," said a colleague after Rice's death.

Yet Rice also had his share of critics. Many thought his flowery prose flew too far over the top. Stanley Walker, a famed *New York Herald Tribune* city editor, wrote in his memoir that "Sometimes the reader had to wade through half a column of this fetching literature and mythology before getting any very clear idea of who won, and how they won. It was magnificent and, may God bless us all, pretty terrible." Robert Lipsyte, the former *New York Times* columnist, thought Rice's stories gave a distorted view of reality: "Painting the lily is not only presumptuous but ultimately destructive. The flower dies. By laying sports with pseudo-myth and folklore, by assigning . . . super natural identities to athletes, the Rice-ites dehumanized the contests."

Rice's writing style would never fly today. Much of current sports coverage aims, in an all-out blitz, to demystify the stars. Tear them down, then tear them down some more. It would have depressed Rice.

Ruth also would have had a tough time in today's media climate. Tales of his legendary womanizing would make perfect kindling for the tabloids. But the writers who covered Ruth and the Yankees wouldn't have dreamt of reporting extracurricular activities—even though many of them witnessed it firsthand.

Back then, writers and teams traveled together, forming bonds during the idle hours on those long train rides. In Holtzman's *No Cheering in the Press Box,* several writers recount what they saw when they traveled with Ruth.

Marshall Hunt talked of accompanying Ruth through Hot Springs, Arkansas, in search of a meal. They looked for a farmhouse with a sign that read CHICKEN DINNER. "What Babe really wanted was a good chicken

Grantland Rice, the most famous sportswriter of the era, didn't write about the Called Shot in his column about the game the next day. However, he celebrated the moment with all his signature flourishes two days later.

dinner and the daughter combination, and it worked that way more often than you'd think," Hunt said.

Richards Vidmar of the *New York Herald Tribune* recalled a time that writers were playing bridge with Ruth in his suite. At one point a woman walked in and went straight to his bedroom. Ruth excused himself, prompting a break in the game. "Pretty soon they'd come out, and the girl would leave," Vidmar said. "Babe would say, 'So long, kid.' Then he'd sit down, and we'd continue our bridge game."

Vidmar added, "Hell, I could have written a story every day on the Babe. But I never wrote about his personal life, not if it would hurt him. Babe couldn't say no to certain things. Hot dogs were the least of them. There were other things that were worse. Hell, sometimes, I thought it was one long line, a procession."

The massive divide between writers and players that exists today didn't then. In fact, in reading the accounts of many of the writers, many thought they were close friends with Ruth. "I never had a cross word with the big baboon," Hunt said in *No Cheering in the Press Box*. "He was no intellectual, you know, but he was an agreeable guy. He really liked baseball, and he liked people. And he tried to be agreeable."

Indeed, the writers weren't as discerning when it came to Ruth in particular or the teams they covered in general. Objectivity wasn't at a premium then, according to Major League Baseball historian John Thorn. "They were virtual employees of the club. Their road expenses were taken care of by the team, not the paper. To call them newspapermen by today's standards would be a stretch. They were more glorified PR men."

Something deeper was also at play. After the gloom of World War I, the Roaring Twenties encapsulated society's desire to let loose and forget its cares. The good times permeated into sports coverage. Fans wanted to read about heroes, and writers were only too happy to deliver.

"I belonged to the gee-whiz group," Paul Gallico said. "I was impressed by athletes, by what I was seeing. We had an overwhelming innocence in those days. We were so naive. Not only sportswriters, but the entire country. We had fought a World War and supposedly won, and thought we saved the world. There was a big boom. Everybody was happy. You could let yourself go on sports."

Then came the big black cloud of the Great Depression, in which people needed a little light in their lives. The sports pages then assumed a different role. Readers wanted an escape from the onslaught of bleak economic news. They wanted stories about larger-than-life athletes performing larger-than-life exploits. "The nation was looking for a lift," Thorn said. "In 1932 it was the heart of the Depression. It was a dark, dark year. The public was anxious to grab on to something that was frothy and fun."

Nobody delivered better in both departments than Babe Ruth, and the mood of the country fed off how the big slugger was covered. If Ruth did anything of note during a game, the writers practically tripped over their own prose to glorify it to the extreme—and Ruth always made for good copy. As he came to the plate during the fifth inning at Wrigley Field, the men in the press box knew he would be the focus of their stories again.

Ruth had already hit a three-run homer in the first. Now the battle reached a fever pitch, Wrigley Field on the verge of exploding. The reporters leaned forward, futilely trying to hear the byplay between the Cubs dugout and Ruth. Thoroughly engrossed in the drama playing out before them, they were scribbling notes—and then *BOOM!* Ruth's massive homer prompted a collective "Did you see that?" gasp in the press box. Many of the veteran writers had witnessed Ruth's most memorable blows, but none of them could remember one as Ruthian as that homer in Chicago. It took several minutes for the buzz to die down in the press box. The rest of the game proved anticlimactic, allowing the writers to home in on Ruth. Even before the final out was called, typewriters were clacking away with game stories.

There are no surviving play-by-play clips from the radio announcers. In 1989 the *New York Times* printed a letter by a fan who recalled listening to the game on radio. "When the announcer said that Babe Ruth was calling his shot, I held my breath in hope and disbelief," the fan wrote, but the radio announcers wouldn't have been able to hear what Ruth was saying. Perhaps the reader mistakenly was recalling one of the many play-by-play recreations that dramatically left nothing to doubt.

No, it was up to the men in the press box to provide the record on the Called Shot. Their dispatches have since become valuable evidence in the debate about the famous homer. Those writers also became part of a misconception embraced by many baseball historians: If Ruth really did call his shot, why didn't they write about it? Indeed, more than one historian points out that the writers covering the game didn't mention the Called Shot or Ruth pointing in their initial stories. It wasn't until several days—or in some cases even weeks—later that the story began to circulate, they contend.

Holtzman, a legendary Chicago baseball columnist and Major League Baseball historian before his death in 2008, adamantly debunked the notion that Ruth called his shot, basing a large part of his opinion on newspaper coverage of the game. In *Baseball, Chicago Style,* he wrote, "More than likely as many as 100 baseball writers covered the Series, but only one, Joe Williams of the *New York World Telegram*, reported in his game story, written on deadline, that Ruth had pointed to centerfield. But Williams later recanted."

Holtzman had an unparalleled knowledge of baseball history, but in this case he was perpetuating one of the myths about the homer. Williams, in fact, wasn't the only person to make reference to Ruth's gesture during the fifth inning. Others did, too.

John Evangelist Walsh exhaustively compiled the coverage. An author of books on Abraham Lincoln and Edgar Allan Poe, among others, Walsh wrote of the famous homer for *Sports Illustrated* in 1965. In his piece he refutes that the men in the press box didn't write about the Called Shot, finding examples to the contrary. "It was tantalizing to wonder what a systematic search of all the country's newspapers for October 2, 1932, would reveal, but having turned up three new contemporary mentions I felt I had gone far enough."

The question clearly lingered in Walsh's mind, though. Nearly three decades later, for the summer 1994 edition of *Wisconsin Magazine of History*, he wrote a 21-page article examining what was written in the wake of the Called Shot. Walsh boiled his analysis down to 38 reporters representing 27 different newspapers. His conclusion:

> *Viewing the 38 sportswriters as a group, without regard for the weight to be assigned each, the most striking fact is the way they split almost equally on the question. While 21 have nothing to say about a Called Shot, 17 others either definitely record Ruth's pointing to the stands in centerfield, or in some manner strongly imply a similar prediction.*

Why the split? Walsh offers a possible reason. Perhaps the reporters who didn't mention the Called Shot simply didn't see it. Maybe they were writing about the byplay when Ruth made his gesture. If Ruth did point, the whole scene happened much more quickly than how Hollywood portrayed it. "A flick of the eyes away from the plate, even for a second or two, and the watcher would have lost the rapid flow of the action, could easily have had his perceptions blurred without being quite aware of it," Walsh noted.

Gordon Cobbledick, writing for the *Cleveland Plain Dealer*, mentioned that Ruth merely "grinned and saluted" before hitting the homer. The great Damon Runyon also exhibited restraint. He wrote that Ruth "engaged in brisk repartee with the fans. He made gestures with his hands in case his voice was not heard." No mention of explicit pointing, though. Jimmy Isaminger of the *Philadelphia Inquirer* had an interesting interpretation. According to him, Ruth "made a satiric gesture to the Cub bench and followed it with a resounding belt." Are we to understand "satiric gesture" to mean "flipping the bird" to the Cubs? A distinct possibility.

Several writers reported that Ruth's gesture meant that he only had two strikes against him. Vidmar of the *New York Herald Tribune* detailed Ruth mixing it up with the Cubs in his account:

As the Babe moved toward the plate with one out in the fifth inning, swinging three bats over his shoulder, a concerted shout of derision broke out in the stands, a bellowing of boos, hisses and jeers. There were cries of encouragement for the pitcher, and from the Cubs dugout came a series of abuses leveled at the Babe.

But Ruth grinned in the face of the hostile greeting. He laughed back at the Cubs and took his place, supremely confident. Charlie Root whistled a strike over the plate. Joyous outcries filled the air and Babe held up one as though to say, "That's only one. Just wait."

Root threw another strike and the stands rocked with delight. The Chicago players hurled their laughter at the great man, but Ruth held up two fingers and still grinned, the super-showman. On the next pitch, the Babe swung. Straight for the fence soared on a line, clearing the farthest barrier, 436 feet from home plate.

Before Ruth left the plate and started his swing around the bases, he paused to laugh at the Chicago players, suddenly silent in their dugout. As he rounded first, he flung a remark at Grimm; as he turned second, he tossed a jest at Billy Herman.

John Drebinger of the *New York Times*:

A single lemon rolled out to the plate as Ruth came up in the fifth inning and in no mistaken motions the Babe notified the crowd that the nature of his retaliation would be a wallop right out of the confines of the park.

Root pitched two balls and two strikes while Ruth signaled with his fingers after each pitch to let the spectators know exactly how the situation stood. Then the mightiest blow of all fell. It was a tremendous smash that tore straight down the center of the field in an enormous arc, came down alongside the flagpole and disappeared behind the corner formed by the scoreboard and the end of the right-field bleachers.

It was Ruth's 15th homer in the world's series competition and easily one of his most gorgeous.

Irving Vaughn of the *Chicago Tribune*:

> *There was something more surprising about the wallop than the distance it traveled or the fact that it was made off a slow pitch. That was the condition under which Ruth turned it loose.*
>
> *Root got him in the hole with two strikes. Guy Bush and Bob Smith, two excellent jockeys, were leaning out of the Cub dugout doing the best they could to capture the Babe's goat. Bush's line of attack was a lot of choice names he figured would make the Babe a pretty mad fellow. Smith made gestures indicating he was trying to put the whammy on the Babe.*
>
> *Babe listened to this and yelled back, apparently annoyed. "That's only two strikes, boys. I still have one coming," he cried, meanwhile holding up two fingers. And when the next one came, Ruth sent it to distant parts. Root still insists that it was a perfectly pitched ball.*

Walsh believes that the writers who went with the two-strikes theory "clearly implied" that Ruth intended to do something grand with Root's next pitch.

Despite reports to the contrary, some journalists wrote what became legend. That is, they specifically said that Ruth called his shot. Warren Brown of the *Chicago American*: "Jurges scored in the fourth the run that tied the count at 4 to 4. It remained that way until Ruth came up again. This time he called his shot, theatrically, and with derisive gestures toward the Cubs dugout. That was the long-distance wallop of all time at Wrigley Field."

Westbrook Pegler, famed baseball writer for the *Chicago Tribune*, was clear about what he saw:

> *Guy Bush, the Cubs' pitcher, was on the top step of the dugout, jawing back at him as he took his turn at bat. Bush pushed back his big ears, funneled his hands to his mouth, and yelled raspingly at the great man to upset him. The Babe laughed derisively and gestured at him, "Wait, mugg, I'm going to hit one out of the yard." Root threw a strike past him and he held up a finger to Bush, whose ears flapped excitedly as he renewed his insults.*

*Another strike passed him and Bush crawled almost out of the hole
to extend his remarks. The Babe held up two fingers this time. Root
wasted two balls and the Babe put up two fingers on his other hand.
Then, with a warning gesture of his hand to Bush, he sent him the sign
for the customers to see. "Now," it said, "this is the one. Look." And that
one went riding in the longest home run ever hit in the park.*

*It was a privilege to be present because it is not likely that the
scene will ever be repeated in all its elements. Many a hitter may make
two home runs or possibly three in World Series play in years to come,
but not the way Babe Ruth hit these two. Nor will you ever see an
artist call his shot before hitting one of the longest drives ever made on
the grounds, in a World Series game, laughing and mocking the enemy
with two strikes gone.*

Gallico didn't write his column until the following day, and it appeared
in the *New York Daily News* on October 3, two days after the game. As he
wrote later in *Farewell to Sport,* he always believed that Ruth pointed. In
this piece he transformed Ruth into a swashbuckling swordsman.

*His performance in the third game of the current hippodrome was one
of the most amazing, exciting, and stimulating happenings in the history of baseball. He pointed like a duellist to the spot where he expected
to send his rapier home and then sent it there.*

*The Babe now held up two fingers and shook them so that they
seemed to reach right into the Cub dugout. And this time it was probably the most daring gesture ever made in any game, because it meant
that he intended to knock the next one out of the park. He was promis-
ing the Chicago players and the Chicago spectators that there wouldn't
be any third strike.*

*If you have never played ball you cannot picture the nerve and
confidence it took to do this. Because it wasn't the pitcher but the Babe
who was in the hole. Root still had a couple more balls to waste on
Ruth. He didn't have to give him a good one with a count of two and*

two on him. It was Ruth who had to make the decision that would spell success or the ignominy of a braggart who has failed.

But Ruth apparently had Root so well measured that he figured to hit him anytime he wanted to. Or maybe he didn't. Maybe he was just lucky. But there were no "ifs" "and" "buts" or "maybes" about the ball that he cocked into the stands. For one brief moment he was all hero, the man who delivers in the pinch.

Bill Corum also waited before he addressed the Called Shot in his wrap-up "Men of the Series" column for the *New York Journal*: "Words fail me. When he stood up there at the bat before 50,000 persons, calling the balls and strikes with gestures for the benefit of the Cubs in their dugout, and then with two strikes on him, pointed out where he was going to hit the next one and hit it there. I give up. That fellow is not human."

The sportswriter credited most frequently with starting the legend of the Called Shot is Joe Williams. A longtime baseball writer for the *New York World-Telegram*, he had the assistance of an unnamed editor who became part of the tale by crafting this famous headline: RUTH CALLS SHOT AS HE PUTS HOMER NO. 2 IN SIDE POCKET

The headline appeared in an edition printed the same evening as the game. In the column Williams wrote:

George Herman Ruth, who gets as much dough as Herbert Clark Hoover, seems to be worth it. He certainly gives you more thrills.

The Bambino hit two homers during the day, each of them a record-breaker, and on the occasion of his second round-tripper even went so as to call his shot. He also cross-fired gags with hecklers on the Cub bench to draw rounds of laughs, and almost moved a most unsympathetic gallery to tears when he stretched pathetically on his broad tummy in a vain effort to field a line drive.

The Babe's first homer came in the first inning with two out, a zooming drive that landed high in right center, the longest ball ever to hit that

section in this park. In the fifth, with the Cubs riding him unmercifully from the bench, Ruth pointed to the center field and punched a screaming liner to a spot where no ball ever had been hit before.

When Ruth came to bat in the fifth Bush and Grimes gave him a verbal roasting from the Cubs bench. The first strike was called and the razzing from the Cub bench increased. Ruth laughed and held up one finger. Two balls were pitched and Babe jeered the Cub bench, the fans and Root, grinning broadly all the time. Another strike was called, and Bush ran part way out of the dugout to tell the Babe that he was a tramp. Ruth hit the next pitch farther than any other ball ever was hit in this park.

As Holtzman said, it's interesting to note that Williams eventually debunked his own description of the Called Shot several decades later. In 1953 Williams began a story thus:

The most fascinating stories, unhappily, are not always true. Biographers assure us George Washington felled no cherry tree, the she-wolf did not wet-nurse Romulus and Will Tell wasted no apples off junior's noggin. And now comes reliable testimony that Babe Ruth didn't call that celebrated home run.

Then in 1965 Williams addressed the issue again:

I think I was as close to the Babe as any sportswriter of the era. Probably closer. I was often a houseguest. I sensed early it was fruitless to try to draw him out on matters of controversy or personal conflict.

I've always thought it significant that he never once stated in my presence that he had called THAT home run off Charlie Root—except possibly by inference.

Casually, I remarked: "I guess you'd have to say the home run you hit after pointing to the center-field stands in Chicago was your biggest thrill."

"Hell no," the Babe roared. "It was the time I struck out Cobb, Crawford and Veach with the bases full. That was some pitching, you gotta admit."

Why the change of heart? Hearing evidence to the contrary from players like Root, Gabby Hartnett, and others through the years obviously influenced Williams. Plus, he never heard Ruth talk about it. Absence of evidence isn't always evidence of absence—but to Williams it was in this case. He also admitted that he might have been guilty of going along with a good story. In the 1953 column he said that "It was just as easy to believe Ruth had actually called the shot as not and it made a wonderful story, so the press box went along with it."

Indeed, a reporter named Davis J. Walsh may have unwittingly influenced the press box. A 1982 article in *The Sporting News* quoted Edgar Munzel, who had covered the game for the *Chicago Herald Examiner*, and described Walsh as an "opinionated" sports editor of the International News Service. Munzel recalled that when Ruth's blow left the park, Walsh leaped to his feet and shouted, "Hey, he hit it exactly where he had pointed."

It certainly seems possible that Walsh's reaction triggered press box chatter that transformed Ruth's gestures to the Cubs into the more dramatic—and therefore more copy friendly—pointing to center field. Which isn't to say that they made it up out of whole cloth, but it does leave room for the possibility that the press men embellished the tale, hardly an uncommon practice. Once their Called Shot accounts hit the papers, the story had the required fuel to lift off and take on a life of its own.

But what of the great Grantland Rice? Where does he fit in?

Rice only added to the mystery. In his syndicated column written the day of the game, he didn't mention a word about Ruth pointing: "Ruth took two strikes as the crowd howled at his impending downfall. All this time the big Babe was exchanging quips and jibes with the Cub bench. And after each exchange the sunny atmosphere was full of sulphur. Then Root turned on a fast one and the Babe took his cut."

So did Rice miss it? It's hard to swallow that he would allow such a mythic moment to pass without rendering it into his purple prose. Sure enough, Rice did address the Called Shot, with all his signature flourishes, the following day.

The big moment of the game—one of the greatest moments of any Series or any competition—came early in the third game when the Babe arrived at bat. . . . The vast majority of 50,000 were either cheering him or jeering him. Both were music to the Babe! The Cub bench was riding him sky high. The Babe was riding back. Two strikes whistled over the plate as the crowd roared. As the second strike swept across, the Babe looked at the Cub bench and held up two fingers. His beaming countenance wore a broad grin. He then pointed to center field. And around five seconds later his famous line-drive lash—not much higher than [Primo] Carnera's head—sailed across the barrier.

The whip-like action of his wrists and arms, working together with a perfect body spin, was as fine a piece of coordination as I have ever seen. . . . He first built up his act with a mixture of comedy and kidding, farce and humor, and then he turned it into drama. . . . No one else in sport could have developed such a plot and then finished the story with such a flaming finale. He called the turn in advance, and then he put everything his 225 pounds carried into the most tremendous swing and lash his big bat had ever known.

This second account raises an obvious question: Why did Rice wait a day to write that column? Walsh points out that Rice was hardly the only writer to have a delayed reaction. Corum and Gallico, among others, did too. According to Walsh:

Most probably, the explanation for the discrepancy rests on the hectic, headlong pace of sports journalism, and in the resulting confusion and sprawl—many reporters at game's end, for example, would rush to catch evening editions.

By pre-arrangement, perhaps, some writers left it to colleagues to report; others may have jealously saved it for fuller treatment the next day—writing the story that same night—when justice could be done.

These are all plausible theories. Keep in mind: Getting a story into a newspaper was much different in 1932 than today. Deadlines were tougher, and computers didn't exist. Reporters couldn't send a story to the copydesk at the push of a button. Columnists like Rice and Gallico also had a habit of saving their best material, knowing a day would come soon when they might need fodder for a column.

Then again, as suggested by historians like Holtzman, who counted the Called Shot a myth, perhaps Rice and the other delayed-reaction writers read or heard about the same-day accounts from Williams and Pegler, who referred to Ruth calling his shot, and figured they needed to jump on the train as soon as possible. Even if Rice hadn't seen Ruth pointing, others were writing about it. Rice might have thought it incumbent on him to write it better than anyone else.

We'll never know for certain about Rice's intentions or others'. The tangled tale could have had a clear focus if all the reporters and columnists in the Wrigley Field press box wrote emphatically about the Called Shot on the day itself, or if none of them did. Instead, the accounts split down the middle, confusing the issue. But either way, they didn't have the last word.

TWELVE

Hollywood Strikes Out

*That movie is one of those things I wish I could go back and do over. It's
like being in that dream when you're in the subway with no clothes on.*
—JOHN GOODMAN ON PLAYING RUTH IN *BABE*

Jerome Holtzman didn't suffer fools, especially when it came to baseball.
A Chicago baseball writer for more than five decades, he had a well-
deserved reputation for being a steward of the game. His dedication
earned him the vaunted nickname "the Dean."

The Dean made rich men of relief pitchers. Seeking a way to quan-
tify the effectiveness of the men in the bullpen, Holtzman was instru-
mental in creating the "save" rule. Every time one of those relievers signs
a multimillion-dollar contract, he should thank the Dean.

Holtzman wrote six books, including the classic *No Cheering in
the Press Box,* an oral history of sportswriting recounted by 24 legends,
including Paul Gallico, Shirley Povich, and Red Smith. Holtzman was
held in such high esteem that when he retired from the *Chicago Tribune*
in 1998, Major League Baseball Commissioner Bud Selig asked him to
become the game's official historian, and Selig paid tribute to Holtzman

when he died a decade later: "Jerome was a Hall of Famer in everything he did, in every sense of the word."

Holtzman's distinguishing characteristics included remarkably bushy eyebrows and a cigar always in his mouth. He may have looked gruff, but friends and colleagues knew that a funny line could reduce him to a puddle of uncontrollable laughter.

He had many opinions on baseball and preserving the sanctity of the game. Few were as entrenched as his view of the Called Shot. He thought it pure fiction. In a 1987 column for the *Chicago Tribune*, he wrote, "Babe Ruth's called-shot home run is a myth, a fairy tale conjured from the imaginative spirit of sportswriters who, of necessity, possess a flair for the romantic and dramatic. If it never happened, why then has this fiction taken root? Because people gild lilies and sometimes remember seeing things they didn't see."

The producers of *Babe*—a movie released in 1992 that starred John Goodman as Babe Ruth—likely didn't know Holtzman's position when they invited him to Wrigley Field on a summer day in 1991. The stands in the classic ballpark stood mostly empty except for the extras playing fans attending the 1932 World Series.

Holtzman watched as director Arthur Hiller and the crew recorded Goodman recreating the Called Shot not once but several times. Holtzman, who took offense at taking liberties with the truth, didn't stay long. In a column the following day, he blistered what he had seen.

Finally, 59 years later, I saw Babe Ruth point. No, that's not true. It wasn't the Babe, it was John Goodman, the heavyweight actor who plays Ruth in the forthcoming film, The Babe, which is expected to be released next spring.

I watched from a seat behind first base. The Babe pointed, for the first take, at 10:56 a.m. and again seven minutes later, for the second take. It was all I could handle. I thanked my host, Rob Harris of Universal Pictures, and explained, hurriedly, it was bad enough that the Cubs were in the grip of a nine-game losing streak. I can live with that. But not with revisionist history.

Of course, revising history is what Hollywood does best, from ancient Egypt to Abraham Lincoln, and the filmmakers' interpretations went a long way in shaping the public's perceptions about the famed homer.

Hollywood's first attempt at tackling Ruth for a feature film was *The Babe Ruth Story*, which shares the name of Ruth's autobiography—but little more. It was rushed into release in 1948 while Ruth still was alive. Quite simply, Ruth deserved better. Critic Leonard Maltin called it "Perfectly dreadful . . . sugar-coated beyond recognition." It isn't just one of the worst sports movies of all time; it is one of the worst movies of all time, period. Indeed, many film buffs contend the film is so bad that it's good.

The movie starred William Bendix as Ruth. A fine character actor, Bendix received much acclaim for his work in *The Life of Riley*. As a young boy in the 1920s, Bendix actually served as a bat boy for the Yankees, giving him an up close look at Ruth in action. In retrospect, Bendix might have been better off playing the bat boy in the film. He was sorely miscast. For starters he was 42 when he film was made. Is there anything sillier than a man in his 40s trying to portray a kid in his teens and early 20s? To make matters worse, Bendix was short and stocky. Ruth had an ample gut during portions of his career, but he definitely didn't look like that as a younger player. Even with a paunch, Ruth moved with an athletic grace. Bendix, meanwhile, looked foolish with every swing and awkward throw.

Robert Creamer, author of *Babe*, once wrote, "For thousands of people, maybe millions, William Bendix in a baseball suit is what Babe Ruth looked like. Which is a terrible shame because lots of men look like William Bendix, but nobody else ever looked like Babe Ruth."

To compound this disaster, director Roy Del Ruth—no relation—approved a script that felt like a fairy tale. The movie supposedly was based on Ruth's autobiography. Bob Considine, the book's coauthor, consulted on the film and is listed as a cowriter. But he gaped at what he witnessed during production. "They kept making things up, things that didn't happen. And when I spoke up they always had the same answer: 'We're trying to make it exciting.'"

Again, it got so bad in certain points, you can't help but laugh. In one scene Bendix, in full uniform, runs into a hospital carrying an injured dog. Even the dog wasn't buying that one. The mystical power of Ruth's mere presence heals young, bedridden children. Suddenly they can walk again. Among the less supernatural inaccuracies, the film completely forgets to note Ruth's first marriage to Helen.

Now, with that in mind, how do you suppose the director handled the Called Shot? With nuance and mystery, leaving open the question of whether Ruth pointed? Fat chance. The Called Shot scene represents the culmination of all that's bad and distorted about the movie.

The director establishes tension between the Cubs and Yankees in a ridiculous scene by placing Bendix literally next to the Cubs dugout at the start of Game One of the series. Remarkably none of the Cubs takes a swing at him as they run onto the field. Bendix pelts them with barbs about how they treated his former teammate Mark Koenig—and what do you know? There's Koenig himself in a cameo. The whole scene is beyond preposterous.

Once the series shifts to Chicago, Bendix, hardly cutting an imposing figure in a New York road uniform, hears the boos from the Wrigley crowd. For some reason lemons weren't good enough, so the movie has the Cubs dugout roll out a cabbage to home plate.

"What's the matter?" Bendix shoots back. "One of yous guys lose your head?"

As Bendix is about to return to the box, Ruth's wife, Claire, played by Claire Trevor, yells from the stands, "Babe, don't forget Johnny!"

Johnny? Yes, Johnny. They tied the Called Shot into the legend of Johnny Sylvester, the sick kid to whom Ruth allegedly dedicated a homer during the 1926 World Series. Sure enough, we next see little Johnny lying motionless in bed, surrounded by his worried parents and a doctor, the game playing in the background. Apparently schmaltz had few limits back then.

Finally the confrontation begins. Charlie Root declined an offer to reprise his role for the movie, so the pitcher never appears. Just before

After Ruth ran the bases and with Gabby Hartnett watching, Gehrig offered his congratulations to the great slugger—before homering himself.
PHOTO COURTESY OF NATIONAL BASEBALL HALL OF FAME LIBRARY, COOPERSTOWN, NEW YORK

each of the first two pitches, Bendix takes his right hand off the bat as he watches them sail by. After each he emphatically indicates that they were strikes.

Then the movie reaches its dramatic climax. Bendix pumps his arm out straight with fingers extended once, then twice, then a third time. No denying Ruth's intentions there. The radio announcer provides clumsy expository: "He pointed to the flagpole in the center field bleachers, plainly indicating that's where he means to park that next pitch."

Bendix, using mostly his arms, swings as if he's trying to swat a fly. In a primitive special effect, the ball—looking like a yo-yo attached to a string—jumps off the bat, soaring over the ivy-covered outfield walls.

You'll also remember that Wrigley didn't have any ivy in 1932, but that's the least of the quibbles we could have with this scene.

As the radio announcer goes crazy, the scene cuts back to the sick boy. It's a miracle! He opens his eyes and smiles. The Called Shot homer has cured him! He clutches a ball signed by Ruth.

The final scenes of the movie depict Ruth, stricken with cancer, vowing to beat the dreaded disease. Ruth did manage to make it to the premiere of the movie in July 1948 in what turned out to be his final public appearance. He died the next month.

It wasn't until the 1990s that Hollywood took another full-blown theatrical swing at Ruth. In 1991 NBC aired the made-for-TV movie *Babe Ruth*. Stephen Lang, a Tony Award–winning actor, played the slugger and much better so than Bendix. In the words of Richard Sandomir, a *New York Times* sports and television columnist, "Lang's physical resemblance to Ruth—with weight, a bulbous fake nose and makeup added—is at times astonishing, especially in the later years. Lang understood that Ruth was a larger-than-life big kid who didn't know how to be a full-fledged adult or how an undisciplined man-child could earn respect for more than swatting homers."

Lang, a right-handed hitter, took lefty lessons from none other than Rod Carew. He also may have received advice from another hitting legend. Pete Rose, the all-time hit king, portrayed the man whose record he surpassed, Ty Cobb. Rose, with his hair slicked back, doesn't do a bad Cobb in a brief scene.

Thanks to Creamer's biography and a more sophisticated approach to the truth in the 1990s, this film depicts a less varnished version of Ruth. It addresses his failed first marriage and details his excesses with women, food, and drink. It also explores his run-ins with manager Miller Huggins, played by Bruce Weitz. Yet for all its attempts at reality, the film, like its 1948 predecessor, doesn't suggest any doubts about the Called Shot. Lang clearly points and then delivers.

John Goodman was supposed to play the role for the NBC movie. However, he had to back out when Universal Films decided to do a big-screen version of Ruth's story. Naturally Goodman was the studio's first choice to play the role. The popular star of the TV sitcom *Roseanne*—who had appeared in the feature films *Arachnophobia, King Ralph,* and *Barton Fink* in the couple of years leading up to *Babe*—was big and burly, giving him the physical ability to take on Ruth's larger-than-life presence.

But during filming Goodman discovered that it wasn't so easy to play the baseball star. "The baseball stuff was really hard because those guys wore these wool uniforms, and we shot in Chicago around 95 degrees. And I had all this rubber on my face."

Much anticipation heralded the film. Everyone had memories of the Bendix disaster. Surely the modern version, based deeper in reality, had to be better. John Fusco, the screenwriter, had a clear mission. "I wasn't interested in doing the William Bendix movie, where they created incidents that didn't happen for sappy dramatic effect. There were so many real incidents that I thought could be incredible."

So what did Fusco write? He wrote a modern version of the Bendix movie—full of clichés, fabricated stories, and brutal distortions of the truth. In fact, the last scene in the movie might have trumped anything in the first film. It shows an aging Ruth struggling in his final days with the Boston Braves. Goodman can barely drag himself around the bases and back to the plate. Ruth's skills may have frayed over the years, but at 40 Ruth was hardly ready for the wheelchair.

Unfortunately it gets worse. In the famous game in Pittsburgh, in which Ruth hit the final three homers of his career, a designated runner takes first base whenever Ruth comes to the plate. Seriously. What game did the director watch that included a designated runner? When Ruth hits the first two homers of the game, he wearily trudges to first base, and then the designated runner completes his turn around the bases. It's hard to believe a movie made just over 20 years ago could do something quite so lame.

After he hits the third homer, Goodman eschews the designated runner and completes the circuit himself. When he reaches home, his teammates surround him. He tells the Braves owner, who had misled him about the opportunity to be a manager, to stick it. Then he throws his hat down and walks off the field ostensibly for the last time. In reality, Ruth played a few more games after his three-homer performance, but, OK, let's give Hollywood some dramatic license here.

As Ruth walks alone in the corridor leading to the locker room, who does he encounter? Why, none other than a grown-up Johnny Sylvester, the boy Ruth visited in the hospital. Little Johnny just happened to be in Pittsburgh on that day and somehow managed to gain access to the visitor's runway. Surely the producers of the Bendix film, assuming any lived to see the Arthur Hiller biopic, wished they had thought up the same dramatic encounter. It was every bit as sappy as the 1948 movie moment that tied the Called Shot to the boy in the hospital.

So how did Hiller, Fusco, and Goodman handle the infamous homer? Unlike the 1948 film, they had access to scores of stories detailing the controversy over whether Ruth predicted the hit. At the very least, we might reasonably expect the scene to contain some mystery and not to resemble the Bendix version in which Ruth's right arm is as straight as a two-by-four. After all, moviegoing audiences were more sophisticated in 1992 than they had been in 1948. Right?

Given how the film ended, it shouldn't come as a surprise that we get another fairy-tale version of the Called Shot. The scene opens with lemons raining down on the field—enough to make lemonade for the entire park. Fans lustily boo Goodman as he walks to the plate, worrying Kelly McGillis, who plays Claire. After taking a strike Goodman holds up a finger and thrusts us into myth mode.

After the second strike, eyeing a heckling Cubs player, Goodman flashes two fingers. Then he raises and extends his arm, aiming those two fingers squarely in the direction of center field. Goodman remains locked in that position for one . . . two . . . three . . . four . . . five full seconds. Even Ruth wouldn't have had the audacity to hold such a controversial gesture that long even if he did do it. Once again, the pivotal scene bore no resemble to reality.

But then the scene grows even more laughable. For the big moment, Goodman makes an awkward lunge at the low, outside pitch. With that kind of swing, he would have been lucky to hit a flare to the shortstop. However, thanks to the wonders of Hollywood, the ball explodes off the bat and goes flying over the center field scoreboard. *Right where Ruth pointed!*

Goodman then starts to run the bases. In the old newsreels Ruth clearly makes repeated mocking gestures at the Cubs bench. But Goodman clasps his hands over his head in a self-congratulatory tribute. When he reaches home plate, his teammates surround him as if it were a game-ending homer. In reality, the score gave the Yankees a 5–4 lead in the top of the fifth. Only Lou Gehrig, the next hitter, greeted him, and Ruth gave him a quick handshake.

The scene concludes with a teammate declaring, "He called his shot." Another says, "He's not human. He's an animal." "No," says yet another, "he's a god."

Not surprisingly the critics trashed the movie. Gene Siskel of the *Chicago Tribune*: "A stunningly bad biography of Babe Ruth that offers none of the joy of baseball and only the surface details of a troubled man's life." Peter Travers in *Rolling Stone*: "Hiller and writer John Fusco pile on so many high-gloss TV-movie contrivances that you reject it all. What could have been the *Raging Bull* of baseball movies becomes the nibble of a mouse on the legend of a giant."

Even Goodman was embarrassed about the film. "That movie is one of those things I wish I could go back and do over," he said in an interview with *Esquire*. "It's like being in that dream when you're in the subway with no clothes on."

It's a shame that someone of Ruth's stature and importance still hasn't had a decent movie made about him. The two major studio productions, with Bendix and Goodman, give us Hollywood at its worst. *Pride of the Yankees* may have had its share of clichés and distortions, but it still possesses a wonderful sense of nobility in the way that Gary Cooper portrays Lou Gehrig. If only someone comparable had played Ruth.

Yet when it comes to the Called Shot, the two Ruth movies likely have had a considerable impact on crystallizing the story. Their depictions of the famous homer have taken on a measure of reality despite the ridiculous myths about other areas of his life. Even if the other material wasn't to be believed, baseball fans had heard tales of Ruth pointing at Wrigley Field, and they finally got to see it for themselves on the big screen, and it influenced public opinion about Ruth's larger-than-life stunt. Feature films are categorically fiction, not documentaries, but for many people if Hollywood says it's so, then it's so. Maybe we're not a more sophisticated audience than moviegoers of 1948—even today. It's little wonder that Jerome Holtzman practically ran from Wrigley Field as soon as he could.

THIRTEEN

Video Footage

When you touch the film, you know it was actually in the ballpark that day.
—KIRK KANDLE

The bridge crossing the Ohio River welcomes visitors with a sign that proclaims Kentucky as "the Birthplace of Abraham Lincoln." Illinois may be "the Land of Lincoln," but its neighbor to the south wants in on the sixteenth president.

The road winds into Louisville and swings past Louisville Slugger Field, where the Triple A Louisville Bats play. The route eventually leads to a charming neighborhood with vintage houses and trendy restaurants. Kirk Kandle is waiting in front of his house with Miya, his dog. The 61-year-old, a robust bike enthusiast, once pedaled coast to coast. He doesn't own a car, preferring to get around on two wheels.

But this visit isn't about bicycles. It is about the Called Shot, of course. In order to get closer to the truth, you have to travel to Louisville and spend time in front of Kandle's computer.

Kandle clicks on the mouse, and there it is: amateur video footage from Game Three of the 1932 World Series that could solve the mystery of whether Babe Ruth pointed to center field and called his shot.

The game occurred long before the creation of television, as we know, and newsreel photographers missed the big moment completely, so what Kandle has in his possession is, if you'll allow the anachronism, the Zapruder film of the Called Shot. In this case it also turns out that an amateur videographer had the most compelling perspective of the famous event.

The lifeline of the film itself is a remarkable story.

"I'm not a sports junkie," Kandle said. "But I am an expert at one thing: a single at bat by Babe Ruth."

Kandle's connection is his great-grandfather, Matt Kandle. Matt took his daughter, Gladys, to Wrigley Field on that sunny October day in 1932. He also brought a borrowed 16 mm camera.

With camera in tow father and daughter walked through the gates to discover that they had two of the best seats in the house. They sat behind the Cubs' on-deck circle on the third base side, either in the upper boxes or just above the aisle in the lower grandstand. This relatively low position gave Matt a decent view to record the game and the great Babe Ruth. He positioned the camera in front of his eye, adjusted the focus, and rolled the film that decades later the game's historians would dissect.

Matt Kandle was an unlikely candidate to play a part in baseball history. After moving from New Jersey to Chicago, he found his niche as a printer. Quite the inventor, he designed printing presses for R. R. Donnelly, now the world's largest commercial printer. Kandle also loved to tinker with gadgets. A 16 mm company camera caught his attention, and his position in the company ensured that he had access to it.

Kandle enjoyed using the camera to record family trips, but the basic family-waving-to-the-camera shots didn't suffice. Instead, he had them play out skits and often ran the film backward to create weird images.

"He was captivated by anything visual," said Kirk Kandle. "He was full of character."

Matt took the camera with him to the one and only World Series game he ever attended. The event made quite an impression him. Kirk pulled out a letter from Matt, dated October 3, 1932, that was passed along to his 10 siblings. It includes this passage (verbatim): "Saturday Gladys and I went to see the World Series and saw the best game ever. I can show you a movie of Babe Ruth slamming out one of his famous home runs. He got two that day. There was a worlds record of six for the game. Chicago team looked much the best to me but were badly managed by letting Ruth hit the ball. His home runs scored 4."

In Kandle's mind he merely had footage of the great Babe hitting a couple of homers in a World Series game. As the letter indicates, it didn't even dawn on Matt that Ruth had done anything out of the ordinary. He knew that Ruth could hit the ball a long way, and that was more than enough to satisfy the amateur filmmaker.

Unfortunately, the 1932 World Series was one of the last times Matt used the camera. In 1933 a car accident left him with several physical limitations. However, his creative mind kept humming along, and he turned his attention to fine art, producing more than 1,000 oil paintings.

Matt Kandle died in 1951. Six months later his grandson, Matt III, became the proud father of Kirk. Like his grandfather, Matt III was a printer. Kirk followed suit, working as a printer to help get through college at Eastern Kentucky University. Kirk eventually gravitated to journalism, though, which led him to a long tenure at the *Louisville Courier-Journal.*

Growing up, Kirk recalled seeing his great-grandfather's old home movies at family gatherings. His father placed a white sheet on the wall and started the projector. The family laughed at all the wacky scenes and visuals, recalling stories about family members from days gone by. Then they watched the footage of Ruth hitting a pair of homers during a World Series game at Wrigley Field.

Matt III changed jobs, so Kirk's family moved around quite a bit. Matt I's amateur movies, including the Called Shot footage, were stored in old, ratty cardboard boxes. In hot attics and damp basements, the lids on the film cans weren't always closed tight—hardly ideal conditions.

"Anything could have happened to the film," Kirk said. "When you think about it, it's amazing that it survived."

But the Called Shot footage was still destined to be seen only at Kandle family reunions. After all, they didn't think they had anything special. While Kirk suffered the slings and arrows of being a Cubs fan, he had many other interests besides baseball and sports.

"In our world we had no idea there was any controversy over the Called Shot," Kirk said. "In our family it was gospel. He pointed."

That changed when he read a story in the *Louisville Courier-Journal* in 1975. The piece, written by Paul Borden, recalls great moments in World Series history and of course includes the fifth-inning homer. Borden, though, wasn't a believer.

"If Ruth actually did point to centerfield and then hit a home run there, it escaped the notice of those who were there," Borden wrote. "The myth is mightier than the fact."

Kirk read the words several times. It was the first time that he realized that some people doubted what Ruth did that day. "But how can it be myth?" he thought. He had seen it all unfold in the film shot by his great-grandfather.

Kirk recalled his reaction to reading the story. "That five-year-old in me jumped up and said, 'Hell yes, he pointed.' I had seen it so many times. I'm sure he pointed at the fence. It never dawned on me that there were questions about Babe calling his shot. I never heard anything else other than the legend."

Kirk telephoned his father and told him about Borden's story. Did he still have the film? Sure, his father said. Kirk quickly collected the valuable reels and invited Borden and a *Courier-Journal* photographer to watch what really happened that day at Wrigley Field.

Kirk borrowed a Bell & Howell projector and nervously ran the film. "It was a risky proposition, because the film was so brittle by then," he said.

The film held up, but Borden wasn't impressed. He passed on writing a follow-up article on the footage. Kirk was disappointed but not deterred. He knew he had a valuable piece of baseball history. Certainly somebody would want to see it.

Kirk next contacted Robert Creamer, who wrote the classic biography *Babe*. An editor and writer at *Sports Illustrated,* Creamer devoted a chapter to the Called Shot in his book. Yes, he replied to Kirk, he was interested in viewing the footage.

In 1976 *Sports Illustrated* invited Kirk Kandle to New York. The magazine sent a car to pick him up at the airport and arranged for a screening of the film in a conference room in their offices. Creamer was very gracious, Kandle said. He verified that what he and fellow staffers were watching was from Game Three of the 1932 World Series.

Creamer and the magazine were intrigued, but they needed pictures for a story. They sent the film to Bud Greenspan to see if he could produce prints from the individual frames. Greenspan, an accomplished filmmaker, is best known for his documentaries on the Olympics. However, despite his vast knowledge, he informed the magazine that he couldn't make any prints. As a result, *Sports Illustrated* also passed on the story.

"I'm crestfallen," Kirk recalled of the moment. "What does it take to get some momentum here? I'm a printer. It didn't seem like it was that impossible to me to make prints."

Kirk went to work at the *Louisville Courier-Journal* in 1978. Once he settled in, he started thinking about how he could tell the story about his great-grandfather's movie. He and a *Courier-Journal* photographer went in the darkroom and managed to make three prints that captured Ruth making his dramatic gestures. The *Courier-Journal* ran a story on Matt Kandle's film, with the pictures, on October 2, 1980.

"It was the first time those pictures ever were published," Kirk said.

The story helped generate some momentum for his great-grandfather's place in baseball history. In October 1982 *The Sporting News* ran the prints in a large story on the 50th anniversary of the Called Shot, paying Kandle $300 for the rights to the pictures. "I thought it was a big achievement," Kirk said.

Shortly after *The Sporting News* story ran, Kirk received a call from the New York Yankees. They wanted to use the Called Shot pictures in

When he took his 16 mm camera to Game Three of the 1932 World Series, Matt Kandle had no idea that his footage would play a key role in the mystery of the Called Shot.

Kirk Kandle examines his great-grandfather's footage of the Called Shot homer. "When you touch the film, you know it was actually in the ballpark that day," he said.

their in-house fan magazine. Kirk said he wanted a fee. The representative said he didn't have a budget for the magazine.

"The richest team in baseball couldn't afford to give me a couple of hundred dollars," Kirk said skeptically.

So what did the Yankees do? They illegally copied the pictures from *The Sporting News* article and ran them in their magazine story about the Called Shot. The images even included a tagline that read, "Copyright: Kirk Kandle."

Livid, Kirk hired a copyright attorney, who contacted the Yankees. Kirk eventually received $300 from the team and signed a nondisclosure agreement, but the incident still ticks him off, even after more than 30 years.

"Put that in your book," he said to me. "When it came to Babe Ruth [and the Called Shot], they were a lousy bunch of cheapskates."

The Yankees theft emboldened Kirk's resolve to keep careful tabs on reproductions of the film and pictures. The issue isn't money. Rather, he wants his great-grandfather's work shown in the best possible light. He has hired a lawyer to track any unauthorized uses of the images. "I'm trying to protect the images," Kirk said. "I don't want them watered down by some third-generation [reproduction]. I'm cautious about where they are circulated."

His great-grandfather's pictures—not the film footage—appeared in the retelling of the Called Shot in Ken Burns's documentary *Baseball*. In 1994 Fox did a 20-minute segment based on the home video for one of its magazine shows. The stills and snippets of the film have appeared elsewhere. In its library the Baseball Hall of Fame also has a copy of the video on DVD available for historians.

A personal high point came when Kirk discussed his great-grandfather's footage with Earle Combs, Ruth's teammate and a Hall of Famer as a center fielder on those great Yankees teams. Kirk actually had lived in Earle Combs Hall when he attended Eastern Kentucky, but he didn't have any idea who the baseball great was until he learned more about the Called Shot.

After discovering the importance of the family film, Kirk arranged to meet with Combs in Paint Lick, Kentucky, shortly before Combs's death in July 1976. Kirk didn't have a suitable projector to show the footage to the Hall of Famer, but in the end it didn't matter. Combs had vivid memories of what transpired.

"He was feeble at the time, but very articulate," Kirk said. "When we talked about the film, he got all excited. It confirmed what he had said, that Ruth called his shot."

Kirk also takes pride in a Louisville connection to the Called Shot. During a visit to the Babe Ruth Birthplace and Museum in Baltimore, he learned about the founding of St. Mary's Industrial School for Boys, where Ruth learned to play baseball. In the mid-1800s Martin Spalding, the bishop of Louisville, opened Catholic schools to assist wayward boys there; later he did the same as archbishop in Baltimore. St. Mary's Industrial was one of those schools.

"If not for him [Spalding], Ruth might have been a tailor," Kirk said. "He never hits that homer, and my great-grandfather never records that film."

Visiting with Combs and meeting a filmmaker like Burns have given Kandle memories to treasure for a lifetime. As for the financial aspect? Well, that's another story. Kirk said he's hardly getting rich off his great-grandfather's handiwork with a movie camera. While he wouldn't disclose how much he has made from licensing fees, he described the amount as "nominal."

The film itself lies in a safe-deposit box in a Louisville-area bank. Assuming nothing happens to the bank, Kirk doesn't see any reason to insure it.

As for the future, Kirk isn't sure what he wants to do with the film. His ultimate dream would be to enlist the efforts of notable baseball fans Billy Crystal and Bill Murray. With Crystal representing his beloved Yankees and the Chicago-born Murray speaking on behalf of his forlorn Cubs, they would moderate a national debate in which fans would weigh in with their views on the Called Shot. Kirk knows the idea is a long shot, but he likes to throw it out there in the hopes that it captures some producer's imagination.

Kirk also contends that the film might contain further secrets. Thanks to modern treatments, the actual film is no longer brittle, but it has yet to be digitally scanned. He believes that with enhanced frame-by-frame analysis it might even be possible to read Ruth's lips to see what he was saying.

Kirk doesn't have the money for that kind of project, though, which makes the more likely route putting the movie up for auction at some point. Again, he stressed that he isn't thinking about the money. He takes great pride in living a simple life in his modest but comfortable two-bedroom condo. Kirk envisions the majority of the proceeds going to a charity that supports youth sports.

"People say you've won the lottery," he said. "I don't think of it in terms of dollar signs. I would like pay off my mortgage, but beyond that

I would like to see kids benefit from this. It would be fitting since Babe Ruth was all about kids."

He doesn't know how much the film is worth, either. "I've never had it appraised. What do you compare it to? Is this a Honus Wagner baseball card? Probably not, but I think there's some value here."

For some people it's not a picture, autograph, or other piece of memorabilia that could be prominently displayed. It's film in a metal tin. Of course, Kirk sees the film's value from another perspective. He believes it represents a chance to own a piece of baseball history from one of the game's most debated and celebrated moments.

"When you touch the film, you know it was actually in the ballpark that day," he said. "It's the actual film that my great-grandfather used to record Babe Ruth. He captured the light that reflected off Babe Ruth himself through the lens and onto the film itself. It's the only tangible thing we have left from the Called Shot."

He paused as if to the digest the notion. "I think that's pretty special."

FOURTEEN

Watching the Kandle

Even when you slowed it down and viewed it frame by frame, you could not tell.
—Major League Baseball historian John Thorn on viewing the Kandle film

Matt Kandle didn't record all of Game Three with his 16 mm camera. Film was at a premium back then, forcing him to pick his shots. Besides, Kandle knew his relatives weren't going to sit through an entire baseball game when he showed it at family gatherings—not when pot roast was waiting on the dining room table.

Kandle's Game Three footage lasts around two minutes, tops. Snippets show various parts of the game. While the film certainly leaves much to be desired, literally, the short bursts of footage offer an incredible portal into a historic moment that previously existed only in our imaginations. The main footage from newsreels is Ruth trotting around the bases after hitting the home run. Thanks to Kandle's film, we have a better sense of what happened on that day in Wrigley Field. However, like everything else about the Called Shot, it hardly provides definitive answers.

I viewed the footage on Kirk's computer. It starts with a panning shot of the ballpark. From his seat along the third base side, he begins in right field, sweeps through to left, and takes in the grandstand. No ivy—planted in the late 1930s—clings to the walls. Instead, as we know, temporary stands in the outfield helped seat the 50,000-plus crowd.

"I've had people tell me that's not Wrigley Field," Kirk said.

It does look different. For example, there's a big wall in center field with nothing behind it. There weren't any bleachers in that area back then. Also, the wall sported a hand-operated scoreboard at field level.

A marching band performs as the players from both teams carry a large American flag onto the field. Ruth presumably participated, although it's unclear from the footage if he did. It's hard to imagine today's multimillion-dollar megastars performing those same duties in a modern World Series.

Next we cut to Ruth at the plate during the first inning. It's still early afternoon, so the sun shines more brightly than it will a few innings later. Ruth takes two pitches from Root for balls. On the next delivery Ruth swings—a little off-balance, certainly not his best effort. But Ruth didn't have to swing perfectly to make solid contact. He did it his way, and it worked. The ball quickly disappears. That was the three-run homer that gave the Yankees their quick 3–0 lead.

Kandle focuses on Ruth doing a lazy home-run trot. Something is tossed onto the field. One of the Cubs' infielders picks it up and throws it away. Was it a ball? A lemon?

What's so striking about this first image of Ruth is seeing him in the context of a game. Much of the footage of his career consists of random shots of him swinging, throwing, mugging for the cameras, surrounded by fans. He's playing, but he's not really playing.

We know it's the first inning of Game Three: Kandle shows Ruth working the count, forcing Root to come in with a pitch he could hit. It's thrilling just to watch the great slugger take a pitch. It provides a wonderful glimpse at his process. Context really is king.

Next comes a brief shot of the Cubs' Kiki Cuyler, who homered in the third inning, running the bases backward. Kandle was having a little fun, but there isn't much to see, and the vignette ends abruptly.

The next scene is why I drove to Louisville. Ruth flashes on-screen again. He's up with one out in the fifth. The setting has darkened, as afternoon shadow has made its way over home plate and infield. More visible now is a heavy metal girder holding up the screen behind home plate.

"If he [Matt] had been a few seats over, that girder might have gotten in his way, and he never would have gotten the Called Shot," Kirk said.

Unfortunately, we don't get to view the entire at bat. It would have been great to see more; to say this is the definitive account of the Called Shot wouldn't be accurate. Perhaps Ruth really did point like Bendix when Kandle's camera was off. We'll never know.

But Kandle did capture the two moments that likely show how the tale of the Called Shot was set into motion. The first produced the famous still of Ruth extending his arm and pointing. The pitch, a ball, dribbles past catcher Gabby Hartnett. This is a key point: Ruth starts to make his gesture here with Hartnett's back turned. The Cubs catcher steadfastly denied that Ruth called his shot, but we can see that he didn't see it all.

With his bat on his left shoulder, Ruth makes two distinctive pointing, waving motions. He appears to be aiming at the Cubs dugout as if to say, "Get your asses back in there." More importantly, he's not looking at center field, and his arm is crossing his body rather than pushing out straight and away.

Kirk didn't dispute my interpretation. But he had his own theory. He suggested there might have been "a double-stroke of the same arm." Kirk stood and demonstrated, showing what Ruth might have done. "Let's say he was pointing to the dugout. With his arm extended, he only would have to move a few degrees [to the right] to point it to center field. It [the gesture] might not have gotten picked up here."

Plausible, but doubtful.

The most important part of this scene, though, is the timing. This *was not* the pitch prior to Ruth hitting his famous homer. Root missed

In this still from Matt Kandle's home video, Ruth makes the famous gesture. Note that Cubs catcher Gabby Hartnett's back is turned as he retrieves the ball. Pitcher Charlie Root also is facing away from Ruth.

the strike zone to set the count to two balls, one strike. Then Ruth goes into pointing mode. Many people assume his dramatic display took place with two strikes on him. The story goes that he pointed and then bashed Root's next pitch for a homer. It didn't happen that way, as we can see.

The next part of the scene shows Ruth taking a strike. Unlike the movie versions, he doesn't lazily eye the pitch so he can get two strikes intentionally. In the footage Ruth shifts his weight as if he means to swing—and why not? It was a hitter's count. Ruth decided to hold off, though.

As Hartnett throws the ball back to Root, Ruth launches through another series of gestures. Hartnett's body obscures Ruth's, but you can clearly see him lifting his right hand almost to chin level. With his arm

Ruth connects on the Called Shot homer, launching the ball into history.

bent it looks like he is raising one, maybe two fingers. Then he pumps his arm once, then twice.

It looks like a warning motion, like someone declaring, "You better watch out." Ruth might have used this gesture to say, "I've got one strike left," as Hartnett maintains. The slugger also could have been directing his ire at Root.

But it's not beyond the realm of possibility that Ruth was saying, "Just watch what I'm going to do with the next pitch." Clearly something significant was taking place. If Ruth wasn't calling his shot to center field, he definitely was telling Root and the Cubs that he was about to lay it on them. It's a highly charged moment. You can feel the intensity. In the perfect clarity of hindsight, the Cubs and their fans had to be crazy to give

Ruth rounds first, sticking it to the Cubs and reveling in his accomplishment. "You lucky bum," he said to himself.

him the extra motivation. If they thought the commotion would distract him, they were wrong. The opposite occurred.

Even though we know what happens next, it's still electric to watch it happen in Kandle's footage. Focused like few other athletes in history, Ruth catches the low and outside pitch clean and sends the ball sailing into the sky. You can see the power and majesty of the hit and the man. He didn't swing off-balance this time, as he had on his first homer of the day. He rotated his hips and murdered the ball.

Kandle then catches an elated Ruth jogging to first base. Shortly after he makes his turn, though, the scene abruptly ends. In an instant we see Kandle's daughter, Gladys, watching the game. We can only guess why Kandle cut away from this historic trot around the bases. Perhaps people in front of him stood up and obstructed his view. It sure would have been great to see Ruth taunting the Cubs.

The remainder of the footage shows Gehrig approaching home plate after he followed the Called Shot with a homer of his own, then a glimpse, after the game, of fans walking on the field as they depart the ballpark. Once again, it's a scene you wouldn't see today.

Kirk and I watched replays of the Called Shot several times at slower speeds. Even then, it's hard to determine the exact nature of Ruth's gestures.

John Thorn shared our opinion. The current official historian for Major League Baseball, Thorn saw the Kandle footage while working for Ken Burns on his *Baseball* documentary. "The angle was bad, and it was rather murky," Thorn said. "Even when you slowed it down and viewed it frame by frame, you could not tell."

Don Bell, a writer for the *Village Voice,* also saw the film. In 1988 he wrote a piece about making the trek to Louisville to get a firsthand look. After close examination Bell went from an entrenched belief that nothing occurred to a conviction that the legend was true:

> *The conclusion? After watching the film some 20 times at various speeds and stopping it at will, there's no doubt in my mind that Ruth actually called his shot four times. Twice in the first sequence, which was more a general statement of intent than a prediction, and more definitely, more precisely, in the two cocking-the-gun-and-shooting gestures just before Root hurled the ball.*

Kirk Kandle also believes. "It's not as clear as the oil painting [of the Called Shot], but he definitely challenges Gabby Hartnett and the Cubs." Kirk is a rational man, though. He can see how people might view it differently. He understands the claims that the Called Shot never really occurred. After years of watching the footage countless times, he is sure of a couple points. Chief among them is that his great-grandfather's film doesn't debunk the legend.

"I believe it leaves open the possibility that he pointed," he said. Kirk also understands that there will never be a universal opinion regarding the Called Shot debate. "You're always going to have a split," he said. "You can look at this film any way you want. People are going to see what they want to see."

SIDEBAR

The Warp Film

It turns out that at least one other person had a 16-millimeter camera at Game 3 of the 1932 World Series. As fate had it, how the footage was recorded and eventually discovered mirrors what happened with Matt Kandle.

Harold Warp, an inventor who started a plastics company in Chicago, wasn't much of a baseball fan. In fact, he went to *one* game during his life. He picked quite a game to attend. Like Kandle, he became part of the tale of the Called Shot.

On October 1, 1932, Warp carried his camera to his seat at Wrigley Field. He squinted while looking through the lens and did the same as Kandle: He recorded what took place in front of him, which included filming Babe Ruth during his famous at bat in the fifth inning.

Then Warp went home and filed the film away with the countless other reels in his collection. He showed the Ruth film, along with other home movies, during annual family reunions in Nebraska every December 26.

Like Kandle, Warp had no notion of the history he had documented on that film. It likely would have been limited to just the Warp family forever if not for James Jacobs. When Warp died in 1994, Jacobs, his great-nephew, took possession of his uncle's films. Initially he planned on doing some edits for better family viewing.

Nor did Jacobs know that he was in possession of something special with the Ruth footage. I spoke with him for a story I wrote in the *Chicago Tribune* in 1999. "I didn't realize the controversy surrounding it," Jacobs said. "I thought there were plenty of newsreels of the homer."

Jacobs showed the film to friends who knew he had something much more than a home movie of a baseball game, though. After some fact-finding, Jacobs eventually consulted with the National Baseball Hall of Fame and the Society for American Baseball Research. They confirmed that the film was authentic and of great historical value.

What next? Jacobs decided to contact ESPN. It just so happened that the network was doing a documentary series, *SportsCentury*, counting down the top athletes of the twentieth century. Ruth obviously ranked high on the list. ESPN eventually placed the slugger second behind Michael Jordan (perhaps in an attempt to continue cashing in on the basketball legend's popularity).

Mark Shapiro, producer of the *SportsCentury* series, was close to wrapping up the Ruth documentary in late 1999. He received a message from Jacobs: Was he interested in new video footage of the Babe Ruth Called Shot homer?

Shapiro couldn't believe it. He thought the only home movie recording the famous homer was shot by Matt Kandle. Now, more than 67 years after Ruth's massive blow, there's another film?

With a tight deadline looming, Shapiro quickly worked to secure the rights to air the video from Warp's son, Harold G. Warp, who runs the family business, Warp Brothers, in Chicago. ESPN agreed to pay Warp $1,000 for the rights. Warp, though, admitted he didn't understand why it was a big deal. "I still don't know if it's that special," Warp said then. "I don't think my father would be too excited. He probably would be more concerned with how much business we did today."

Shapiro was thrilled. Naturally, ESPN heavily promoted the discovery of the new video leading up to the *SportsCentury* documentary on Ruth.

Like the Kandle film, it also was shot from the third-base side, allowing Warp's camera to zero in on the left-hitting Ruth. Unlike Kandle's film, though, the Warp footage follows the flight of the ball—albeit with the camera jiggling—and records Ruth glaring at the Cubs dugout as he rounds third.

The new film confirmed what Shapiro already thought from viewing the Kandle video. "It is obvious that the myth is dead," Shapiro said. "He was clearly pointing at the Cubs dugout. Speaking as a sports fan and not as a producer of the show, I say he wasn't pointing at center field."

Jacobs agreed. "To me it looks as if he was pointing toward the Cubs dugout. If he were pointing toward the seats, his arm would be elevated a bit more." Nevertheless, he was excited that his uncle had a link to the Called Shot. "Personally I think it was kind of meant to be. It was fluke that the video got sent to me in the first place. To think he [Warp] went to one game in his life and now all this is happening—it's pretty incredible."

FIFTEEN

Modern Viewpoints

There's more conclusive real-time evidence about the damned Billy Goat Curse than there is about Ruth's supposed Called Shot.

—KEITH OLBERMANN

Ultimately, it's up to the historians and the baseball experts to render their verdicts on the Called Shot. They have sifted the evidence, examined the pictures, and heard the testimony. In some cases their verdict derives from logic and plausibility as much as anything else.

In interviews and through e-mail, I asked a cross section of broadcast analysts, historians, reporters, and authors to weigh in on what happened during Game Three of the 1932 World Series. Much like the players and fans at Wrigley on that October day, there's a wide variety of opinions and interpretations among this elite group. They all had one thing in common, though: a passion for baseball and for preserving its history.

Bob Costas

Still carrying his boyish looks, Costas—now in his 60s and with more than three decades' worth of deep ties to baseball—has become one of the game's resident sages. He participated in a 1994 Fox TV piece in which he analyzed Kandle's video.

You can argue that maybe there was some gesture that wasn't captured in it [the Kandle film]. From what you see it's obvious that he is clearly gesturing at the pitcher's mound. The angle of his arm is more straight, which means he was pointing at the pitcher. If he had been pointing beyond to center field, the angle of his arm would have been more upward. Then there's the wave of his hand. It's almost like a wave of disgust or disdain.

He's definitely indicating something along the lines of, "I've got one left and it only takes one," or maybe if we indulge in a flight of fancy, "Just wait to see what I do with the next one."

I never saw anything that was 100 percent conclusive. There's no question he is doing something, and there is some bravado. I would infer from the bravado that he was saying, "I'll show you." That's different from saying, "I'll show you, and I'm going to hit this next pitch into the center field bleachers." We would like to believe that. We just don't have the evidence to back it up.

Keith Olbermann
As with everything else from politics to sports, Olbermann, a keen student of baseball, past and present, isn't shy about voicing his opinion about what happened in Wrigley Field that afternoon.

An opinion is one thing, but most of the evidence seems to be pretty clear that this is hyperbole—not home-run hitting—of Ruthian proportions. That marvelous film that turned up 20 years ago shows him gesturing, but he is clearly gesturing not toward the outfield but toward the Cubs' third base dugout. Certainly he might've been *saying* he was going to hit the next ball into the bleachers, but the legend of and the definition of a called shot is Ruth pointing to the spot *and* saying something that translates as, "I'm going to hit the ball right there."

As you've seen (unless you've come up with something I've never seen), there is also a vital missing piece of contemporaneous support. No two identical in-person accounts of this remarkable event appear in any of the same-day coverage in the newspapers. Compare this to the wall-to-wall coverage of Ruth's triumphs, his hospital visits, his rodeo and boxing and football stunts, even to how much the readers of 1932 knew about how the Yankees felt about the Cubs short-shrifting their ex-teammate Mark Koenig with a partial World Series share. There's more conclusive real-time evidence about the damned Billy Goat Curse than there is about Ruth's supposed Called Shot.

George Will
A longtime political commentator as well as a long-suffering Cubs fan, Will had good reason to think about the Called Shot. He wrote A Nice Little Place on the North Side: Wrigley Field at One Hundred *and in it gave his take on what happened during Game Three of the 1932 World Series.*

The only reason for believing that Ruth called his shot is that a small minority of the sportswriters at the game said so, as did a few fans. The two reasons for disbelieving are:

1. Ruth never unequivocally said he did.

2. If he had pointed to the centerfield seats, the pitch he was vowing to hit there would have hit him. Charlie Root, the Cubs' pitcher, didn't need much of an excuse to throw at hitters. Had Ruth provoked him, Root would have decked him.

Tim McCarver
Having called the most World Series games in broadcast history, you'd think McCarver was behind the microphone for the Called Shot. The idea elicited a chuckle from him and prompted him to repeat a favorite trivia question: Who was the only player to play in a World Series and the Masters? Answer below.

I've seen the tape 50 times. The intention may not have been clear. He might have been shrugging his shoulder, as if to say, "Oh, yeah, I'll show you what a home run is." Maybe there was some exasperation in there. If he pointed, whatever happened to wasting a pitch?

It's grown over the years. Television perpetuates this kind of stuff to mythical proportions. It's taken on a life of its own.

The answer to McCarver's question: Sam Byrd. He was a defensive replacement for Ruth in Game Four of the 1932 World Series. Byrd fared better as a golfer, though, winning six tournaments with two top-four finishes in the Masters.

Leigh Montville
Taking on a tough assignment, Montville, an exceptionally talented writer, followed in the footsteps of Robert Creamer and wrote a biography of Ruth in 2006. The Big Bam *became a best seller.*

After the book came out, I remember going around to the talk shows and invariably we would wind up talking about the Called Shot. It's one of those stories: It's whatever you want it to be. All the different participants said different things. All opinions are pretty good because the Babe himself said everything and anything. He talked big and was forever a blowhard. He could be brought into confrontations easily throughout his career. He always was yelling and carrying on. I don't think he called his shot as if he was going to hit a homer to a specific spot. But he was pointing that he was going to hit the ball a long way. It was fortuitous the way it worked out.

If you look at the amateur videos, you can't be sure if he was pointing at the pitcher, the dugout, or if he was putting his hand up for a beer. If he was pointing at the dugout, he was pointing as if to say, "I'm going to do something bad to you guys." That's the way I like to think of how it happened. But as I said, all opinions are valid.

Robert Creamer

Unfortunately Creamer died in the summer of 2013, before I could ask for his verdict on the matter. But it was likely similar to what he wrote in his book, Babe, and how he answered the question numerous times in his life. From the book:

What about the legend? What about the story, often affirmed, often denied, that the Babe pointed to a spot in centerfield and then hit the ball precisely to that spot? It is an argument over nothing, and the fact that Ruth did not point to centerfield before his home run does not diminish in the least what he did. He did challenge the Cubs in front of 50,000 people, did indicate he was going to hit a home run, and did hit a home run. What more could you ask?

John Thorn

The second and current official historian for Major League Baseball, Thorn succeeded Jerome Holtzman. Not only do few people know the game and its history like Thorn, but few can articulate the stories better than he can.

I spent decades as a dogged researcher, trying to strip legend away from fact and arrive at the most accurate retelling of the story. However, as I become older, I have come to respect that legends and fables are more powerful and enduring than facts.

When I worked on Ken Burns's *Baseball*, we did many interviews with older players who told stories of a highly dubious nature. Yet those stories were so glorious that we would all chime in, "Our verdict is that the facts are too good to check." Ultimately, if the element of faith and belief enters into the telling of a story, it's OK. Even if you don't believe it yourself, it's important to have respect for the belief.

From an academic point of view, why do people believe these things? Why do people believe Abner Doubleday invented baseball despite so many of us trying to stuff him back in his grave? All the myths have been knocked down, and yet 85 percent of the public thinks he invented the game. Why do we believe in Santa Claus, the Easter Bunny? Babe Ruth is in that category.

He almost certainly pointed to something. From the angles of the home footage, it's not possible to determine for sure if he was pointing to the Cubs dugout or center field. My best guess is that he was waving his finger at the dugout. He was planning his revenge against the Cubs. That's the more likely scenario than he was pointing at center field. But in the end, I don't fight for this interpretation. The story is too good. If you're blowing bubbles, do I want to be the one to prick the bubble?

Bill Jenkinson

A noted historian, Jenkinson has studied Ruth for more than 30 years. He wrote The Year Babe Ruth Hit 104 Homers *and has done extensive research on the Called Shot, creating a website for his findings: BabeRuth1932.webs.com.*

It's the single most transcendent moment in baseball history. I believe he called his shot. The problem in believability is the issue of location. Nobody, including Ruth, could point to a spot and say, "I'm going to hit a home run there." That was always the problem with the legend. But if you strip away that facetious element that never should have been there to begin with, did he predict he was going to powder the ball with all his might? He did. There's no question about it.

I'm glad the research took me down this path. Previously I had been a naysayer. But the data's there. It's overwhelming.

He stood there in that batter's box, facing a great pitcher under tremendous adversity. The fans and players were all on him. He had two strikes on him. With all that going on, he proclaimed his invincibility by saying, "You can't stop me." Then Root threw him a pitch virtually impossible to hit, and the guy slammed it 490 feet.

I feel sorry for Charlie Root. He seemed like a great guy. But that whole bit about him saying after the fact that he would have knocked Ruth on his ass is garbage. He was just trying to save face. The fact is, Babe Ruth did call him out. Ruth did everything but stand on his head.

The people who say he didn't [call his shot] are reacting to the legend. They are basing their opinions on inaccurate data.

If you look at the facts, yeah, he called his shot.

Tim Wiles

As the director of research for the Baseball Hall of Fame in Cooperstown, Wiles has studied Babe Ruth and the Called Shot extensively. He also says that Thorn influenced his view.

I grew up in Peoria. I had the "bittersweet" opportunity to participate in a Yankees retrospective of their 27 World Series titles. I volunteered for 1932 and 1938 because they involved the Cubs. (The Yankees swept them both times.) When you're a Cubs fan, you'll take any connection to the World Series you can get.

John Thorn gave a talk here. He's very good with words. He said something like, "It doesn't matter whether Ruth called his shot. What matters is that we're still talking about it." The fact that we're still talking about it indicates what sort of a person Babe Ruth was, and that it is entirely plausible that he could have called his shot. He had that outsized talent and personality to be able to do what he said he was going to do.

It's like what Reggie Jackson did with his three-homer game. He didn't have the same personality as Ruth, but he had enough personality to come through and rise to the occasion.

John profoundly affected me. As a historian you find so many contradictory elements, pieces of evidence, and pieces of conjecture about this subject. Unless some crystal clear film or photograph emerges, or some new source that is qualitatively different, we are never going to know.

Gabriel Schechter

Author of several books on baseball history, Schechter was a researcher at the Baseball Hall of Fame from 2002 to 2010.

I've been thinking about the Babe and how to express my mixed feelings about it. Having read many eyewitness accounts, I found that the vote was split just about down the middle about whether Ruth called that home run. Perhaps the least biased observer, home plate umpire Roy Van Graflon, said that Ruth did call the shot. On the other hand, whenever I look at the film, it appears clear to me that Ruth was pointing at the Cubs dugout, not at center field.

The reasons for the animosity between Ruth and the Cubs have been well documented, and it certainly would be in his character for him to point at where he'd hit the ball. The uncertainty is a big part of the myth, though the biggest factor is that it was Ruth. Ted Williams historian John Holway says he can document more than a dozen times when Williams called a home run, but nobody cares. As famous as Williams is, there's only one Babe, and his calling his shot in such a flamboyant way on the game's biggest stage simply multiplies his aura as baseball's most prodigious slugger.

My considered view is that Ruth did call the home run but didn't point to center field. I buy the "It only takes one" interpretation—that Ruth took two strikes and yammered to the Cubs about it only taking one pitch, looking into the dugout and pointing one finger at them for emphasis. The implication is: Only one pitch to do what? Bunt? Hit the highest pop-up they've ever seen? No, only one pitch to hit his second home run of the game and stick it to them. If that isn't calling your shot, what is?

Michael Gibbons
Executive director of the Babe Ruth Birthplace and Museum in Baltimore, Gibbons is constantly asked about the Called Shot.

It's far more complicated than black or white, yes or no. Most fans, investigators, scholars who come through here agree something profound occurred during the fifth inning of Game Three. Most people don't feel like he pointed to center field.

The angle of the home movie leaves us inconclusive. He does point; there's no question about that. But is he pointing at the Cubs bench? Charlie Root? Center field?

I don't think he is pointing at center field. With that said, I also think Ruth was greatly influenced by being in that moment. There was pure animosity between the two teams. The bottom line for me is that I believe he felt he needed to do something significant. I don't think he necessarily pointed to center field, but he did let the Cubs know, "I'm going to ram it down your throat."

He orchestrated the whole thing. He took two called strikes to make it more dramatic. He challenged them, and he delivered. As he rounds the bases, he's clearly saying, "See, I got you." He called his shot through those gestures and the dynamic of the moment. I just don't think he called his location.

Tom Verducci

A multimedia machine, Verducci reports on baseball for Sports Illustrated, *MLB Network, and Fox Sports.*

We've mapped the moon and the human genome. A little uncertainty, even mythology, is good for the soul in this age of hyperanalytics. I don't know if Babe Ruth really called his home run in the 1932 World Series, and I'm okay with not knowing. I've read the accounts from Joe Sewell, Burleigh Grimes, Billy Herman, Gabby Hartnett, Bill Dickey, and Ruth—all of whom were on the field or in the dugout that day—and it's still not certain. It seems what we do know is that Ruth made a gesture of some kind with a raised hand to the center field area.

There is no debate that there was bad blood between the teams. The Cubs and Yankees were heckling one another so viciously that Judge Landis sent a letter to Yankees manager Joe McCarthy after the game explaining that any player using profanity (much of it could be heard in the stands) would be fined $500. Bench jockeying was a crude art form back in that day, so it's reasonable to think Ruth wanted to respond to the heckling from the Cubs. You can believe Ruth was telling the Cubs he still had another strike left in the count, that he was motioning to Charlie Root not to quick-pitch him again, that he was pointing in a general direction to signify he was going to get a hit somewhere, or that he called his shot of more than 440 feet to center field. Believing he called his shot—and Ruth seemed to encourage this belief as time went on, recognizing the value of the story—is more fun than believing he didn't.

Marty Appel
You would be hard-pressed to find a greater expert on the Yankees than Appel. The Yankees PR director in the 1970s, he wrote an exhaustive 600-page history of the team: Pinstripe Empire: The New York Yankees from Before the Babe to After the Boss.

Because even those on the field that day disagree about "yes" or "no," it's impossible for me to render an opinion. I will say that he was smart enough never to deny it, knowing a great story and a great moment when he had one.

When the home movie of his pointing was uncovered, everyone went, "What a find." But even that was inconclusive. He was certainly capable of pulling off such a stunt.

Glenn Stout
Stout examines the team's dominance in Yankees Century: 100 Years of New York Yankees Baseball.

I don't think he called his shot. I don't think it matters any more than it really matters whether his stomachache was caused by hot dogs, VD, or alcoholism. With Ruth, myth—far more than reality—has always been more important. He's the rare kind of player for whom the literal truth hardly matters because nothing factual we ever learn ever seems to diminish him. He just becomes more outsized, more legendary, more mythic, more of the cultural presence he has been since about 1920.

He wasn't just a player, but a *time,* damn near his own epoch, someone whose oversized presence, like a black hole, bends and absorbs everything around him and takes us to another place. In this case a home run warped the events around it into a story that, even though untrue, fit him more snugly than his uniform. You could say he did call his shot—he just went back in a time machine to do it, and no other player has that ability.

Ken Rosenthal
Starting at the Baltimore Sun, *Rosenthal also wrote for* Sports Illustrated *in the 1990s and since 2005 has been a familiar fixture on Fox Sports and MLB Network.*

I don't know if he pointed, but I love the story. The story certainly has some legitimacy to it if you believe he pointed. If you look at it from a modern perspective, players wouldn't do that today. Can I think of players who are confident enough in their abilities to do that? Yes, but it just isn't the thing to do. However, if you go back through the years, before all the modern etiquette and sportsmanship came into play, can you imagine Babe Ruth doing it? Certainly. It matches what we know of his personality. Whether it actually happened I have no idea, but it definitely fits the vision I have of him.

Brian Kenny
The MLB Network host has become a strong advocate for Sabermetrics in baseball. However, analyzing numbers doesn't help with interpreting the Called Shot, so Kenny had to go the subjective route.

Some version of it happened. Bench jockeying was a serious thing back then. Those guys were rough on Ruth, and he had an answer for them. It was the early version of "How do you like me now?"

Did he stand and point to center field? We would have seen that on film somewhere. It would have been more obvious. Still, it definitely is how we remember him. It boils down everything about him into one clean moment: his awesome power, his flamboyance, his ability to rise to the occasion. It was all there. It's all part of his legend and myth. Why not buy into it?

Buster Olney
Olney covered the Yankees for the New York Times *before becoming a baseball reporter for ESPN.*

I don't think Ruth called his shot based on the moving images we have. If he was standing in the box and pointing toward the center field fence, as if to take note of something in the distance, I think he would've raised his hand and arm much higher. I do think he was jabbering at Charlie Root, and giving him "what for," to use Babe's words, and he may have said something along the lines of, "You throw the ball in here, and I'll kill it."

But either way, the guy was a sports god, among very few: Thorpe, Ali, Gretzky. I have always loved the images of Ruth talking down the Cubs bench as he rounds the bases.

Roger Snell
Author of Root for the Cubs: Charlie Root and the 1929 Chicago Cubs, *Snell visited Kirk Kandle in Louisville to view Kandle's footage from the game as part of his research.*

When you see it, even in slow motion, it's not conclusive. Kirk Kandle sees it as, "Yeah, he did call his shot." I can see it as, "This is what Hartnett was talking about." Ruth was yelling at the dugout. To me he's responding to the third base side.

Why it has lived so long is amazing to me. Hartnett and Root, who had their views, were as honest as can be, but so was Lou Gehrig. Why would he lie and say the opposite? There are so many sides to the story.

I want to believe Charlie and Della [Root's daughter]. If there was any way in the world Root thought Ruth was showing him up, you know where the next pitch would be. He was tough guy. He wouldn't have put up with that. He would have taken care of Ruth.

Jonathan Eig

Author of the definitive biography on Lou Gehrig, Luckiest Man, *Eig provides the perspective from "the Iron Horse."*

Gehrig was on the on-deck circle. He was closer than anybody but the pitcher and catcher. He initially said it didn't happen. I always take the most credence in what somebody initially says. As the myth began to grow, Gehrig went along with whatever everyone else wanted to believe.

He must have known something dramatic happened. He saw Ruth calling attention to himself. He saw Ruth yelling at Root and the Cubs bench. Then he hit the next pitch for a homer. All of that was spectacular enough. I'm sure Gehrig saw it and appreciated it. He didn't want not to defend the Babe. He wasn't going to call him out as a liar.

I suspect when Ruth talked about the Called Shot, he did it with a wink. You can't count on these guys to tell the truth. The fact is, things tend to get exaggerated. It wasn't good enough just to hit a homer in the World Series. It gets embellished, and before you know it it becomes the Called Shot. The better the story, the happier everyone is—the facts be damned.

Rob Neyer

The baseball writer for SB Nation, Neyer wrote Rob Neyer's Big Book of Baseball Legends: The Truth, the Lies, and Everything Else, *which includes a chapter on the Called Shot.*

It all depends on one's definition of "called." Do I think he stepped out of the batter's box, then pointed to the center field fence in the distance before hitting a home run over that fence? No, I don't. I do believe that Ruth did something more brazen than most players would have dared and that if he hadn't done *something* fairly incredible, we wouldn't still be talking about it today.

Not many players had the gall to make such a public display (whatever it was), and not many men owned the power or the skill to hit a home run to center field off Charlie Root. But the Babe had it all and showed everyone on professional sports' biggest stage.

Phil Rogers
A longtime baseball writer for the Chicago Tribune, *now writing for MLB .com, Rogers also wrote a biography of Cubs great Ernie Banks.*

Baseball has always been a hard game played by hard men. It was certainly a tough crowd in 1932. I don't think a hitter could have made such a grand gesture without getting beaned by the pitcher.

While we all love great stories, I side with Charlie Root with this one. I believe Ruth's gesture was far less grand than it has become over the passing of time. More than likely, he waved his bat at Root after a quick pitch or for some other minor crime. But God, what a moment that must have been. A Cubs–Yankees World Series at Wrigley Field? In and of itself, that stretches the boundary of my imagination.

Ed Hartig
Hartig has chronicled the ups and mostly downs of the Cubs as a longtime team and Wrigley Field historian.

I don't think he called his shot. Ruth was responding to bench jockeying from Guy Bush. I've seen the footage. Ruth obviously is making a series of gestures—but to me it looks more like a sweeping motion, as if pointing back and forth between the Cubs dugout and the mound. That would support the claim that Ruth was actually gesturing at Guy Bush, the Cubs' scheduled starter for Game Four of the series; that Ruth couldn't wait till it was Bush's time on the mound on the next day.

Ruth likely did say that he still had one strike coming, but that doesn't mean he said he was going to homer. If he did call a home run . . . I think it's plausible that he said that he'd homer off *Bush* the next day. He just so happened to complete the current at bat with a home run off Root.

By the way, Bush hit Ruth with a pitch on his first at bat in the next game!

David Fletcher

A passionate student of the game, Fletcher is the founder of the Chicago Baseball Museum.

The Called Shot still reverberates and is still relevant today. The incident has a prime mythological place in baseball history involving the greatest baseball player of all time and also because of its location—the pre-ivy confines of Wrigley Field.

Babe Ruth was robbed of an opportunity to hit at Wrigley Field in September 1918 for the Cubs–Red Sox World Series. The Cubs were afraid that their very short right field fence at the four-year-old ballpark would be a launching pad for the pitcher-outfielder. The team also wanted to sell more seats to the fans at the more spacious Comiskey Park. So Ruth finally got a chance to hit in the place he called "a dump."

In essence, the Babe Ruth Called Shot is a wonderful fable, but that's all it is—a fable. Put in the context of the time, Ruth "calling" his homer could not have happened. Bench jockeying of the most virulent, ethnically insensitive, and racist type was part of baseball at the bottom of the Depression. But showing up an opponent by pointing to the stands to call your homer? Taboo to the 10th power.

Ruth was the game's greatest-ever showman, but he adhered to the age-old code of the game. You couldn't even point to the faraway bleachers now in the demonstrative, flaps-down, slo-mo home-run-trot, show-off twenty-first century. Providing even more insurance to the concept that Ruth gestured only to the Cubs dugout is the fact that pitcher Charlie Root was a notorious headhunter. Root would have been judge, jury, and executioner on the spot had Ruth seriously violated baseball decorum by calling his shot.

I have seen the two Zapruder-like home movies that show Ruth that fateful fifth inning on October 1, 1932. Like Kennedy assassination conspirator theorists, one can attempt to make a case that Ruth called his shot by pointing. But all evidence shows he pointed at the Cubs bench amid the bench jockeying over Ruth's outsized personality and his protests of Cubs players' granting former Yankees teammate Mark Koenig just a partial World Series share.

SIDEBAR

Mickey Says Yes, Reggie Says No

Mickey Mantle and Reggie Jackson, combined, hit 1,099 regular-season homers and added another 33 in postseason play, so the two legendary sluggers earned the right to make their determination over whether Babe Ruth called his shot at Wrigley Field.

In the winter of 1994, a Fox magazine-style TV show, *Front Page,* did a 20-minute report on the Called Shot, broadcasting Kandle's footage on television for the first time. On the show Mantle and Jackson analyzed the actions of their fellow slugger. Mantle watched the footage at his baseball camp in Florida alongside Johnny Blanchard, Ron Guidry, Jim "Catfish" Hunter, Bobby Murcer, and Bill Skowron. Illness was descending on Mantle, who died in August 1995, but he appeared in fine spirits for the show, exhibiting the aw-shucks humor that made him so popular among fans and teammates.

"I called my shot against the Cardinals in the 1964 World Series," Mantle said. "He [Elston Howard] was on the on-deck circle. I said, 'Elston, you're going back in. I'm going to hit a home run.'"

Sure enough, Mantle hit a walk-off homer to give the Yankees a 2–1 victory in Game Three. However, he didn't wallow in the moment during the *Front Page* story. "I called them about 500 times. That was the only time I did it. Usually, I struck out."

Front Page then showed Mantle and his old Yankees pals watching the video footage. In Mantle's view the key moment occurred when Ruth cocked his arm and gestured while Cubs catcher Gabby Hartnett was throwing the ball back to pitcher Charlie Root.

"That's when he called it," Mantle said. "This is it." Mantle watched Ruth unload on Root's pitch. "It looks like a home run swing. That's gone. I think he called it." Mantle concluded by paying tribute to Ruth. "He built the house we lived in," he said honorably, referring to Yankee Stadium.

After Mantle, Jackson had his turn, and their comments couldn't have differed more. While Mantle was self-deprecating, Jackson brimmed with the cocky bravado that constituted the trademark of his career. "It had to be a Reggie Jackson–type, Babe Ruth–type, Muhammad Ali–type athlete" to pull off the Called Shot, Jackson said, placing himself in rather elite company. "I can't think of another athlete that was like that."

Jackson talked about how he used to run his mouth at everyone and anyone, particularly the pitcher, when he was at the plate. "When I was in my prime, I was mean and vocal. I'd do what he [Ruth] is doing now. I'd tell the guy, 'You're full of crap.'"

Then Jackson watched the sequence of Ruth's at bat against Root. "Look at that transfer of weight," he said as he watched Ruth connect.

However, Jackson didn't think Ruth called his shot. "There is no extended arm, no pointing. This is much more realistic when you see it like this. He's jawing now. 'I've got one, two.' I don't see a Called Shot here."

Two of the game's greatest sluggers watched the same film and came away with two different interpretations—which comes as little surprise. It's just another example of the split of opinion over the legendary homer.

SIXTEEN

What Does It Mean?

If anybody could be inclined to do it, it would be him. So the story matches the legend of the man.

—Bob Costas

It was a sunny day—not that there are any cloudy days in the life of Ernie Banks.

He was at his second favorite place in the world: a golf course. He loves the game both as a participant and a fan and avidly follows the PGA Tour. Banks made it a point to be at the Augusta National when Tiger Woods made history with his epic first victory at the 1997 Masters.

Banks worked the clubhouse as the golfers prepared to hit the course. His knees long ago betrayed him, and the once sleek frame of his youth has acquired some extra padding. Yet his contagious smile and the ever-present twinkle in his eyes remain. Banks continues his lifelong mission to cheer up the world with his infectious personality. He is the Babe Ruth of making people feel good.

"Let's play two," a man says, echoing Banks's trademark line about always wanting to play a doubleheader.

"I'm ready," Banks shoots back. "I'm always ready."

Inevitably, the conversation turns to baseball, giving Banks the perfect opportunity to share his thoughts on the Called Shot homer.

Nobody knows Wrigley better. It's his favorite place in the world. He ruled the ballpark during an illustrious 19-year career. The slim shortstop had incredibly strong hands, launching balls out of the park seemingly with a flick of his wrists. He finished his Hall of Fame career in 1971 with 512 homers, a notable achievement when hitting 500 homers meant something. He represented the lone shining light in nearly two decades of bleakness for the Cubs, winning two National League MVP awards while playing on losing teams. Banks also knows a thing or two about power.

When asked whether a player could call a homer, Banks thought for a moment. "I never thought of doing something like that. I just wanted to hit it hard and hope it goes out." Banks then considered the question in the context of Ruth. "Yes, it is possible to do it. It's just the feeling of the player, the pitcher, the park, and the game itself. I believe he could do it." The notion took hold of Banks's imagination. "I believe he did it. I wish I would have been there to see it."

Not only was Banks one of the game's all-time best hitters, he is also one of its supreme eternal optimists. The man who never lost his smile—despite playing so many losing seasons for the Cubs—is a dreamer, and that's what's required for this story. In order to appreciate the totality of the Called Shot, you have to view it from two perspectives: reality and myth. Objectively, sure, you could knock holes in the legend. Plenty have and will continue to do so as the tale passes along to future generations.

The home videos show no direct evidence of him making the dramatic gesture that some claim he made. Fans in the stands and people in the press box interpreted Ruth's waving as a destination call. Once he delivered and the reporters wrote about it, then of course he called his shot. But the videos clearly indicate that Ruth was gesturing at the Cubs players, telling them to simmer down. All things considered, it's amazing that the umpires didn't halt the game to return events to order.

Also, Ruth's initial comments don't indicate that he pointed. In his heart of hearts, he knew you couldn't hit a baseball to a specific spot far in the distance. After all, this wasn't golf. Ruth had a bat in his hands, not a 5-iron. If Ruth had pointed, all of his teammates would have recalled him boasting about it immediately after the game. Never one for bashfulness, he wouldn't have kept his achievement quiet in the clubhouse. Ruth bought into the story only after hearing it repeated so many times. If people wanted to believe it, who was he to spoil a good tale?

At the same time, to say that Ruth didn't predict that he would homer against Charlie Root is also wrong. While he didn't specifically point to center field, his actions clearly imply that he planned to stick it to the Cubs—which of course he did. As Gehrig said, it might have been along the lines of telling Root, "I'm going to knock the next one down your goddamn throat."

The telling gesture occurs after Ruth takes his second called strike. With his arm cocked and finger pointing, he is definitely warning the Cubs. *Pitch at your own risk, Charlie.* Clearly, something big happened. He delivered. Boy, did he deliver.

After losing the first two games and falling behind early in Game Three, thanks to Ruth's three-run homer in the first, the Cubs finally had some momentum, rallying for a 4–4 tie going into the fifth. A different outcome, such as a strikeout, and who knows what would have happened? Ruth's homer effectively sealed the Cubs' doom.

Bill Jenkinson, a noted historian who has done extensive research on Ruth's career and on the Called Shot, tried to envision a similar confrontation taking place in today's game. "Put the Called Shot in a modern situation, and take away the element of direction. Name your guy . . . Albert Pujols, someone else. Put it in a modern World Series with the friction between the two teams, with opposing players calling for his head. It's a pressure situation with an ace pitcher on the mound. Then this player steps out of the batter's box and gestures defiantly. Then he goes ahead and hits a home run.

"If that happened today, the world would stop. Nobody would talk about anything else for a month. People would be incredulous. It would be the story to end all sports drama."

It happened in 1932, though, and people were incredulous. Ruth's career needed the Called Shot. His vast reputation called for a singular blow to serve as the ultimate symbol of prowess. Without the Called Shot Ruth would have lacked the instantly identifiable trip to the plate that we have discussed and dissected seemingly forever. He hit hundreds of homers, but he never delivered a grand slam to win a World Series game. John Thorn, official MLB historian, notes that even when Ruth hit his 60th homer in 1927, it broke his own existing record only by one run—and that mark was only six years old.

Ruth hit the first homer in All-Star history. However, as Bob Costas says, that moment wasn't remotely as dramatic as Ted Williams crushing a game-winning homer in the 1941 All-Star Game. His last swing—a homer in Fenway Park in his final at bat—will always define Williams's entire career. While Ruth had a three-homer game in 1935, he still played more games before hanging up his glove, and that game took place in Pittsburgh in a forgettable Boston Braves uniform, not in Yankee Stadium in the unforgettable pinstripes. The Called Shot gave Ruth his signature moment. When fans talk about Ruth, the conversation usually starts in Wrigley Field in 1932 when he achieved the incredible.

"It was the theatrical capstone of his career," Thorn said.

"I've been researching Babe Ruth for 30 years," Jenkinson said. "He never seems to disappoint. The canvas is so vast it defies rational analysis. The Called Shot was his pièce de résistance."

Perhaps the best element of the Called Shot, though, was that it occurred in 1932. TV cameras and commentators didn't yet exist to dissect every action and reaction. "One of the reasons that this has endured is that it predates television," Costas said. "If this happened in 1952, even though all you would have had is black-and-white kinescope-type film, you'd have something. Back then, you had nothing but word of mouth, newspaper accounts.

"Even they [amateur movies] suggest something, but that doesn't prove anything. If anything, it adds to the legend."

Costas insists the term requires some clarification, however. "I've often said this: People misuse the word 'legendary' in the modern era when they really mean celebrated or noteworthy or much acclaimed. For example, if you said, 'Who is the more legendary figure, Satchel Paige or Michael Jordan?' I would say Satchel Paige. Not that he was a greater pitcher than Jordan was as a player. But almost everything Jordan did is well documented. The shot on Bryon Russell [in the 1998 NBA Finals] was incredible, iconic. But it was not legendary, at least not in the full sense of legendary.

"If something is a legend, that means it has been handed down. It's been embellished. There are different versions. Satchel Paige clearly is a legend. With Jordan you have videotape from every angle."

Marty Appel's father makes for a case in point. Appel, an erstwhile PR man for the Yankees, wrote a telling passage about his father in his book *Pinstripe Empire*.

My father was born in Brooklyn but wasn't much of a baseball fan and didn't attend a game until he took me to Ebbets Field in 1955. It was the first game for both of us. Once, when we were discussing Hank Aaron breaking Ruth's home run record, he said to me, "Oh, but Ruth used to call his home runs." So for the average American, the story made it into popular culture; the translation wasn't always perfect, but no one can really be sure what happened that afternoon.

That's the essence of a legend. Appel's father didn't follow baseball. He didn't know about the conflicting evidence concerning the Called Shot. All he knew were the stories told over and over again. He believed that on one beautiful early fall day in Chicago, Ruth pointed and hit the ball there.

The legend becomes even more believable because of the man standing behind it. As Costas notes, people wouldn't have bought into the notion if Lou Gehrig had been in Ruth's position. The low-key star certainly had athleticism comparable to Ruth, but as Costas says, "It wouldn't have been true to him as a person."

The Called Shot "represented something that was essentially true," Costas said. "When you talk about Ruth with his outsized personality and bravado, it's something where you could say, 'It could be true.' If anybody could be inclined to do it, it would be him. So the story matches the legend of the man."

Legend morphs into myth. Thorn calls Ruth "Paul Bunyan–like." "He almost did not exist while he still was playing the game. His records were so far ahead of everyone else."

Indeed, Ruth, a larger-than-life character, all but transcended the bounds of physical limitations. He ate more hot dogs than anyone else, drank more beer than anyone else, had more sex than anyone else, hit the ball farther than anyone else, and so on. Stories about him are almost the stuff of fable. In some cases they actually are.

Tim Wiles, a historian for the Baseball Hall of Fame in Cooperstown, says Ruth often crosses the line between reality and fiction, especially in regards to the Called Shot. He notes the scene in the movie *The Natural* in which young Roy Hobbs confronts a Ruth-like character named "the Whammer." The slugger points, but unlike what happened in Wrigley Field, the young pitcher fans him on three pitches. "Ruth is a folkloric hero," Wiles said. "Babe Ruth was obviously real, but he works as a fictional, literary character, and the Called Shot is his prime moment in that regard. There is so much fiction written about this moment—not journalism, but in kids' novels, adult novels, movies. This moment has been seized upon by both fiction and nonfiction writers.

"This guy was capable of either doing it or creating the mystique that he could do it. It's the same process that makes historical heroes. Go back to David and Goliath or King Arthur. Nobody knows if these guys really existed, but their stories had such an intrigue about them. Ruth fits that mold."

Is the story as good if Goliath defeats David in five rounds? Hardly. We need to believe that our heroes are capable of defying imagination by performing superhuman feats of excellence at a time when we most want them to deliver. The Called Shot was that moment for Ruth.

Kirk Kandle maintains a website about the famous homer, TheCalled Shot.com. It includes a section asking readers to share their views. In 1998 one such reader, Jeremy Schoenike, was 14. Even though Ruth had died 50 years earlier, the slugger's life and career fascinated Schoenike. He knew all about the legend of the Called Shot, and he didn't want reality intruding on what his mind envisioned took place when Ruth faced Root in 1932. Schoenike wrote:

> *I have searched the web for hours just to find more on the BABE. I found your website very enjoyable to look through. I believe that Babe called his shot. I don't care if he didn't, that's what I believe. I love to hear both sides of the story. Even if he didn't really call his shot, what a story to tell and read. It truly is my favorite story and legend. LONG LIVE THE BABE!!!*

Perhaps you need the wonder of a 14-year-old boy or the wide-eyed optimism of Ernie Banks to buy into the legend of the Called Shot completely—or maybe you needed to see him step to the plate, swing that heavy bat, and hit the ball into the deep blue sky. Then he did it again and again.

Waite Hoyt, the great Hall of Fame pitcher on the 1927 Yankees, wasn't at Wrigley Field for that game. But he had seen Ruth perform so many great feats of showmanship that he had no doubts about the Called Shot. "I always believed he did do it," Hoyt said.

Hoyt's view speaks to Creamer's favorite quote about Ruth. It succinctly captures the majesty of the career. "One of the old ballplayers told me, 'All the lies about Ruth are true,'" Creamer said. The Called Shot may have been a lie, but it was true.

APPENDIX A

The Called Shot in Pop Culture

Babe Ruth's most celebrated home run has appeared in nearly every medium from advertising and a children's book to movies and television. Here is a short survey.

TOOTSIE ROLL

To coincide with the release of *The Babe Ruth Story* in 1948, Tootsie Roll did a cartoon ad featuring the Called Shot. It's told through the eyes of the movie's star, William Bendix. Sadly he looks more believable depicting Ruth in a cartoon than he did on the big screen. But the artist has the epic event occurring in the wrong inning, the fourth instead of the fifth.

SATURDAY NIGHT LIVE

A 1978 episode of the sketch-comedy show spoofs the Called Shot and the promise to hit a homer for the dying kid. Unlike the gushy Hollywood version, though, Ruth fails and the kid dies. The host for that episode was O. J. Simpson.

THE NATURAL

An early scene in the 1984 film features "the Whammer," ostensibly Ruth, facing a young Roy Hobbs, portrayed by a too-old Robert Redford. The Whammer points with his bat, as if calling his shot. Hobbs, though, fans him on three pitches. The scene makes quite an impression on sports-writer Max Mercy.

MAJOR LEAGUE

In this terrific 1989 baseball movie, it comes down to the final at bat. Cleveland Indians catcher Jake Taylor points to the outfield. The gesture angers the Yankees pitcher, who promptly knocks Taylor down with a pitch. Undeterred, Taylor gets up and points again. However, instead of swinging for the fences, he bunts, and Willie Mays Hayes scores the winning run from second base.

THE SIMPSONS

In the 1992 episode "Homer at the Bat," Homer, playing in a softball game, does his version of Ruth pointing. He then hits the ball to the opposite side of where he pointed. Naturally.

GEORGE CARLIN

The legendary comedian had fun with the Called Shot in his 2001 book *Napalm and Silly Putty*. "Contrary to popular belief, Babe Ruth did not call his famous home run shot. He was actually giving the finger to a hot dog vendor who had cheated him out of 12 cents."

BABE & ME

Dan Gutman's 2002 young adult novel features a boy going back in time to prove the truth about the Called Shot.

BUD LIGHT

Echoing the same theme as Carlin, a beer ad in the mid-2000s suggested that Ruth pointed because he spotted a Bud Light vendor.

CHEVROLET

In 2011 the carmaker released a youth baseball commercial in which Little Leaguers imitate the most famous homers of all time. One kid waves the ball fair like Carlton Fisk in the 1975 World Series; another pumps his arm with joy like Kirk Gibson in the 1988 World Series. The final scene features a stocky boy wearing the number 3 on his jersey. He extends his right arm and points with two fingers to center field. The kid takes a swing, and there it goes . . .

APPENDIX B

Game Three Play by Play

Starting Lineups (in Batting Order)	
Yankees	**Cubs**
Earle Combs, CF	Billy Herman, 2B
Joe Sewell, 3B	Woody English, 3B
Babe Ruth, LF	Kiki Cuyler, RF
Lou Gehrig, 1B	Riggs Stephenson, LF
Tony Lazzeri, 2B	Johnny Moore, CF
Bill Dickey, C	Charlie Grimm, 1B
Ben Chapman, RF	Gabby Hartnett, C
Frank Crosetti, SS	Billy Jurges, SS
George Pipgras, P	Charlie Root, P

TOP 1

Earle Combs reaches first on an error by Billy Jurges. Joe Sewell walks. Babe Ruth hits homer to right field, scoring Combs and Sewell. Lou Gehrig grounds out. Tony Lazzeri strikes out. Bill Dickey singles. Ben Chapman singles. Frank Crosetti flies to deep left. **Yankees 3, Cubs 0.**

BOTTOM 1

Billy Herman walks. Woody English flies out. Kiki Cuyler doubles, scoring Herman. Riggs Stephenson grounds out. Johnny Moore walks. Charlie Grimm grounds out. **Yankees 3, Cubs 1.**

TOP 2

George Pipgras strikes out. Combs flies out. Sewell walks. Ruth flies out to deep right. **Yankees 3, Cubs 1.**

BOTTOM 2

Gabby Hartnett grounds out. Billy Jurges singles. Charlie Root strikes out. Billy Herman flies out. **Yankees 3, Cubs 1.**

TOP 3

Gehrig hits lead-off homer to right. Lazzeri grounds out. Dickey flies out. Chapman walks. With Crosetti at bat, Chapman caught stealing for third out. **Yankees 4, Cubs 1.**

BOTTOM 3

English grounds out. Cuyler hits homer to right. Stephenson singles. Moore hits into fielder's choice; Stephenson out at second. Grimm doubles, scoring Moore. Hartnett hits foul pop-up to third. **Yankees 4, Cubs 3.**

TOP 4

Crosetti grounds out. Pipgras strikes out. Combs strikes out. **Yankees 4, Cubs 3.**

BOTTOM 4

Jurges doubles to left. Root grounds out. Herman pops up to second. English reaches first on error by Lazzeri; Jurges scores. With Cuyler at bat, English caught stealing for third out. **Yankees 4, Cubs 4.**

TOP 5

Sewell grounds out. **Ruth homers to deep center.** Gehrig hits homer to right. Pat Malone replaces Root. Lazzeri walks. Dickey walks. Chapman grounds out. Crosetti given intentional walk. Pipgras strikes out. **Yankees 6, Cubs 4.**

BOTTOM 5

Cuyler singles. Stephenson grounds into double play. Moore grounds out. **Yankees 6, Cubs 4.**

TOP 6

Combs lines out. Sewell flies out. Ruth walks. Gehrig strikes out. **Yankees 6, Cubs 4.**

BOTTOM 6

Grimm grounds out. Hartnett flies out. Jurges grounds out. **Yankees 6, Cubs 4.**

TOP 7

Lazzeri grounds out. Dickey reaches first on error by Jurges. Chapman strikes out. Crosetti singles to right; Dickey to third. Pipgras strikes out. **Yankees 6, Cubs 4.**

BOTTOM 7

Marv Gudat, pinch-hitting for Malone, pops out. Herman grounds out. English walks. Cuyler grounds out. **Yankees 6, Cubs 4.**

TOP 8

With Frank "Jakie" May pitching, Combs strikes out. Sewell hit by pitch. Ruth grounds into double play. **Yankees 6, Cubs 4.**

BOTTOM 8

Stephenson flies out. Moore pops out. Grimm grounds out. **Yankees 6, Cubs 4.**

TOP 9

Gehrig pops out. Lazzeri reaches first on error by Hartnett. Dickey reaches first on error by Herman. Chapman doubles, scoring Lazzeri. With Bud Tinning replacing May, Crosetti pops out. Pipgras strikes out. **Yankees 7, Cubs 4.**

BOTTOM 9

Hartnett homers to left. Jurges singles. Herb Pennock replaces Pipgras. Rollie Hemsley, pinch-hitting for Tinning, strikes out. Herman grounds out. English grounds out. **Yankees 7, Cubs 5.**

APPENDIX C

1932 World Series Recap

GAME ONE

Wednesday, September 28, 1932
Yankee Stadium I
Attendance: 41,459

	1	2	3	4	5	6	7	8	9	R	H	E
Chicago Cubs	2	0	0	0	0	0	2	2	0	6	10	1
New York Yankees	0	0	0	3	0	5	3	1	x	12	8	2

Pitchers: Cubs: Bush, Grimes (6), Smith (8)
                  Yankees: Ruffing

                  WP: Ruffing   LP: Bush
                  Save: none

Home Runs: Cubs: None   Yankees: Gehrig

GAME TWO

Thursday, September 29, 1932
Yankee Stadium I
Attendance: 50,709

	1	2	3	4	5	6	7	8	9	R	H	E
Chicago Cubs	1	0	1	0	0	0	0	0	0	2	9	0
New York Yankees	2	0	2	0	1	0	0	0	x	5	10	1

Pitchers: Cubs: Warneke
Yankees: Gomez

WP: Gomez   LP: Warneke
Save: none

Home Runs: Cubs: none   Yankees: none

GAME THREE

Saturday, October 1, 1932
Wrigley Field
Attendance: 49,986

	1	2	3	4	5	6	7	8	9	R	H	E
New York Yankees	3	0	1	0	2	0	0	0	1	7	8	1
Chicago Cubs	1	0	2	1	0	0	0	0	1	5	9	4

Pitchers: Yankees: Pipgras, Pennock (9)
Cubs: Root, Malone (5), May (8), Tinning (9)

WP: Pipgras   LP: Root
Save: Pennock

Home Runs: Yankees: Gehrig (2), Ruth (2)
Cubs: Cuyler, Hartnett

GAME FOUR

Sunday, October 2, 1932
Wrigley Field
Attendance: 49,844

	1	2	3	4	5	6	7	8	9	R	H	E
New York Yankees	1	0	2	0	0	2	4	0	4	13	19	4
Chicago Cubs	4	0	0	0	0	1	0	0	1	6	9	1

Pitchers: Yankees: Allen, Moore (1), Pennock (7)
Cubs: Bush, Warneke (1), May (4), Tinning (7), Grimes (9)

WP: Moore   LP: May
Save: Pennock

Home Runs: Yankees: Combs, Lazzeri (2)
Cubs: Demaree

SOURCE: BASEBALL-REFERENCE.COM

APPENDIX D

Babe Ruth's Milestone Homers

May 6, 1915: Jack Warhop earns his place in history as the Yankee gives up Ruth's first homer. Ruth batted ninth as the starting pitcher for the Boston Red Sox. Despite his big day at the plate, Boston lost the game 4–3.

May 1, 1920: Ruth hits his first homer for the Yankees at the Polo Grounds. It comes at the expense of Herb Pennock and his former team, the Red Sox.

July 12, 1921: Ruth homers off Dixie Davis of the St. Louis Browns. It is the 137th of his career, eclipsing the all-time mark set by Gavvy Cravath in the 19th century. From that day forward Ruth, just 26 years old at the time, remained all-time home run leader until Hank Aaron surpassed him in 1974.

April 18, 1923: Ruth fittingly hits the first homer at Yankee Stadium, which became known as the House That Ruth Built. Again Boston is the victim, with Howard Ehmke serving the pitch.

Sept. 2, 1927: Ruth hits number 400 off Rube Walberg of Philadelphia.

Sept. 30, 1927: Ruth hits his 60th homer of the season off Washington's Tom Zachary. That single-season record stood until 1961, when Roger Maris hit 61.

Aug. 11, 1929: Ruth hits number 500 against Cleveland's Willis Hudlin.

Aug. 21, 1931: Ruth hits number 600 against George Blaeholder of the St. Louis Browns.

Oct. 1, 1932: Ruth hits his 15th and final World Series homer in Game Three against the Cubs. It proved to be the signature homer of his career.

July 6, 1933: Ruth hits the first All-Star homer off St. Louis Cardinal pitcher Bill Hallahan at Comiskey Park in Chicago.

July 13, 1934: Ruth lands number 700 off Detroit's Tommy Bridges.

May 25, 1935: Playing for the Boston Braves, Ruth has his last big day, hitting his final three homers against Pittsburgh. The last two come courtesy of Guy Bush, the former Cubs pitcher who had played a key role in the Called Shot. Number 714, a mammoth shot, cleared the right field grandstands at Forbes Field. Circling the bases, Ruth nodded at Bush, his old adversary. Even Bush had to admit that he had met his match. "He got ahold of that ball and hit it over the triple-deck, clear out of the ballpark in right-center," Bush said. "I'm telling you, it was the longest cockeyed ball I ever saw in my life. I tipped my cap just to say, 'I've seen everything now.'"

APPENDIX E

Babe Ruth's Salaries

By modern standards Babe Ruth was the biggest bargain in baseball history. Adjusted for inflation, his peak salary would have reached roughly $3 million—barely the wage for a .250-hitting second baseman nowadays.

Year	Team	Salary	Equivalent Today
1914	Baltimore Orioles	$600	$27,100
1914	Boston Red Sox	$1,300	$58,700
1915	Boston Red Sox	$1,300	$61,200
1916	Boston Red Sox	$3,500	$143,000
1917	Boston Red Sox	$5,000	$169,000
1918	Boston Red Sox	$7,000	$213,000
1919	Boston Red Sox	$10,000	$270,000

Year	Team	Salary	Equivalent Today
1920	New York Yankees	$20,000	$514,000
1921	New York Yankees	$30,000	$957,000
1922	New York Yankees	$52,000	$1.57 million
1923	New York Yankees	$52,000	$1.45 million
1924	New York Yankees	$52,000	$1.46 million
1925	New York Yankees	$52,000	$1.37 million
1926	New York Yankees	$52,000	$1.32 million
1927	New York Yankees	$70,000	$1.81 million
1928	New York Yankees	$70,000	$1.77 million
1929	New York Yankees	$70,000	$1.73 million
1930	New York Yankees	$80,000	$2.22 million
1931	New York Yankees	$80,000	$2.58 million
1932	New York Yankees	$75,000	$3.03 million
1933	New York Yankees	$52,000	$2.25 million
1934	New York Yankees	$37,000	$1.45 million
1935	Boston Braves	$25,000	$914,000

SOURCES: *NEW YORK TIMES*, BASEBALL-ALMANAC.COM, MEASURINGWORTH.COM (2012 CONTEMPORARY STANDARD OF LIVING VALUES)

ACKNOWLEDGMENTS

I have to start with thanking Supreme Court Justice John Paul Stevens. His interview in 2008 catalyzed my thinking that I could do a book on the Called Shot. Stevens was more than gracious with his time, and it was a thrill to be in a justice's chambers in the Supreme Court.

It staggered my imagination that I could talk to Babe Ruth's daughter nearly 100 years after he played his first major league game. Thanks also to Julia Ruth Stevens's son, Brent, for arranging the interview and providing his own insights. My conversations with Linda Ruth Tosetti, Ruth's granddaughter, were highly entertaining and also proved important for the book.

I am grateful, too, that Lincoln Landis gave a memorable interview about attending the game with his famous uncle.

Initially, I wavered on making the trip to Louisville to view Matt Kandle's Called Shot video. Now I'm glad I did. Kandle's great-grandson Kirk was a terrific host and shared terrific stories and opinions about what happened that day in Wrigley Field.

Special thanks go to Bill Jenkinson as well, who did outstanding research on the 1932 season and the Called Shot for his website, a valuable resource in writing this book. I also want to acknowledge John Evangelist Walsh's comprehensive research and analysis on the press coverage. Roger Snell, Charlie Root's biographer, provided me with wonderful insights about the Cubs pitcher.

It was a thrill to be able to include the insights of my mentor, the late, great Jerome Holtzman. His book *No Cheering in the Press Box* is a classic.

Speaking of classics, it's hard to top the Babe Ruth biographies written by Robert Creamer and Leigh Montville, two power hitters in their own right. A bow goes to baseball historians John Thorn, Marty Appel, Tim Wiles, Michael Gibbons, and others for their insights.

I am grateful to the assistance from David Fletcher, founder of the Chicago Baseball Museum. He provided me with the fan letter to Charlie Root, which added great context to the story.

As always, the Baseball Hall of Fame was a tremendous resource. Thanks to John Horne for assisting with the photos.

I can't say enough about the Society for American Baseball Research (SABR). Their research aided the cause. Thanks to Jacob Pomrenke for putting me in touch with several historians.

It's always a pleasure to talk baseball and history with Bob Costas and Keith Olbermann, whose passion runs so deep for the game.

I am indebted to my agent, Jonathan Lyons. He guided me along the way, giving me an education on what it really takes to write a book. Thanks for everything, Jonathan. My editor, James Jayo, skillfully took my writing to another level. His editing and care for the story taught me important lessons. It was a pleasure to work with you, James. Many thanks to Meredith Dias for her work on the project. I am grateful for the job done by copyeditor Sarah Zink.

I owe a huge thanks to Richard Rothschild. My former colleague at the *Chicago Tribune* who now writes sports history for *Sports Illustrated* read through the entire text to make sure I had crucial facts correct. I can't tell you how reassuring it was to have Richard on the case.

Thanks also to my special advisors, Jody Rein, Josh Karp, Gene Wojciechowski, and Shari Wenk, for all their guidance and advice. My good friends Ira Cohen and Joe Logan always offered their encouragement if not extra strokes on the golf course.

For me, it always begins and ends with my family. My father, Jerry, gave me his love for baseball. He would have loved this book. My mother, Susan, continues to be my biggest fan. I couldn't imagine having better in-laws than Phil and Judy Goldstein. Their support means so much to me. I enjoyed sharing tales of the Called Shot with my younger son, Sam, my chief advisor in all things fantasy sports. My oldest son, Matt, and my wife, Ilene, assisted in copyediting the manuscript, finding what other editors already knew: I'm not perfect. As usual, they made me look better. Indeed, the biggest thrill of doing the book is that it truly was a family project. Ilene, Matt, and Sam were with me every step of the way, and I know they always will be.

SOURCES

BOOKS

Alexander, Charles. *Breaking the Slump: Baseball in the Depression Era.* New York: Columbia Press, 2002.

Anderson, Dave, ed. *Story of the Yankees.* New York: Black Dog & Leventhal Publishers, Inc., 2012.

Appel, Marty. *Pinstripe Empire: The New York Yankees from Before the Babe to After the Boss.* New York: Bloomsbury USA, 2012.

Aron, Paul. *Did Babe Ruth Call His Shot? And Other Unsolved Mysteries of Baseball.* Hoboken, N.J.: John Wiley & Sons, 2005.

Blake, Mike. *Baseball Chronicles.* Cincinnati: Betterway Books, 1994.

Connor, Anthony J. *Voices from Cooperstown: Baseball's Hall of Famer's Tell It Like It Was.* New York: Galahad Books, 1998.

Creamer, Robert. *Babe: The Legend Comes to Life.* New York: Simon & Schuster, 1974.

Didinger, Ray, and Glen Macnow. *The Ultimate Book of Sports Movies.* Philadelphia: Running Press, 2009.

Ehrgott, Roberts. *Mr. Wrigley's Ball Club: Chicago & the Cubs during the Jazz Age.* Lincoln: University of Nebraska Press, 2013.

Eig, Jonathan. *Luckiest Man: The Life and Death of Lou Gehrig.* New York: Simon & Schuster, 2005.

Fountain, Charles. *Sportswriter: The Life and Times of Grantland Rice.* New York: Oxford University Press, 1993.

Freedman, Lew. *Going Yard: The Everything Home Run Book.* Chicago: Triumph Books, 2011.

Gallico, Paul. *Farewell to Sport.* New York: Alfred A. Knopf, 1937.

Garner, Joe. *And the Crowd Goes Wild.* Naperville, Ill.: Sourcebooks, 1999.

Golenbock, Peter. *Wrigleyville: An Oral History of the Chicago Cubs.* New York: St. Martin's Press, 1996.

Ham, Eldon. *Broadcasting Baseball.* Jefferson, N.C.: McFarland & Company, 2011.

Holtzman, Jerome. *The Jerome Holtzman Baseball Reader.* Chicago: Triumph Books, 2003.

———. *No Cheering in the Press Box.* New York: Holt, Rinehart and Winston, 1973.

———. *On Baseball: A History of Baseball Scribes.* Champaign, Ill.: Sports Publishing, 2005.

Holtzman, Jerome, and George Vass. *Baseball, Chicago Style: A Tale of Two Teams, One City.* Chicago: Bonus Books, 2001.

Meany, Tom. *Babe Ruth.* New York: A.S. Barnes and Company, 1947.

Montville, Leigh. *The Big Bam: The Life and Times of Babe Ruth.* New York: Doubleday, 2006.

Neyer, Rob. *Rob Neyer's Big Book of Baseball Legends: The Truth, the Lies, and Everything Else.* New York: Fireside, 2008.

Povich, Shirley. *All Those Mornings . . . at the* Post. Cambridge, Mass.: Perseus Books Group, 2005.

Ritter, Lawrence. *The Glory of Their Times: The Story of the Early Days of Baseball Told by the Men Who Played It.* New York: Macmillan and Company, 1966.

Ruth, Babe, and Bob Considine. *The Babe Ruth Story.* New York: E.P. Dutton & Co., 1948.

Shea, Stuart. *Wrigley Field: The Unauthorized Biography.* Washington, D.C.: Potomac Books, 2004.

Smith, Red. *The Red Smith Reader.* New York: Random House, 1982.

———. *To Absent Friends.* New York: Atheneum Publishers, 1982.

Snell, Roger. *Root for the Cubs: Charlie Root and the 1929 Chicago Cubs.* Nicholasville, Ky.: Wind Publications, 2009.

Stevens, Julia, and George Beim. *Babe Ruth: A Daughter's Portrait.* Dallas: Taylor Publishing Company, 1998.

Stevens, Julia, and Bill Gilbert. *Babe Ruth: Remembering the Bambino in Stories, Photos & Memorabilia.* New York: Stewart, Tabori & Chang, 2008.

Stout, Glenn. *Everything They Had: Sportswriting from David Halberstam.* New York: Hyperion, 2008.

———. *Yankees Century: 100 Years of New York Yankees Baseball.* New York: Houghton Mifflin, 2002.

Tygiel, Jules. *Past Time: Baseball as History.* New York: Oxford University Press, 2000.

Veeck, Bill. *Veeck—As In Wreck.* Chicago: University of Chicago Press, 2001.

Vorwald, Bob. *Cubs Forever: Memories from the Men Who Lived Them.* Chicago: Triumph Books, 2008.

Williams, Peter, ed. *The Joe Williams Baseball Reader.* Chapel Hill, N.C.: Algonquin Books, 1972.

MAGAZINES

Baseball Digest
The Sporting News
Sports Illustrated

SPECIAL MENTION

BabeRuth1932.webs.com
Walsh, John Evangelist. "Babe Ruth and the Legend of the Called Shot," *Wisconsin Magazine of History* 77, no. 4 (1993–1994).

NEWSPAPERS

Chicago Sun-Times
Chicago Tribune
New York Daily News
New York Post
New York Times
New York World-Telegram

WEBSITES

BabeRuthCentral.com
Baseball-Almanac.com
BaseballHall.org
BaseballLibrary.com
Baseball-Reference.com
ESPN.com
MLB.com
PBS.org
SI.com
TheCalledShot.com
TheTrueBabeRuth.com
YouTube.com

INDEX